Bloom's Modern Critical Views

Bloom's Modern Critical Views

Bloom's Modern Critical Views

NORMAN MAILER

Edited and with an introduction by
Harold Bloom
Sterling Professor of the Humanities
Yale University

CHELSEA HOUSE
PUBLISHERS
A Haights Cross Communications Company

Philadelphia

Printed and bound in the United States of America.

10   9   8   7   6   5   4   3   2   1

Library of Congress Cataloging-in-Publication Data

Norman Mailer / edited and with an introduction by Harold Bloom.
    p. cm. -- (Bloom's modern critical views)
Includes bibliographical references.
  ISBN: 0-7910-7442-0
  1. Mailer, Norman--Criticism and interpretation. I. Bloom, Harold.
II. Series.
  PS3525.A4152 Z818 2003
  813'.54--dc21

                                    2002153652

Chelsea House Publishers
1974 Sproul Road, Suite 400
Broomall, PA 19008-0914

http://www.chelseahouse.com

Contributing Editor: Pamela Loos

Cover designed by Terry Mallon

Cover: © Douglas Kirkland/CORBIS

Layout by EJB Publishing Services

Contents

Editor's Note

My Introduction attempts canonical judgement upon Mailer's work.

Alvin B. Kernan's essay in *Of a Fire on the Moon* sees Mailer as an elegist marking the death of Romantic art at the hands of scientific myth.

My review essay upon *Ancient Evenings*, that vast panoply of humbuggery and bumbuggery, centers itself upon Mailer's highly individual phantasmagoria of death, copulation, and rebirth.

Richard Poirier also concerns himself with *Ancient Evenings*, which he surprisingly compares to William Faulkner and Joseph Conrad, not in my judgement an elevation Mailer's novel can sustain.

In a retrospective view Stacey Olster commends Mailer for his agonistic spirit, after which Gabriel Miller finds in the early work a similar sense of defiance.

Nigel Leigh goes back to the Trotskyite *Barbary Shore*, as anarchistic as it is Marxist, while Peter Balbert juxtaposes *The Deer Park* with D.H. Lawrence's *Lady Chatterley's Lover*, another comparison, I fear, that diminishes Mailer.

In a brilliant essay on *The Executioner's Song*, Mark Edmundson uncovers Mailer's renewal of High Romantic self-creation, after which Joseph Tabbi praises Mailer's career, while noting its limitations in addressing psychological and technological issues.

Mailer's imitation of the detective traditions is judged by Robert Merrill to be a success, which seems to me overpraise of *Tough Guys Don't Dance*. Kathy Smith centers upon Mailer's quest to convert nonfictional writing to literary possibilities.

Michael K. Glenday takes us back to Mailer's first novel, *The Naked and the Dead*, in order to trace the seeds there of all future Mailer.

In this volume's final essay, John Whalen-Bridge discusses the myth of the American Adam in later Mailer, connecting this to the perpetual agon of God and the Devil in Mailer's literary cosmos.

Introduction

I

Mailer is the most visible of contemporary novelists, just as Thomas Pynchon is surely the most invisible. As the inheritor of the not exactly unfulfilled journalistic renown of Hemingway, Mailer courts danger, disaster, even scandal. Thinking of Mailer, Pynchon, and Doctorow among others, Geoffrey Hartman remarks that:

> The prose of our best novelists is as fast, embracing, and abrasive as John Donne's *Sermons*. It is polyphonic despite or within its monologue, its confessional stream of words....
>
> Think of Mailer, who always puts himself on the line, sparring, taunting, as macho as Hemingway but deliberately renouncing taciturnity. Mailer places himself too near events, as science fiction or other forms of romance place themselves too far....

Elizabeth Hardwick, a touch less generous than the theoretical Hartman, turns Gertrude Stein against Mailer's oral polyphony:

> We have here a "literature" of remarks, a fast-moving confounding of Gertrude Stein's confident assertion that "remarks are not literature." Sometimes remarks are called a novel, sometimes a biography, sometimes history.

Hardwick's Mailer is "a spectacular mound of images" or "anecdotal pile." He lacks only an achieved work, in her view, and therefore is a delight to biographers, who resent finished work as a "sharp intrusion," beyond their ken. Her observations have their justice, yet the phenomenon is older than

1

Mailer, or even Hemingway. The truly spectacular mound of images and anecdotal pile was George Gordon, Lord Byron, but he wrote *Don Juan*, considered by Shelley to be the great poem of the age. Yet even *Don Juan* is curiously less than Byron was, or seemed, or still seems. Mailer hardly purports to be the Byron of our day (the Hemingway will do), but he might fall back upon Byron as an earlier instance of the literary use of celebrity, or of the mastery of polyphonic remarks.

Is Mailer a novelist? His best book almost certainly is *The Executioner's Song*, which Ms. Hardwick calls "the apotheosis of our flowering 'oral literature'—thus far," a triumph of the tape recorder. My judgment of its strength may be much too fast, as Ms. Hardwick warms, and yet I would not call *The Executioner's Song* a novel. *Ancient Evenings* rather crazily is a novel, Mailer's *Salammbô* as it were, but clearly more engrossing as visionary speculation than as narrative or as the representation of moral character. Richard Poirier, Mailer's best critic, prefers *An American Dream* and *Why Are We In Vietnam?*, neither of which I can reread with aesthetic pleasure. Clearly, Mailer is a problematical writer; he has written no indisputable book, nothing on the order of *The Sun Also Rises, The Great Gatsby, Miss Lonelyhearts, The Crying of Lot 49*, let alone *As I Lay Dying, The Sound and the Fury, Light in August, Absalom, Absalom!* His formidable literary energies have not found their inevitable mode. When I think of him, *Advertisements for Myself* comes into my memory more readily than any other work, perhaps because truly he is his own supreme fiction. He is the author of "Norman Mailer," a lengthy, discontinuous, and perhaps canonical fiction.

II

Advertisements for Myself (1960) sums up Mailer's ambitions and accomplishments through the age of thirty-six. After a quarter-century, I have just reread it, with an inevitable mixture of pleasure and a little sadness. Unquestionably, Mailer has not fulfilled its many complex promises, and yet the book is much more than a miscellany. If not exactly a "Song of Myself," nevertheless *Advertisements* remains Mailer at his most Whitmanian, as when he celebrates his novel-in-progress:

> If it is to have any effect, and I can hardly look forward to
> exhausting the next ten years without hope of a deep explosion of
> effect, the book will be fired to its fuse by the rumor that once I
> pointed to the farthest fence and said that within ten years I

would try to hit the longest ball ever to go up into the accelerated hurricane air of our American letters. For if I have one ambition above all others, it is to write a novel which Dostoyevsky and Marx; Joyce and Freud; Stendhal, Tolstoy, Proust and Spengler; Faulkner, and even old moldering Hemingway might have come to read, for it would carry what they had to tell another part of the way.

Hemingway in 1959 reached the age of sixty, but was neither old nor moldering. He was to kill himself on July 2, 1961, but Mailer could hardly have anticipated that tragic release. In a letter to George Plimpton (January 17, 1961) Hemingway characterized *Advertisements for Myself* as the sort of ragtag assembly of his rewrites, second thoughts and ramblings shot through with occasional brilliance." As precursor, Hemingway would have recognized Mailer's vision of himself as Babe Ruth, hitting out farther than Stendhal, Tolstoi, *et al.*, except that the agonistic trope in the master is more agile than in the disciple, because ironized:

> Am a man without any ambition, except to be champion of the world, I wouldn't fight Dr. Tolstoi in a 20 round bout because I know he would knock my ears off. The Dr. had terrific wind and could go on forever and then some....
> But these Brooklyn jerks are so ignorant that they start off fighting Mr. Tolstoi. And they announce they have beaten him before the fight starts.

That is from a letter to Charles Scribner (September 6–7, 1949), and "these Brooklyn jerks" indubitably refers to the highly singular author of *The Naked and the Dead* (1948), who had proclaimed his victory over Hemingway as a tune-up for the Tolstoi match. Hemingway's irony, directed as much towards himself as against Mailer, shrewdly indicates Mailer's prime aesthetic flaw: a virtually total absence of irony. Irony may or may not be what the late Paul de Man called it, "the condition of literary language itself," but Mailer certainly could use a healthy injection of it. If Thomas Mann is at one extreme—the modern too abounding in irony—then Mailer clearly hugs the opposite pole. The point against Mailer is made best by Max Apple in his splendid boxing tale, "Inside Norman Mailer" (*The Oranging of America*, 1976), where Mailer is handled with loving irony, and Hemingway's trope touches its ultimate limits as Apple challenges Mailer in the ring:

"Concentrate," says Mailer, "so the experience will not be wasted
on you."

"It's hard," I say, "amid the color and distraction."

"I know," says my gentle master, "but think about one big
thing."

I concentrate on the new edition of the *Encyclopedia
Britannica*. It works. My mind is less a palimpsest, more a blank
page.

"You may be too young to remember," he says, "James
Jones and James T. Farrell and James Gould Cozzens and dozens
like them. I took them all on, absorbed all they had and went on
my way, just like Shakespeare ate up Tottel's *Miscellany*."

There are no such passages in Mailer himself. One cannot require a
novelist to cultivate irony, but its absolute absence causes difficulties,
particularly when the writer is a passionate and heterodox moralist. Mailer's
speculations upon time, sex, death, cancer, digestion, courage, and God are
all properly notorious, and probably will not earn him a place as one of the
major sages. The strongest aesthetic defense of Mailer as speculator belongs
to Richard Poirier, in his book of 1972:

> Mailer insists on living *at* the divide, living *on* the divide, between
> the world of recorded reality and a world of omens, spirits, and
> powers, only that his presence there may blur the distinction. He
> seals and obliterates the gap he finds, like a sacrificial warrior or,
> as he would probably prefer, like a Christ who brings not peace
> but a sword, not forgiveness for past sins but an example of the
> pains necessary to secure a future.

This has force and some persuasiveness, but Poirier is too good a critic
not to add the shadow side of Mailer's "willingness not to foreclose on his
material in the interests of merely formal resolutions." Can there be any
resolutions then for his books? Poirier goes on to say that: "There is no
satisfactory form for his imagination when it is most alive. There are only
exercises for it." But this appears to imply that Mailer cannot shape his
fictions, since without a sacrifice of possibility upon the altar of form,
narrative becomes incoherent, frequently through redundance (as in *Ancient
Evenings*). Mailer's alternative has been to forsake Hemingway for Dreiser, as
in the exhaustive narrative of *The Executioner's Song*. In either mode, finally,
we are confronted by the paradox that Mailer's importance seems to

transcend any of his individual works. The power of *The Executioner's Song* finally is that of "reality in America," to appropriate Lionel Trilling's phrase for Dreiser's appropriation of the material of *An American Tragedy*. Are we also justified in saying that *An American Dream* essentially is Mailer's comic-strip appropriation of what might be called "irreality in America"? Evidently there will never be a mature book by Mailer that is not problematical in its form. To Poirier, this is Mailer's strength. Poirier's generous overpraise of *An American Dream* and *Why Are We In Vietnam?* perhaps can be justified by Mailer's peculiarly American aesthetic, which has its Emersonian affinities. Mailer's too is an aesthetic of use, a pragmatic application of the American difference from the European past. *The Armies of the Night* (1968), rightly praised by Poirier, may seem someday Mailer's best and most permanent book. It is certainly not only a very American book, but today is one of the handful of works that vividly represent an already lost and legendary time, the era of the so-called Counterculture that surged up in the later 1960's, largely in protest against our war in Vietnam. Mailer, more than any other figure, has broken down the distinction between fiction and journalism. This sometimes is praised in itself. I judge it an aesthetic misfortune, in everyone else, but on Mailer himself I tend to reserve judgment, since the mode now seems his own.

III

Mailer's validity as a cultural critic is always qualified by his own immersion in what he censures. Well known for being well known, he is himself inevitably part of what he deplores. As a representation, he at least rivals all of his fictive creations. *Ancient Evenings*, his most inventive and exuberant work, is essentially a self-portrait of the author as ancient Egyptian magician, courtier, lover and anachronistic speculator. Despite Poirier's eloquent insistences, the book leaves Mailer as he was judged to be by Poirier in 1972, "like Melville without *Moby Dick*, George Eliot without *Middlemarch*, Mark Twain without *Huckleberry Finn*." Indeed, the book is Mailer's *Pierre*, his *Romola*, his *Connecticut Yankee in King Arthur's Court*. At sixty-two, Mailer remains the author of *Advertisements for Myself*, *The Armies of the Night* and *The Executioner's Song*.

Is he then a superb accident of personality, wholly adequate to the spirit of the age? Though a rather bad critic of novelists, he is one of the better critics of Norman Mailer. His one critical blindness, in regard to himself, involves the destructive nature of Hemingway's influence upon him.

Hemingway was a superb storyteller and an uncanny prose poet; Mailer is neither. Essentially, Mailer is a phantasmagoric visionary who was found by the wrong literary father, Hemingway. Hemingway's verbal economy is not possible for Mailer. There are profound affinities between Hemingway and Wallace Stevens, but none between Mailer and the best poetry of his age. This is the curious sadness with which the "First Advertisements for Myself" reverberates after twenty-five years:

> So, mark you. Every American writer who takes himself to be both major and macho must sooner or later give a *faena* which borrows from the self-love of a Hemingway style ...
>
> For you see I have come to have a great sympathy for the Master's irrepressible tantrum that he is the champion writer of this time, and of all time, and that if anyone can pin Tolstoy, it is Ernest H.

By taking on Hemingway, Mailer condemned himself to a similar agon, which harmed Hemingway, except in *The Sun Also Rises* and in *The First Forty-Nine Stories*. It has more than harmed Mailer's work. *The Deer Park* defies rereading, and *An American Dream* and *Why Are We In Vietnam?* have now lost the immediacy of their occasions, and are scarcely less unreadable. In what now is the Age of Pynchon, Mailer has been eclipsed as a writer of fictions, though hardly at all as a performing self. He may be remembered more as a prose prophet than as a novelist, more as Carlyle than as Hemingway. There are worse literary fates. Carlyle, long neglected, doubtless will return. Mailer, now celebrated, doubtless will vanish into neglect, and yet always will return, as a historian of the moral consciousness of his era, and as the representative writer of his generation.

ALVIN B. KERNAN

The Taking of the Moon: The Struggle of the Poetic and Scientific Myths in Norman Mailer's Of a Fire on the Moon

At the center of the institution of literature there is, I have argued earlier in Chapter I, a world-view or myth which informs the various activities of the institution and is in turn objectified by them. To speak of *the* myth of literature, as Frye does, is probably a mistake since no two minds seem to conceive literature in exactly the same way, and since the dialectic interaction of world and mind results in constant change in the myth. Nevertheless, the great central statements about the nature of literature during a given period tend to hang together well enough to permit us to speak of a governing world-view or myth of literature of that particular time. Within the romantic period with which we are concerned, from Wordsworth's *Prelude* to Shade's "Pale Fire" the major works of literature, for all their individual differences, join with the major works of criticism such as Arnold's *Culture and Anarchy* or Frye's *Anatomy of Criticism*, to create a romantic myth of a vast and mysterious universe, filled with the magic of the unexpected, which is therefore a perpetual source of wonder and joy, never quite to be explained. Its world is a plenum of many things endlessly different from one another, individuals, each with its own special quality and beauty. But in this infinity of variety all the parts are ultimately linked with all other parts in organic ways which can only be apprehended by intuition, imagination, or powerful sensory excitement—not by reason and logic. Only by paying careful

From *The Imaginary Library: An Essay on Literature and Society.* © 1982 by Princeton University Press.

attention to the unique being of each person or thing, only by responding to its "thou" of being with the "thou" of its own deep being, can imagination hear the music of the spheres. In this romantic cosmology, the world is not static as in the Great Chain of Being, or circular, as in a Myth of Eternal Return, but is in movement, through struggle, towards some only dimly perceived but surely glorious future. Its plot is a titanic struggle of opposites, God and the Devil, thesis and antithesis, Apollo and Dionysus, Id and Ego, poet and society. The great enemy is passivity, stasis, the lack of energy, entropy. In this struggle mighty Promethean heroes emerge, charged with divine or daemonic energy, to carry the fire through great apocalyptic battles with the forces of darkness.

Despite the various forms of the myth of literature, it provides, however differently it may be conceived in different minds, the enabling charter of the remainder of literature. So long as it is believed in, thought of as a true picture of the world, so long the texts, the poets, the word craft, the criticism and all the other many activities which compose the institution of literature are valid and worth the labor expended on them. Attacks on the myth questioning its usefulness or its truth come therefore very close to the heart of literature. Such attacks, usually centered on the fictional aspect of literature, have been fairly constant from Plato to the present, and have been met in the usual way of institutions by assimilation, as Aristotle adjusted poetry to meet Plato's objections, or at times by a radical change in the myth to accommodate itself to changed social conditions, as the romantics redefined poetry in the face of the new society brought about by the democratic and industrial revolutions. Recently, as we have earlier seen, that romantic myth of poetry, as modified over the two centuries since its construction in the late eighteenth century, has been coming under increasingly heavy attack from Marxists who see it as merely an instrumentation of class interests, from philosophical critics who are deconstructing the logic of its assumptions, and from radical changes in the beliefs of the society which deny the basic literary principles. In *Of a Fire on the Moon*, a description of the landing of two Americans on the moon in 1969, Norman Mailer dramatizes these attacks on literature in a conflict of two great myths, science and poetry, for the control of reality.

In identifying the basic threat to the believability of poetry's myth as another myth, that of science, Mailer is following a long line of distinguished romantic predecessors—Blake, Carlyle, Arnold, and Ransom, to name only a few—who well understood that the social world is always an arena of competing systems of belief or myths and that literature's great competitor for belief has been, at least since the late eighteenth century, science. From

Aristotle through Pope, poetry was usually defined by its difference from philosophy on one hand and history on the other as more specific than the first, more general than the second. But in the eighteenth century, at about the same time that the more universal term "literature" began to replace the older "poetry," a new social paradigm of the arts began to develop. The crucial first step, described by Paul Kristeller in a remarkable article, "The Modern System of the Arts," was the full statement of a long-developing concept of Art as consisting of five fine arts—poetry, architecture, sculpture, painting, and music—distinguished from other activities by a shared purpose, the creation of pleasure through beauty, and by their total lack of any workaday function such as imitation or instruction. Poetry had, of course, long been loosely associated with music and painting, but only in the mid-eighteenth century were the various arts joined together in systematic form and the conception of Art created. As Kristeller explains the change:

> The various arts are certainly as old as human civilization, but the manner in which we are accustomed to group them and to assign them a place in our scheme of life and of culture is comparatively recent. This fact is not as strange as may appear on the surface. In the course of history, the various arts change not only their content and style, but also their relations to each other, and their place in the general system of culture, as do religion, philosophy or science. Our familiar system of the five fine arts did not merely originate in the eighteenth century, but it also reflects the particular cultural and social conditions of that time. (226)

Kristeller goes on to show that this conception of the identity of the arts under the concept of Art was spread through the *Encyclopédie*, and a philosophical and psychological basis for the special status of the arts was provided by Kant, in whose *Critique of Judgment* "Aesthetics, as the philosophical theory of beauty and the arts, acquires equal standing with the theory of truth (metaphysics or epistemology) and the theory of goodness (ethics)." (223)

If poetry, and later literature, has been defined by its similarity to the other arts, within the broad category of art, or, as Raymond Williams would have it, culture, it also has found its opposite, as we have seen, in a utilitarian industrial society, and chiefly in its principal philosophy, science. In good structuralist fashion, then, literature has been known, and has known itself, by those things it is like, the other arts, and by what it is unlike, science. The warfare between science and poetry, or C. P. Snow's two cultures, has from this structuralist point of view been long and fruitful in that it has enabled literature to define itself in the great system of social institutions by contrasting its subjectivity to science's objectivity, imagination to reason, connotative language to mathematics, and its sense of the mysterious uniqueness of events and things to the scientific assumption of the uniform behavior of particles of charged matter. But the opposition of science and poetry remains functional only so long as the poets can maintain in the face of science at least the possibility that their myth can describe or create a reality as true and believable as the scientific myth. In fact, of course, the poets have been far more nervously aware of science than the scientists of poetry, and the poetic myth telling of a world organized in conformity with human desire has long been on the defensive because the opposing scientific myth has proved so extraordinarily powerful in the control it gives over nature that it has by its achievements increasingly discredited the poetic myth. *Of a Fire on the Moon* dramatizes what it conceives of as the last battle in this long war, for in the late 1960's, Mailer feels, the scientific conception of the world has all but triumphed, and the landing on the moon will demonstrate conclusively the enormous power of science, validate its myth, and complete its dominion over the minds of men. The world will now become what science makes it, a world of objects moving in relationship to one another in accordance with immutable laws, coming from nowhere and going nowhere, lost in an infinity in which being is only relative. Literature and its humanistic conception of a world corresponding to human desire, organically related and metaphysically purposive, will disappear. As if to make clear its final assault on literature, science has now appropriated the myths of poetry: the mission is named Apollo 11, claiming for a rocket the name of the god of poetry and art, and it will land on and seize the traditional symbol of the poetic imagination, the moon, transforming it into a dead object, another scientific fact, "alien terrain where no life breathed and beneath the ground no bodies were dead." (32) The uncannily accurate prophecy of the poet Keats at the beginning of the nineteenth century will at last be fully realized:

> Do not all charms fly
> At the mere touch of cold philosophy?
> There was an awful rainbow once in heaven:
> We know her woof, her texture; she is given
> In the dull catalogue of common things.

> Philosophy will clip an Angel's wings,
> Conquer all mysteries by rule and line,
> Empty the haunted air, and gnomed mine—
> (*Lamia*, II, 229-36)

Against this scientific imperialism, this desacralization of the myths of a weaker culture by a stronger one, stands the poet Aquarius, Norman Mailer's persona, commissioned by a magazine to write a factual description of the moon-shot, but using the occasion to fight what he sees as the last battle between science and poetry, the Armageddon of art. But before we turn to a consideration of Aquarius and the myth he tries to make work once more, let us look at the beliefs of science as Mailer defines them in a typically romantic fashion, making them the exact opposite of poetic beliefs.

NASA-land, "the very center of technological reality (which is to say that world where every question must have answers and procedures, or technique itself cannot progress)" (47) is almost overwhelming in its power, its complexity, its effectiveness. Its machines are made of millions of parts, all of which are perfectly designed to interact smoothly with each other in flawless perfection and perform the most complex tasks without fail. Its buildings are taller than cathedrals, and its booster rockets as large as destroyers. The rocket fuel is maintained at fantastically low temperatures, where gases change to liquids, and when the fuel burns at thousands of gallons per second it produces fires with such enormous thrust power as to overcome the earth's gravity. The capsules sent into the vastness of space are navigated with pinpoint precision from the earth to the moon and back again. Every detail of the flight is monitored, every variation corrected with exactitude, by thousands of men working together with the same emotionless efficiency as their machines. Voices and images are transmitted clearly over thousands of miles of space, emergencies are handled with case, and no contingency among millions of possible variables is not foreseen and procedures for dealing with it worked out beforehand. No one, not even the poet Aquarius, can remain unimpressed when the great rocket leaves its launching pad to journey into space:

> two horns of orange fire burst like genies from the base of the rocket. Aquarius never had to worry again about whether the experience would be appropriate to his measure. Because of the distance, no one at the Press Site was to hear the sound of the motors until fifteen seconds after they had started. Although the rocket was restrained on its pad for nine seconds in order for the motors to multiply up to full

thrust, the result was still that the rocket began to rise a full six seconds before its motors could be heard. Therefore the lift-off itself seemed to partake more of a miracle than a mechanical phenomenon, as if all of huge Saturn itself had begun silently to levitate, and was then pursued by flames.

No, it was more dramatic than that. For the flames were enormous.... Two mighty torches of flame like the wings of a yellow bird of fire flew over a field, covered a field with brilliant yellow bloomings of flame, and in the midst of it, white as a ghost, white as the white of Melville's Moby Dick, white as the shrine of the Madonna in half the churches of the world, this slim angelic mysterious ship of stages rose without sound out of its incarnation of flame and began to ascend slowly into the sky.... (99-100)

There is a good deal of the poet as well as the rocket in this lyric passage, particularly in its imagery, which tries to keep the humanistic world in play with the rocket, but the event in itself is powerful enough to be impressive in its own right.

But elsewhere, though he is always respectful of the power of the event he is witness to, Aquarius is more often repelled by than attracted to the marvels of science and its technological creation, NASA-land. Like the America out of which it comes, NASA-land is "An empty country filled with wonders." (103) For all of its intricacy and efficiency, it presents a smooth, emotionless face to the observer, gives off no smells—a particularly important sense for Aquarius—no signs of mystery or vitality. Its buildings are bleak and windowless, usually placed in some barren setting, its atmosphere air-conditioned, its procedures developed from abstract rules rather than from human needs.

Aquarius first sees the astronauts at a press conference behind a screen of glass—to protect them from germs—and they never appear close up and in the flesh, but always as some distant, removed image, seen from far away as they move in their plastic helmets to the launch, are projected on television, and, finally, are glimpsed in a quarantine box on the carrier *Hornet* after they have landed. The personalities of these "shining knights of technology" are as removed and alien as their distant images. "What we can't understand, we fear," says the wife of one of them, and their internalization of scientific understanding relieves them of fear, of excitement, of pleasure, even of competitiveness. Like interchangeable parts of the machines they design and operate, one astronaut seems much like the other, and each could in fact exchange roles with the others and function effectively. The third astronaut, Collins, who does not land on the moon but remains in the command ship circling the moon while Armstrong and Aldrin land, could equally well have been chosen to walk on the moon, and he insists that his failure to be chosen doesn't bother him at all since he is merely part of the team, and it is the mission, the group, not the individual which counts.

This emphasis on the group, on the project, on the field, as it were, rather than the individual is close to the center of the scientific myth which empowers NASA. Behind Apollo 11 lies a vast bureaucracy, a host of contractors, an army of scientists and engineers, all working together like one of their machines with a minimum of friction and a predictable outcome. Individuality, the unique or unpredictable, is frowned on, and the men who make up NASA are, according to Aquarius, all cut from the same cloth of middle America, short-sleeved shirts of synthetic material with several pencils in the pocket, crew-cut hair, muscular and trim, humorless, WASP, intent, rational, the statistical norm. The astronauts themselves are the farthest extensions of this human machine, and any hint of the unusual about them, physically or mentally, would disqualify them for the mission. Neil Armstrong, the leader, is particularly without any irregularities or psychic bumps. He comes from a small town in Ohio, worked hard as an errand boy to earn the money to learn to fly, waited long to marry a school teacher, served as a Navy pilot in Korea and then as a test pilot. Although he has known difficulties and tragedy in the death of a young child, he is still the American Dream personified, small-town poor beginnings, hard work and determination, courage in the face of danger, intelligence and hard training, and now the biggest of all pay-offs, the first man to walk on the moon. Perfectly programmed for this mission, following their learned routines exactly and almost never called on for individual decisions, linked at all times to Mission Control in Houston, with even their heartbeats monitored, watching their thousands of instruments, locked into and entirely dependent for their lives on the complicated machinery of which they have become parts, the astronauts in their plastic helmets and protective space suits are the perfect image of scientific man when they step clumsily and uncertainly out onto the surface of the moon, unable to live or move except within the vast support system that extends back to earth. And though they are the principal figures in the trip to the moon, they can never become heroes, to the intense frustration of the millions who watched them, because systems emphasize teamwork, and heroes are romantic individuals. And they know this, are perfectly programmed to this pattern, so that every remark they make plays down their own importance and emphasizes that success is the result of joint effort, just as their smooth quiet exteriors and calm voices efface all traces of personality.

Aquarius has been charged with being unfair to the astronauts and purposely dehumanizing them in order to sharpen his point. But since their return from the moon there have been several books about these astronauts which substantiate Mailer's analysis of them. Two of the books were "ghost-written," but the ghosts are not mysterious romantic spooks, only the familiar professional writers, specialists of the PR team which is the "communication arm" of the technological society. The official book, characteristically a team effort of all three astronauts, *First on the Moon, A Voyage with Neil Armstrong, Michael Collins, Edwin E. Aldrin, Jr.* (1970), is said to be "written with" Gene Farmer and Dora Jane Hamblin, with, significantly, an epilogue by the science-fiction writer Arthur C. Clarke which tries to make the voyage to the moon exciting and meaningful by the application of some imaginative dreaming about the future. The book was carefully read and approved in final draft by a NASA official. The royalties were distributed in equal shares to the members of the team, all the astronauts in the program at the time, not just the three who went to the moon first; when an astronaut left NASA, as Armstrong, Aldrin and Collins all eventually did, his share in the royalties ceased. The book makes a considerable effort to humanize the moon venture by having Armstrong worry about his mail as the rocket is launched, by cutting to the nervous wives and families at home during the landing, and by showing Vince Lombardi telling his football players to pray for the astronauts because the voyage to the moon is even more important than football. But the book is flat, its touches of human interest only the stock-in-trade of the professional "flack," and the entire venture seems as meaninglessly dreary in this official version as Mailer depicted it in his book.

Colonel Edwin Aldrin was for Mailer the most curious of the astronauts, an engineer and a pure product of technology, but still "with the hint of unpredictability," (23) and his book, *Return to Earth*, "written with Wayne Warga," (1973) proves in many pathetic ways Mailer's point that men cannot yet live as machines within machines. After the return from the moon, the astronauts were handed over to another mechanism, the PR machine, which sent them to endless ceremonies and banquets, on friendship tours and visits of state around the world. Under these pressures the relationship of the astronauts broke down, and Aldrin, the super-achiever, began to drink, to have affairs, and to spend long hours simply staring at a wall, communicating with no one. At last he completely broke down and was hospitalized until a psychiatrist provided a conventional but very romantic explanation of Aldrin's profound existential anxiety:

I had gone to the moon. What to do next? What possible goal
could I add now? There simply wasn't one, and without a goal I
was like an inert ping-pong ball being batted about by the whims
and motivations of others. (303)

In the midst of his troubles Aldrin remembered a book, probably by Jules
Verne, he had read as a boy about a voyage to the moon which encounters
great difficulties and from which one of the astronauts returns insane. How
delighted Mailer-Aquarius would have been to know that a romantic fiction
would eventually be needed to organize and give meaning to the life of an
astronaut! In the end, by the aid of ministers, friends, modern medicine, and
a faithful family, Aldrin's "dysfunction" is corrected and there is a
conventional happy ending; but the power of his book derives from the
pathos generated by the contrast between the extraordinarily simplistic
understanding of life it projects in all its language and values and the
powerful and profound human needs at work in the man but baffled by and
unable to find expression or understanding in the strange machine-like world
in which he must live.

Language is, we now believe, the central structure of meaning and
values in a culture, and it is the NASA language which generates its scientific
myth and its social manifestation, the impersonal world of technology. When
the reporters in an interview press the astronauts for "disclosure of emotion,
admission of unruly fear—the astronauts looked to give replies as proper and
well-insulated as the plate glass which separated them." (38) Their words
never yield much—"Our concern has been directed mainly to doing the job"
(38)—and the famous phrase uttered by Armstrong as he first stepped on the
moon, "That's one small step for a man, one giant leap for mankind," (399)
is so neat, so flatly delivered, so patently manufactured on Madison Avenue
for the event that it reverberated with not even the slightest heartfelt spontaneous delight of a man doing something truly extraordinary. The language
of the astronauts and of the NASA administrators, always carefully
controlled to eliminate or conceal emotion, is further insulated by the jargon
Aquarius calls "computerese."

The use of "we" was discouraged. "A joint exercise has
demonstrated" became the substitution. "Other choices" became
"peripheral secondary objectives." "Doing our best" was
"obtaining maximum advantage possible." "Confidence" became
"very high confidence level." "Ability to move" was a "mobility
study." "Turn off" was "disable"; "turn on" became "enable." (39)

Computerese tends toward abstraction and the stripping away of emotional content, subjective responses, and the historical accretions words have gathered over the centuries as a result of their involvement in the lives of men. Much of the vocabulary of computerese is made up of acronyms, EVA for "extra-vehicular activity," i.e., walking on the moon; PTC equals "passive thermal control." VAB, the acronym for the Vehicle Assembly Building where the great rockets are readied for flight could be, Aquarius remarks,

> the name of a drink or a deodorant, or it could be suds for the washer. But it was not a name for this warehouse of the gods. The great churches of a religious age had names: the Alhambra, Santa Sophia, Mont-Saint-Michel, Chartres, Westminster Abbey, Notre Dame. Now: VAB. Nothing fit anything any longer. The art of communication had become the mechanical function, and the machine was the work of art. What a fall for the ego of the artist. What a climb to capture the language again! (55-56)

But the dull language of fact, the acronyms, the jargon, the scientific cant, the plain but still somehow pompous statements of the astronauts and their spokesmen, these are only the various *paroles* of a *langue* whose alphabet is ultimately number, numbers which because they are "abstracted from the senses ... made you ignore the taste of the apple for the amount in the box, ... shrunk the protective envelope of human atmosphere...." (138) The paradigm underlying computerese is finally that simplest and most reductive of all mathematical forms, the binary system in which all things are ultimately plus or minus, one or zero, yes or no, go and no go, a flash of energy or its absence. Computers are built upon this *langue*, and computers are the very heart of Apollo 11, plotting its orbits and vectors, tracking its progress, monitoring the heartbeats of the astronauts and the consumption of fuel, and doing all these in an infinitesimal fraction of the time it would take human beings to work out the problems. Without computers there would have been no moon walk, but the price paid for their service is that every question "fed" to them, every problem they solve, every pattern they work out has to be reduced to "bits." As a result this particular reductive structure of "thought" informs all the activities of NASA, the language of men as well as its technical procedures. And so NASA and the astronauts think of things as yes or not yes, presence or absence, fear or no fear, go or no go, success or no success, true or not true. Computerese does not work in terms of the old romantic dualisms such as good *and* evil, or true *and* false, where the second term has an existence in its own right, but in terms of one *or* zero, the presence of a thing or its not presence, like Orwell's "Newspeak" in *1984*, or like the orthodox but little-believed Christian theology which tried to eliminate evil by making it merely the absence of good. For Aquarius this radical monism of the computer makes it "some species of higher tapeworm ... quietly ingesting the vitals of God." (352) As it is applied to more and more situations "to simulate what had hitherto been out of the range of simulation," it solves "problems whose outer margins would be lost as the center was sucked into the binary system." (355)

The binary language of the computer is at the heart of NASA and by its simplification of everything to presence or absence makes finally possible the achievement of the ultimate "world-vaulting ... assumption that sooner or later everything would be understood—'I paid a trip to death, and death is a pleasant place and ready for us to come in and renovate it.'" (108-109) Computerese eliminates misunderstanding and mystery to create a universe that is "no majestic mansion of architectonics out there between evil and nobility, or strife on a darkling plain, but rather an ultimately benign field of investigation...." (109) Beauty in this world is merely "system perfection," and truth only the possession and structuring of clear, uncontroversial data.

But as the contradictions disappear, so does what Aquarius calls "firm sense of magnitudes," (302) by which he means the architectonics of the romantic world, the existence of many things in relationship to other things by virtue of their firmly established uniqueness. It is just this firm sense of magnitudes that the country as a whole lacks—"the American disease: Focus on one problem to the exclusion of every other" (386)—and which is personified by the astronauts who "like narcissists, like children, like old people, ... all exhibited a single-minded emphasis on each detail which arrived before them, large or small." (273) In the empty space in which they journey, all orders of human magnitude disappear, and on the moon as the astronauts see it through the eyes of technology there is no sense of scale, and therefore no differences, for a crater may be as large as New York or as small as a house. Everything blurs into a sameness which, according to Aquarius, Cézanne, followed by Picasso and Cubism, prefigured when he abandoned the traditional emphasis on particular surfaces, "the sheen and texture, the hairs, the dust, the flickering motes of light on the surface of a drape," (300) for a vision in which "the similarities between surfaces [are] now more profound than the differences." (301)

An organization so internally consistent and coherent as NASA has no teleology and needs none. It is in a condition of homeostasis, runs in order to run, is entirely self-sufficient; therefore so long as it continues to function—and who will raise troublesome questions about it internally?—it really needs no purpose outside itself. To go to the moon, yes, but why? Collins, the most perceptive of the astronauts, realizes that something is lacking, "It's been one of the failings of the Space Program ... that we have been unable to delineate clearly all the reasons why we should go to the moon." (341) But Armstrong when pressed with the question of why all this expense and effort can only come up with the flat, canned cliché used a thousand times to explain activities that have no purpose outside themselves: "I think we're going to the moon because it's in the nature of the human being to face challenges." (42) And to other questions outside the system defined by computerese—"What will you do if you find the moon inhabited?" or "Will landing on the moon create any psychic disturbances on earth?"—NASA can only respond with a polite shrug of incomprehension.

Aquarius perceives that there is something pointless, tautological, about the entire venture, "a meaningless journey to a dead arena in order that men could engage in the irrational activity of designing machines which would give birth to other machines which would travel to meaningless places...." (152) Perhaps the best image of this monolithic quality, this enclosed system which reduces the world to itself and then blankly ignores whatever remains outside, giving off no odors of vitality, no hints of meaning, is a painting by Magritte, which Aquarius sees in a house in Houston, "a startling image of a room with an immense rock situated in the center of the floor ... it was as if Magritte had listened to the ending of one world with its comfortable chairs in the parlor, and heard the intrusion of a new world, silent as the windowless stone which grew in the room, and knowing not quite what he had painted, had painted his warning nonetheless." (133-34) Solidly there, immensely powerful, impervious, self-contained, the rock gives visible form to what Aquarius had earlier felt, "The horror of the Twentieth Century was the size of each new event, and the paucity of its reverberation." (34) As more and more happens and events get bigger and bigger, wars, mass murders, famines, GNP, speed, they come somehow to mean less and less, to simply be, like the trip to the moon of Apollo 11.

Of a Fire on the Moon quite obviously presents science in the images of NASA and Apollo 11 in a hostile fashion, but the undeniable power of technology, its perfect confidence, the ability of its system to manage events and bring them to the desired end give it a solid and impressive reality. It is there, it is real, and somehow the literary artist like Mailer must deal with *it*, not the other way round. His commission from *Esquire* magazine is simply to write a lively but factual description of the moon landing, and Mailer fulfills his contract, managing at the same time to criticize the venture very sharply for its banality and lack of what he as a good romantic would call meaning. Werner von Braun, the genius of the rockets that powered the space program, may describe the landing of two men on the moon on July 20th, 1969, as "equal in importance to that moment in evolution when aquatic life came crawling up on the land" (72-73), but for Norman Mailer writing about and trying to comprehend the event, "something was lacking, some joy, some outrageous sense of adventure."

> Strong men did not weep in the streets nor ladies copulate with strangers.... It was as if on the largest stage ever created, before an audience of half the earth, a man of modest appearance would walk to the center, smile tentatively at the footlights, and read a page from a data card. The audience would groan and Beckett and Warhol give their sweet smiles. (385-86)

But Mailer is not content with merely analyzing the reasons why the moon shot was so disappointing to him and to millions of viewers of the event on TV. Instead, and this is what makes his book so remarkably interesting, he attempts to make literature out of the fact of science, to impose the romantic literary myth on the very "reality" which denies its efficacy and truth. The center of *Fire on the Moon* is a confrontation of the poet with science in a titanic struggle to restore "magic, psyche, and the spirits of the underworld to the spookiest venture in history, a landing on the moon, an event whose technologese had been so complete that the word 'spook' probably did not appear in twenty million words of NASA prose." (131) In the most obvious terms, Mailer's immediate problem is to lift the book "like a boulder out of the mud of the mind," (470) by making the moon shot, as we would say, "interesting," in the face of its resolutely mechanical quality, its lack of mystery, its elimination of danger, its determination not to allow personality to intrude, in short, its objectivity. This difficult problem is approached by facing it squarely and making the real plot of the book the struggle of the poet to humanize, and thereby make interesting, the stone of the fact itself, to sieve "the transcript for lunar gold." (314) The task is, however, a Herculean one, for events had, Mailer realizes, developed "a style and structure which made them almost impossible to write about." (88)

In the pursuit of his task, Mailer is, it is important to note, severely handicapped from the beginning by his inability to transform the fact of the moon shot into the fiction of literature. Fictionality has long been the most prominent, perhaps the defining, characteristic of literature—"the poet nothing affirmeth and therefore never lieth," as Sidney puts it—and the poets have paradoxically maintained that though their fictions mirror the world obliquely, they reveal it more truly than do other more literal modes of description. The defenses of fiction range all the way from Aristotle's preference for poetry's probable over history's actual, or Boccaccio's explanation that fictions are necessary covers of sacred truths which prevent them from becoming known to the vulgar, to the modern view, dramatized most effectively by writers like Borges and Nabokov, that *all* views of the world are fictional orderings of events which in themselves have no absolute meaning or form, and that therefore the creation of fictions in literature openly reveals the essential process by which men make the world. However its truth has been justified—and the ways are many—fiction has remained not only the primary method of the artist but the expression of his belief that the poetic imagination can create a truer world than that of muddy fact. But where less troubled romantic writers, like Jules Verne and later writers of science fiction, simply imagine voyages to the moon, filling the bleakness of space with color and animating it with humanoids, Mailer's imaginative vision is blocked by the unavoidable fact of NASA, which prevents him from making up his own fictional world and denies the validity of his other literary techniques. "The world," he realizes, "*had* changed, even as he had thought to be pushing and shoving on it with *his* mighty ego. And it had changed in ways he did not recognize, had never anticipated, and could possibly not comprehend now. The change was mightier than he had counted on." (55) This overwhelming factuality saps the confidence of the poet who faces the encounter with NASA, the Armageddon of poetry. He is aware of and frankly talks about both the tremendous power of his antagonist and of his own consequent disorientation and lack of secure belief in his heartfelt artistic values: "he no longer had the remotest idea of what he knew.... He was adrift." (141) His mind is "a pit of wrenched habits and questions which slid like snakes," and with uncertainty and confusion comes a frequent loss of confidence in the ability to write—"It was a terror to write if one wished to speak of important matters and did not know if one was qualified." (435) Old, fat, tired, depressed, at times he accepts the final triumph of science over poetry, "the heroes of the times were technologists, not poets, and the art was obliged to be in the exceptional engineering, while human communication had become the routine function." (151) This artistic weakness in the face of fact had already been evident in Mailer's earlier work, where his artist-heroes regularly fail, and his own writing had already yielded to the "real" world in that he had abandoned fiction—that mark of confidence in the writer's ability to create reality out of his own imagination—and turned to the writing of "novels of fact" in which the events are supplied by the objective world but interpreted, i.e., given meaning, by the methods and subjectivity of the artist.

This invasion of the "real" into art continues in *Fire on the Moon*, where Mailer is prevented by the overwhelming scientific facts from writing fiction, and his narrative is swallowed up entirely by fact in numerous places where he simply gives in and reprints PR handouts and verbatim transcripts of long radio conversations between the astronauts and their Houston base. But elsewhere in *Fire on the Moon*, though denied the freedom of fiction by a reality grown too real to permit it, Mailer tries to transform scientific fact into literature by imposing upon it the romantic myth, using the rhetorical strategies which instrument and embody the values of the myth.

He begins, in good romantic fashion, by putting an artist into the scene, himself in the persona of the writer Aquarius—a name with the associations of astrological magic and life-giving wetness in a dry land. *Of a Fire on the Moon* begins with a lament for the suicide of Hemingway, "the greatest living romantic," (4) who while he was alive had made it still possible to believe that fear could be kept at bay by courage and style. But Aquarius-Mailer's romantic affinities extend far beyond Hemingway, for the poetic persona Mailer creates to dramatize himself and his views in the confrontation with science derives primarily from the entire radical wing of romanticism, the energetic, tough, revolutionary line that leads from Blake and Byron, for all their differences, through such poets as Rimbaud to Sartre and Genet. Like an existentialist hero, he has without motive stabbed his wife at a party. He is a strutting, swaggering macho lover, a brawler and a drinker. He admires blacks, ethnicity, athletes, charismatic figures, the poor, but has no interest in rich and powerful but dull people, the managers, the bureaucrats, the pious, the middle-class. His politics are leftish—he has run for mayor of New York and lost badly—but although his instincts take him in this direction they do so not so much because he has any theoretical political-philosophic leanings as because it is on the left that he finds those romantic values he prizes above all else, energy, generosity, strong emotions, action, a desire for change, a sense of deeply felt engagement with the world, some suffering at its hands, and the consequent awe of its unpredictable powers.

Aquarius is a very old-fashioned, very standard romantic poet: "his philosophical world" is a place ultimately of mystery and uncertainty, built "on the firm conviction that nothing was finally knowable." (7) Although trained as an engineer, he is intensely suspicious of reason and science as ways of dealing with his enigmatic universe, and his distrust of machinery and scientific ways of knowing descends directly from such writers as Carlyle and Arnold. "He has little to do with the immediate spirit of the time," (4) and trusts instead, in a Keatsian manner, to his senses, particularly to his sense of smell, to put him in communication with the real and vital nature of things, to tell him where life is present and where it is not. In characteristic romantic fashion, the senses in turn lead him to feeling the identity of things and their ultimate relationship in some great unified whole. But despite his close association with the poets of the romantic tradition, Aquarius is at the end of that heroic line of great imaginers, and his own reality, actually the reality of Norman Mailer, weighs as heavily upon him as the reality of science presses down upon his imagination. Forty-six years old, overweight, with his fourth marriage breaking up, subject to fits of deep depression, uncertain of his own powers, witty, vulgar, self-conscious enough to be able to laugh at his own egocentricism, baffled by his world but still feeling it deeply, envious that *he* is not the center of the moon adventure, he is partly Childe Harold and partly Sancho Panza. His sweaty clumsy appearance in the same scenes with the cool, effortless efficiency of the astronauts and engineers immediately enlarges the world of NASA enormously and complicates it with the presence of something familiarly human, with an individual "I," to oppose the collective "we" of NASA. With his appearance on the scene all the complexities and the poetic beliefs he embodies become real, and what was monolithically one immediately becomes differentially two. A rudimentary plot that can confer poetic meaning on events then becomes possible: a struggle between Aquarius and NASA, poetry and science, good and evil.

As the book proceeds, the human context is constantly expanded as the poet's art populates the NASA world with the ghosts of the old Indians who once walked the land where the rockets are now launched, with the memory of older adventurers—Odysseus, Columbus, Magellan—with the faces of poor blacks representing all mankind deeply etched by life:

> the faces of saints and ogres, of emaciated angels and black demons, martyrs, philosophers, mummies and misers, children with the eyes of old vaudeville stars, children with faces like midgets and witches, children with eyes which held the suffering of the lamb. But they were all faces which had gone through some rite of passage, some purification of their good, some definition of their remaining evil. (93)

No scene in *Fire on the Moon* is more powerful, more deeply rooted in the human stuff of life, than the description of the people who gather to watch the great Saturn rocket of Apollo 11 fired at Cape Canaveral. The cars they drive, the cheap whisky they drink, the fears of losing their jobs, the despair, the sexaul urgencies, the hero worship, the deep antagonisms between husband and wife, the play of the children, all surround the launch with a Breughel-like fullness of life, culminating in the most earthbound of images: "Out a car window projected the sole of a dirty foot. The big toe pointed straight up to Heaven in parallel to Saturn V." (63)

It is not only people who make up the fullness of the poetic world Aquarius creates, but things as well, rendered in all their variety and their specificity, in contrast to the abstractions of science. Aquarius furnishes the void of every NASA scene with careful description of objects, the canteens, the food-serving machines that don't work, the red tiles, the broken-down dusty bus, the plastic webbing of the chairs, the round bed and floor-level bath of the luxury motel, the bleakness of the Venetian blinds, the color and quality of the land, the trees, and the sun rising and setting over the sea. All of this is partly the descriptive realism of a careful craftsman, but it ultimately functions in the book to create the solidity and reality, the sensuous plenum, of a cluttered landscape that gives the feel of the real world as human senses know it.

Aquarius' copious style is a typically romantic response to the monolithic quality of the event. His flood of words, his willingness to follow up every detail and raise every possibility of meaning, his relentless naming of parts and exploration of technological matters, his constant analysis of his own thoughts and feelings, his evocation of a vast world, past and present, around NASA, all are a frantic, at times excessive, verbal effort to give the landing on the moon some meaning, to break its self-contained isolation and pierce its stony sameness. But the copious style also suggests Aquarius' lack of certainty about his ability to deal with NASA—it is as if all the words in the world would somehow never be enough to humanize the technological fact by surrounding it with the variety and plenitude of the world and thus giving it the desired romantic magnitude.

These large-scale attempts to find meaning in, or force meaning on, NASA are backed up by the constant use of a variety of typically romantic rhetorical devices which work on a smaller scale, but at higher frequency, to achieve the same end. "To regard the world once again as poets," says Aquarius, we must "behold it as savages who knew that if the universe was a lock, its key was metaphor rather than measure." (471) Metaphor, the central trope of romantic poetics, is employed steadily and with great skill by Aquarius, who is nothing less than a genius at finding the striking and the telling comparison which brings objects to life in a sudden flash. His

metaphors, various and numerous as they are, all tend to perform the same
task: to translate the mechanical world of technology into immediately
human terms, and to bind the abstract world of science into a larger
continuum with the existential world of men. The Saturn rocket at takeoff
consumes as much oxygen as half-a-billion people, a sixth of the world's
population, drawing breath at once; "physics was love and engineering was
marriage" (178); the procedures of science resemble efforts to bring together
a couple compatible except that the husband has a body odor repugnant to
the wife; the safety precautions in the space vehicle are designed on a
principle like the 613 laws of the Talmud; the astronauts on the moon walk
with "about as much coordination as a two-year-old in three sets of diapers."
(387)

    If metaphor creates or discovers meaning by reassembling those
isolated things which belong together in the romantic world view, ultimately
building the world into a great whole, then the symbol, that other primary
romantic trope, intensifies the power of a chosen object until it radiates the
meaning it contains or loses its opacity and focuses a world of meaning lying
behind it. The computer, the machine, and the rock are transformed from
things into symbols which reveal to Aquarius the nature of NASA; an old car
buried at the end of the book—about which more later—manifests the
condition of modern industrialism; and the rocket itself reveals the phallic
worship of the technological society. Like other romantics, Aquarius assumes
that objects "are shaped in a way which offers meaning, not only scientific
meaning, but existential meaning," (302) and he follows the painters in
believing that "form is a language which seeks to express itself by every
means." (292) He looks carefully at every object, like some "medieval
alchemist rubbing at a magic stone whose unfelt vibration might yet speak a
sweet song to his nerve," (293) hoping that the arrangement of its parts will
speak to him of its nature and its history in miraculous language. He
speculates that even "the face of the moon might be a self-portrait which
looked to delineate the meanings of its experience in that long marriage with
the earth and its long uninsulated exposure to the solar system and the stars."
(292) There is very little that is not made a symbol by the romantic Aquarius,
and his ability to turn objects into symbols by focusing language on them
until meaning flares out is one of his major techniques for attempting to
enlarge the world of scientific fact.

    Working in this fashion, Aquarius surrounds the rock of NASA with an
extensive context, verbal, human, cultural, and historical, and by bringing it
into opposition with the poet puts it into the movement of a rudimentary
plot. But the monolith itself remains as yet intact, and to extend and

demonstrate the truth of his romantic view of things, Aquarius must somehow split it, break into its center. To do so he must probe until he finds within NASA the conflicts, paradoxes, ambiguities, and mysteries which the romantic mind considers essential to reality. But these are the same qualities NASA has eliminated; like the machine its parts all work toward the same end and its components are interchangeable; co-operation not conflict is its guiding principle; and it moves toward the achievement of clarity and certainty in the place of mystery and ambiguity. So tight is its organization and so coherent are its theories that it is nearly impenetrable, but Aquarius believes that he can split the monolith if he can find the slightest aperture for his imagination to enter in: "where there is a little magic, there can be a mighty magic." (163) He notes that the maiden name of one of the astronauts' mothers was "Moon," hoping that it may indicate some astrological influence; he eagerly seizes on each malfunction of the machinery as an indication of mysterious non-scientific forces at work; he expands on the possibilities of fate manifesting itself in the lightning which strikes an oak in Collin's yard on the night before the launch; he extensively pursues the possibilities of visionary foreknowledge in a dream that Armstrong had when he was young of holding his breath and being able to hover motionless above the earth; he tries to relate the apocalyptic figure Apollyon in *Revelations* to Apollo 11, even though logic tells him that the names are etymologically unrelated. By continuing to probe and lever in a thousand little ways, he keeps opening the cracks wider and wider until he finds contradictory elements within NASA, ghosts in the machines, unconscious forces at work deep in the minds of the astronauts beneath their bland exteriors, apocalyptic tendencies in the emotionless efficiencies of science, and a metaphysical message in the smell of the dry dust of the moon. Using "every effort ... to find an edge of the sinister in this first expedition to the peculiar soil of the moon," (409) Aquarius ultimately locates a mystery concealed behind all the confidently reductive terms of science: what is electricity finally? or magnetism? or gravity? We know how to make these forces work, but their ultimate nature remains an enigma. Huge answerless questions are thus raised to cast their shadows over NASA's clarity.

The deep powers of the mind posited by romanticism as the source of true knowledge, the imagination, the collective unconscious, the Dionysiac, the id, "the mansions, theaters, and dungeons of the deepest unconscious where knowledge of a more poetic and dread-filled nature may reside," (156) have been a fortress of literature long after science and rationalism conquered the surface of the daylight world. Psychology therefore inevitably becomes one of Aquarius' most powerful methods for opening up the depths of NASA and discovering concealed mysteries and latent conflicts. By investigating their dreams and looking deep into all the peculiarities of their personal lives, he hopes to discover "how much at odds might be the extremes of [the astronauts'] personality. From their conscious mind to their unconscious depth, what a spectrum could be covered!" (46) Aquarius is very much a Freudian, and wherever he locates or creates a psychology, he assumes that it will have unconscious energies which will be individualistic, willful, freedom-seeking, and in conflict with the controls exerted by the reality principle. He tries therefore by means of hints and guesses to endow every person he meets in NASA with a psychology, a mind internally at war, and in one of his most desperate efforts to psychologize the world even tries to demonstrate a psychology of machines, "for if machines have psychology, then technology is not quits with magic." (161) By demonstrating the uncertainties of science about how its apparatus ultimately works, and by showing that even the simplest machines are not always predictable, Aquarius is able to animate the machines and find "some all but undetectable horizon between twilight and evening where [the machine] is free to express itself, free to act in contradiction to its logic and its gears, free to jump out of the track of cause and effect." (162)

Aquarius does not, however, try to impose his desired meaning on the moon shot merely by revealing the possibilities of latent conflicts and mysteries which the scientific myth ignores. To achieve his goal of making literature out of the science which denies its validity, he must put NASA into some great dialectical struggle, some romantic plot which moves it toward an end that will explain the mystery of existence and tie it to the order of the universe. NASA has, of course, its own plot derived from the linear logic of the computer: to go to the moon and return. But the inability of NASA and the astronauts to explain satisfactorily even to themselves just why they are going to the moon suggests the inadequacy of this plot, a lack of meaning felt by Aquarius and most of the people who looked at its climax on TV.

In the failure of the scientific plot, Aquarius finds his opportunity to impose on the event his own larger romantic plot. A sense of history, of the organic relationship of present things to the past and the development of the future from them, has always been central to the romantic consciousness, and Aquarius labors mightily to give the trip to the moon this kind of history. It is a very romantic history he constructs, a *Geistesgeschichte* of titanic forces involving the spirits of peoples and the struggle of mighty powers for the control of the universe. The frontier has at last disappeared in America, and now the people, half afraid and half eager, are ready for new adventures in space. The motive power driving the mission forward is twentieth-century corporate capitalism, and its *deus ex machina*, the German engineer Werner von Braun, is literally dropped into a meeting on the eve of the launch by a helicopter. After developing the German rockets fired at London in World War II, von Braun brought his crew of rocket experts to America and developed the big boosters which power the exploration of space. Aquarius plays with the idea that there is some meaning in the similarity of NASA and Nazi, but the *geist* that really creates NASA and shapes it in its own image is modern capitalism, "the marriage of huge profit with huge service, of teamwork ... and of detestation of contradiction." (183) In the Aquarian view of history, corporate capitalism has "run amuck" in the twentieth century, producing a flood of shoddy goods, spending its money on advertising rather than on crafting its products well, and in the process has wasted the earth, gagging "the bounty of nature" with "plastic wastes," polluting the atmosphere, and burdening the people with factory work death-heavy in its pettiness. But the corporations have lost their nerve, their own ideas having gone dead in triviality and in fear of what has been done, and now in the 1960's, a fierce reaction, of which Aquarius is a part, has taken the offensive: "for years, the forces of irrationality had been mounting into a protective war against the ravages of corporate rationality run amuck." (189) The voyage to the moon is a last effort by "corporate rationality" and the political system which mirrors and serves it: "to save itself [corporate capitalism] would commit the grand, stupendous, and irrational act (since no rational reasons of health, security, wisdom, prudence or profit could be given) of sending a ship with three men to the moon." (189)

This earthly history is only a part of a much greater war in heaven between good and evil which Aquarius imposes on the venture. He draws attention to his own Manichean inclinations early in the narrative, and throughout the book he poses the metaphysical question: "was our venture into space noble or insane, was it part of a search for the good, or the agent of diabolisms yet unglimpsed?" (140) "Man," he says, "was voyaging to the planets in order to look for God. Or was it to destroy Him?" (79) Whether God or Satan is at the helm of this new *Pequod* becomes for Aquarius the most crucial issue of his entire attempt to understand Apollo 11, but the question is never answered to his own satisfaction, though in the end, as we shall see, he asserts that in the long run the venture into space is on the side of good, even if those who create it do not know what they are doing and he cannot specify what the good will be.

Aquarius continues to insist throughout his book that this cosmic plot is his chief instrument for transforming "a conceptual city of technologese to one simplicity—was the venture worthwhile or unappeased in its evil?" (131)

But the cosmic plot never quite succeeds in actually becoming the plot of *Fire on the Moon*. It remains merely one of Aquarius' many attempts at sympathetic magic, and the actual plot emerges as a conflict between science and poetry, personified in NASA and Aquarius, for control of the book. If NASA wins, the book need not, cannot, be written at all, since the official version of the astronauts' journey to the moon will provide the needed record of the facts, or it can be merely a reprint of PR handouts and transcripts of communications between the astronauts and Houston base. If Aquarius wins, the book will be written and will transform the moon shot into the new Jerusalem of the poetic myth embodied in Blake's prophetic books, Shelley's *Prometheus Unbound*, or, at the least, Byron's *Don Juan*. No such poetic triumph takes place, and instead we get a fragmented, disordered narrative of a poet lacking any firm *a priori* grasp of events, trying confusedly to impose his romantic ways of understanding on events he cannot control. Baffled by NASA, he must use a process of blind and furious association, a seizing of any stray possibilities, "sifting of haystacks of technological fact for the gleam of a needle or a clue." (467) Going back again and again over the details of the flight and his own responses to it, like the detective to whom he frequently compares himself, he hopes that somehow with enough words and enough feeling he can write a book that will eventually animate the trip to the moon and make it shine with a light which sears the senses and satisfies the human desire for meaning to fill the void.

The hero-poet as underdog, the Miltonian single just man isolated from his fellows, doing battle with a fearsome enemy, is a standard romantic plot, *The Prelude* retold in modern terms. But the feelings of the inadequacy and failure of the poetic vision are far deeper in *Fire on the Moon* than in Wordsworth, and there is, as we shall see, a very real question of whether they are finally overcome. Nothing causes Aquarius-Mailer more distress and more doubt about his values than his allies in the great battle against corporate capitalism and its technology. At the end of his time as an observer of events in Houston and at Cape Canaveral, Aquarius returns to Provincetown to try to write his book. His friends, the artists and swingers of that intellectual community, have been drunk or stoned out of their minds all the summer during which NASA has taken the moon. As Aquarius looks at these late inheritors of the romantic tradition, though he loves them still, they disgust and frighten him:

> they had used their years, drinking, deep into grass and all the
> mind illuminants beyond the grass, princelings on the trail of hip,
> so avid to deliver the sexual revolution that they had virtually

strained on the lips of the great gate. They had roared at the blind imbecility of the Square, and his insulation from life, his furious petulant ignorance of the true tremor of kicks, but now it was as if the moon had flattened all of his people at once, for what was the product of their history but bombed-out brains, bellowings of obscenity like the turmoil of cattle, a vicious ingrowth of informers, police agents, militants, angel hippies, New Left totalists, entropies of vocabulary.... (440)

This is the counter-culture, the burnt-out ends of the romantic tradition in the summer of 1969. The poet feels betrayed on all sides by the course it has taken: the hippies, those "outrageously spoiled children who cooked with piss and vomit," Teddy Kennedy at Chappaquiddick, the Manson family, and Woodstock. What disturbs Aquarius most is the utter futility of all this "while the Wasps were quietly moving from command of the world to command of the moon," (440) and his sense of hopelessness is perfectly concentrated in a scene at the end of the summer when some radical-chic friends give a party at which a car is buried. An old wreck used for summer transportation has broken down, and now a hole is dug for it in the sand— the work done by a very technological bulldozer of course—and amid much drinking and laughing the car is pushed in backward so that it rests on its trunk. Sand is pushed around it, but the front end remains pointing upwards above the sand like some sad broken monument of technology. Passages from Vergil and the *Song of Songs* are intoned, the children animate it by painting ribs and belly on its underside in green luminescent paint, and a sculptor welds pieces of it into odd angles to transform it into a piece of statuary. It is a tribal ceremony, one of the rituals of sympathetic magic about which Aquarius has been reading all summer in *The Golden Bough*, and it is a recapitulation of what he has been trying to do with the voyage to the moon, the humanization of the machine by means of art expressing romantic values. But Aquarius knows that this is weak magic, which finally has no more effect on the world than an earlier Provincetown ritual with the same import in which the image of a vagina with fluttering lips is superimposed on the TV screen and the image of the face of Richard Nixon, the political manifestation of the technological society and the robot man, as he speaks in the political version of computerese about the journey to the moon. In this attempt to instrument the romantic dream, love, or at least sexuality, replaces politics, the living organ the machine; but in the end it is only an illusion, for the substitution doesn't hold in the real world. Technology has conquered the moon.

Fire on the Moon portrays the possible death of art, romantic art at least, its disappearance into fad and joke, as a result of its failure to control the world, to grasp reality and to shape it in the image of its own desires, to be, to put it most simply, any longer believable. Aquarius suspects that the end has come—"what if radio, technology, and the machine had smashed the most noble means of presenting the Vision [of the Lord] to the universe?" (469)—but he ends the book which has been so difficult to write on a small note of affirmation. He returns to Houston "looking for the smallest sign" and finds there "a true object, a rock from the moon," (470) the last appearance of the monolith he has been trying to breach. Through two layers of glass deep in the "plastic vaults" of NASA he *smells* the rock, "tender as the smell of cleanest hay ... like the subtle lift of love which comes up from the cradle of the newborn," (472) and this evidence of the senses tells him that some living thing is there, gives him his sign and "certitude enough to know he would write his book and in some part applaud the feat and honor the astronauts because the expedition to the moon was finally a venture which might help to disclose the nature of the Lord and the Lucifer who warred for us...." (471)

On the whole, this final note of affirmation is a noble effort, and characteristic of *A Fire on the Moon* in its hard-working, intense effort to come to grips with issues of fundamental importance, to assert despite doubts that art and the values it carries can still shape the world. But the scene in which the rock is made to give off smell seems contrived, imposed on a book whose only slightly concealed doubts about itself are sounded again in the words "might help to disclose." Throughout the book the large metaphysical schemes and meanings that Aquarius has sought to fasten on the voyage to the moon have not been asserted as fact but smuggled in as subjunctive possibilities or as questions. Events "*suggested* that it was in the nature of structures to address each other." (370) "*Was* the world more polluted" because a great novel had not been written? "The astronauts *could* even be men with a sense of mission so deep it was incommunicable even to themselves." (316) *Did* an ape sent into orbit "sicken and die because of some drear but most recognizable message its animal senses had received from space ...?" (421) "*Was* a curse building like the curse of the Pharaohs on the explorers who would open their tomb?" (174) Suspense is built by such means, but when almost every major statement of meaning, metaphysical, moral, psychological, is bracketed as only a possibility, such deep uncertainty is not overcome by the joyous proclamation of the smell of a moon rock, through two layers of glass.

It is not, of course, a question of NASA and the technological world it represents having some absolute claim on reality, of being themselves "real" in some absolute sense, while the poet is only a dreamer of what might be, some heroic wish-fulfiller. Mailer sees science and poetry as alternative world-views, myths, struggling for the human mind and the right to shape the world throughout the nineteenth and twentieth centuries. Science has at last almost triumphed because its machines are capable of delivering such awesome power. What the steam engine and the spinning jenny started, the great rockets and the computers finally achieve, the authority to organize society, to create a new language, and to define the individual as another machine, mechanical or electronic. The conquest of the moon is the supreme achievement of the technological society, and its power in the world reveals that the romantic conception of the world and of meaning, far from being inevitable human ways of thinking, however "natural" they may by now seem, are rather a particular set of values, one way among many of organizing the phenomena of the world into a myth which endows the parts with meaning. Literature, or art in general, is not, *Of a Fire on the Moon* reveals, some unchanging, immutable thing, some eternally privileged way of writing about reality whose authority is located in some perennial psychological power—genius, imagination, sensitivity—or in some especially true way of writing—fiction, plot, hero, character, organic form—or in some special form of language—verse, metaphor, symbol. It is rather the expression of a set of values, a humanistic way of looking at and under-standing the world, which has selected and stressed, made the essence of poetry, those ways of thinking and writing that, among all the many possibilities available, express its values and satisfy its needs: metaphor which binds diverse things together, fiction which creates new worlds from old, plots which bring the struggle of opposites to meaningful conclusions, heroes who express human individuality, symbols which contain infinity in a grain of sand, the sublime which reveals the mysterious wonder of the world, and organic form in which each thing speaks in its structure and development of its own essential nature. These ways of thinking and writing which constitute the romantic myth of literature exist, *Fire on the Moon* tells us in striking ways, in society where they must compete with other great systems of belief and their institutional organizations for power and continued existence.

HAROLD BLOOM

Norman in Egypt

"Crude thoughts and fierce forces are my state." With this artful sentence, Norman Mailer begins his Book of the Dead. Our most conspicuous literary energy has generated its weirdest text, a book that defies usual aesthetic standards, even as it is beyond any conventional idea of good and evil. Like James Merrill, with whom he has in common absolutely nothing else, Mailer finds one of his occult points of origin in the visionary Yeats, but unlike Merrill, Mailer truly shares Yeats's obsession with the world of the dead. Merrill's spirits, in *The Changing Light at Sandover*, are representations of our lives, here and now. But Mailer has gone back to the ancient evenings of the Egyptians in order to find the religious meaning of death, sex, and reincarnation, using an outrageous literalism, not metaphor. What the subscribers to the Literary Guild will find in it is more than enough bumbuggery and humbuggery to give them their money's worth.

But there is also spiritual power in Mailer's fantasy (it is not the historical novel that it masks itself as being) and there is a relevance to current reality in America that actually surpasses that of Mailer's largest previous achievement, *The Executioner's Song*. More than before, Mailer's fantasies, now brutal and unpleasant, catch the precise accents of psychic realities within and between us. *Ancient Evenings* rivals *Gravity's Rainbow* as an exercise in what has to be called a monumental sado-anarchism, and one

From *The New York Review of Books* 30, no. 7 (April 28, 1983): 3-5. © 1983 by NYREV, Inc.

aspect of Mailer's phantasmagoria may be its need to challenge Pynchon precisely where he is strongest. Paranoia, in both these American amalgams of Prometheus and Narcissus, becomes a climate.

Ancient Evenings goes on for seven hundred large pages, yet gives every sign of truncation, as though its present form were merely its despair of finding its proper shape. The book could be half again as long, but no reader will wish it so. Thomas Mann proudly remarked of *his* Egyptian novel, *Joseph and His Brothers*, that "as the son of a tradesman I have a fundamental faith in quality.... The song of Joseph is good, solid work." Mann gave his life to the book for sixteen years, and its quality is durable. Mailer has given *Ancient Evenings* a decade, and it is wild, speculative work, but hard work nevertheless. Its quality is not durable, and perhaps does not attempt to be. Mailer is desperately trying to save our souls as D.H. Lawrence tried to do in *The Plumed Serpent* or even as Melville did in *Pierre*. An attentive reader ought to bring a respectful wariness to such fictions for they cannot be accepted or dismissed, even when they demand more of the reader than they can give. Mailer wishes to make his serious readers into religious vitalists, even as Lawrence sought to renew our original relationship both to the sun and to a visionary origin beyond the natural sun. Mailer's later works thus strain at the limits of art.

Mailer's readers will learn rather more ancient Egyptian mythology than they are likely to want or need, but the mythology is the book, and seems more than mythology to Mailer. Like his ancient Egyptian nobles, Mailer hunts, slays, roasts, and devours his gods, in order to increase his share in courage, sexual potency, immortality. I assume that a reading of *The Book of the Dead (The Papyrus of Ani)* first alerted Mailer to the Egyptian analogues to his own ongoing obsessions, but whether that is true or not, it is of some interest to look at the translation of the ancient text by E.A. Wallis Budge[1] alongside Mailer's nightmare of a book.

The Book of the Dead exists in many versions, some of which may go back thousands of years before the 190 covered in Mailer's book (1290-1100 BCE). But they tend to tell the same stories concerning the gods and the afterlife, stories that center upon the death, mutilation, and resurrection of the god Osiris. Even as Osiris triumphed over death, so the Egyptians hoped to emulate him, and indeed to achieve a virtual identity with that king of eternity, who in his resurrection had taken on aspects of Ra, the sun god. And even as Osiris had risen in his reassembled corporeal body, so the ancient Egyptians conceived that they would live again in more than the spirit. As resurrected gods, they would feast and love forever.

Unfortunately, the great hazards of passing through the various stages and places that lay between the tomb and heaven made this vision of resurrection difficult even for those handfuls of monarchs and great nobles who could afford properly monumental and well-stocked tombs. The *duad* or Land of the Dead swarmed with hideous monsters, and only a proper combination of magical preparation, courage, and plain good fortune was likely to get one through. This is essentially the given material that Mailer appropriates.

What Mailer adds are his own emphases upon scatology, buggery, and the war between women and men, but the fundamental material on the wavering border between the human and the divine, and on the world of the dead, is already there in Egyptian mythology for him to develop. His book's peculiar and disturbing sincerity is its strength. The reader is likely to be numbed by the repetition of charnel-house horrors, and even the most avid enthusiasts of buggery, whether heterosexual or homosexual, may flinch at confronting Mailer's narrative exuberance in heaping up sodomistic rapes, but the religious seriousness of all these representations is rather humorlessly unquestioned and unquestionable.

"Crude thoughts and fierce forces are my state" because Mailer's narrator is the Ka—or surviving double of a dead young nobleman—who had been named Menenhetet the Second. This unfortunate Ka takes us on a ghastly tour of the necropolis, where it encounters the Ka of the young man's great-grandfather, Menenhetet the First (henceforth I shall emulate Mailer in calling both these personages by their shortened name, Meni). Great-grandfather Meni is Mailer's central character, and has just died out of his fourth life, at a still monstrously vigorous sixty. We are at about 1100 BCE in an Egypt all too like the United States in the 1970s, but now we are hearing the song, not of the executioner, but of the magician.

Great-grandfather Meni, a devourer of bat dung, has mastered all the mysteries, including a rather lively one of Mailer's own invention (which rather peculiarly is attributed to Mosaic esotericism). In this occult performance, one becomes one's own father, by begetting one's own next incarnation upon a woman who thus in some sense already is one's mother. Meni the First selects his own granddaughter, Hathfertiti, for the honor, which in some other sense has to be regarded as very nearly one's dying act. But I don't intend to give an elaborate plot summary, since if you read *Ancient Evenings* for the story, you will hang yourself. There is a lot less story than any summary would indicate, because this is a book in which every conceivable outrage happens, and yet nothing happens, because at the end everything remains exactly the same.

There are only two characters who matter in the book, and they not inaccurately could be termed versions of Hemingway (I mean the novelist, not one of his characters) and of Mailer himself, the heroic precursor and his vitalistic follower and son. One is the great pharaoh Ramses the Second, victor over the Hittites at the battle of Kadesh, and the other is the three-times reincarnated magician Meni the First, who fought at Kadesh as the pharaoh's first charioteer.

Ramses the Second is a beautiful and potent male god, usually called Usermare, while the scarcely less potent Meni is condemned to be the perpetual worshipper of his pharaoh, a condemnation enacted by way of a ferociously divine bumbuggering of Meni the First by Ramses, which in true Maileresque terms sets up the dilemma that all Meni's magic will never resolve. To have been bumbuggered by one's precursor is a sublime new variant on the sorrows of literary influence, but evidently it does not inhibit the strong sons of strong fathers from bumbuggering the Muse, a delicious revenge carried out by the magician Meni upon the queen and goddess Nefertiti, prime wife of Ramses the Second.

Most of the magician's story is told by him to the reigning pharaoh, a descendant of the great Ramses, in the course of an endless night of banqueting, which together with the inserted lives of Meni the First consumes about five hundred of Mailer's seven hundred pages. There is an unsolved problem of form here, but that is minor compared to defects of texture, to hopelessly unresolved inconsistencies of tone and of badly mixed imagery. Mann found a style for Joseph in Egypt, but Mann's strength was irony and Mailer's strength is never ironic. There are some horribly grand set pieces, most notably the battle of Kadesh, but there are also immense stretches through which the poor reader must crawl with an unrewarded patience, including the entire "Book of Queens," which occupies 135 pages of harem intrigues. Nothing else Mailer has published is so hopelessly listless as the "Book of Queens," which might have been entitled. "The Prisoner of Sex Revisited, or The Radical Feminists' Revenge." In fairness to Mailer, I offer a single representative passage, honestly chosen at absolute random:

> Disloyalty stirred then in Menenhetet, and his breath became hushed as the water. He was ill with desire for the little queens. It was vivid as shame to be alone among so many women with not even a boy about older than ten, but then by that age, the children born here were off to the priests for schooling. All he heard were the voices of women who had no husband nor friend nor any lover but the Good and Great God Usermare. Worse.

About him were all the plump eunuchs with their black muscles enriched by the air of their easy life. Thereby they were appealing to all—the hundred women and Menenhetet—attractions powerful to his senses. His loins ached, his throat was gorged, and his mouth was so hungry he would not look through their windows at the beerhouse these little queens were making. In the dark, like the horse that hears a murderous beast in the rustle of a leaf, he started at each breeze. At this hour, there were eunuchs everywhere in the gardens, fondling one another with their fingers and their mouths, giggling like children, and the flesh of Menenhetet was inflamed.

But poor Meni's flesh is inflamed for pretty much all of these seven hundred pages, and ultimately the inflammation is the lust to be Usermare-Ramses, pharaoh and god, and so never to die except as a rapid transition between incarnations. The actual magical and physical process by which Meni begets a fresh incarnation is rather obscure. He must be able, "during an embrace, to ride his heart right over the last ridge and breathe his last thought as he passed into the womb of the woman and thereby could begin a new life, a true continuation of himself; his body died, but not the memory of his life." Whatever that gallop over the last ridge truly is, Meni the First still comes to a very bad end. Unlike Scheherazade, Meni finally runs out of stories, and is graciously allowed to cut his own throat with the pharaoh's own knife. Where has Mailer's fantasy of his magician brought us? On the Stevensian aesthetic principle that "It Must Change," Meni, once a general, can find his epitaph in Stevens:

> *Nothing had happened because nothing had changed.*
> *Yet the general was rubbish in the end.*

Why are we in Egypt? Where else could we be? Mailer's dialectics of sex and death have found their inevitable context, though the world of Usermare and Meni may not be wholly distinct from the world of Gary Gilmore. Pynchon and this newest Mailer are what Vico called "magic primitives," giant bards who try to deify themselves by the ancient praxis of divination, but Pynchon scatters himself even as he finally scatters his hero Slothrop in *Gravity's Rainbow* quite literally, by having him undergo a parody of the fate of Osiris, or as Yahweh scattered the builders of the Tower of Babel. Mailer, like his American ancestors from Poe through Hemingway, resists the scattering of his self and name. *Ancient Evenings* thus fulfills the critical prophecy of

Richard Poirier's book on Mailer (1972) which found in the emphasis upon buggery a dialectic by which meaning is both de-created and restituted. Poirier argued that it is almost as though in the Kabbalah of Norman Mailer, buggery constitutes the trope of the breaking of the vessels, as a negative creation that is a prime Gnostic image.

Mailer, as a fictive theologian, has been developing a private version of an American gnosis for some time now, in the sense that Gnosticism can be a doctrine insisting upon a divine spark in each adept that cannot die because it never was any part of the creation anyway. Such a doctrine resigns history and mere nature to the demons or bad angels, and identifies what is immortal in the self with the original abyss, from which the Yahweh of Genesis stole in order to form his bad creation. Libertine and antinomian, since it identifies the law of the Torah with a catastrophic creation, such a faith is the antithesis both of normative Judaism and of orthodox Christianity. In Jewish Gnosticism or Kabbalah, the catastrophe that ruins creation is imaged as the breaking of the vessels, the shells of the cosmos and the body that becomes riddled with divine light. Consciously or not, Mailer has substituted buggery for the breaking of the vessels.

Buggery even as a word has Gnostic origins, alluding as it does to the Bogomils or Bulgar Manichaeans. As a metaphysician of the belly (self-titled), Mailer had some earlier inclination toward regarding buggery as an antinomian act—a transgression of all the rules of a deeply false order that would reveal a higher truth (see the buggering of Ruta, the German maid, in *An American Dream* and "The Time of Her Time"). In *Ancient Evenings* he has emancipated himself, and seems to be verging upon a new metaphysic, in which heterosexual buggery might be the true norm (as it may have seemed to the Lawrence of *Lady Chatterley's Lover*), and more conventional intercourse perhaps is to be reserved for the occult operation of reincarnating oneself in the womb of the beloved. Here we may recall an analysis of the Marquis de Sade that was carried out by Horkheimer and Adorno in their chapter on *Juliette* in *The Dialectic of the Enlightenment*, in which they observed that the harangues of the Sadean heroes marked a final perfection in the rationality of the Enlightenment. Yet this seems more appropriate to the sado-anarchism of Pynchon's paranoid rationalists than to the Egyptian mysteries of Mailer-Meni, who has striven so mightily to wrench himself away from post-Enlightenment reality.

Mailer's is too formidable a case of an authentic literary drive to be dismissed, and dismissal is certainly not my intention. *Ancient Evenings* is on the road of excess, and what Karl Kraus said of the theories of Freud may hold for the speculations of Mailer also—it may be that only the craziest parts are true. Mailer probably is aware that his Egyptian obsessions are in the main tradition of American literature, carrying on from much of the imagery of the major writers of the American renaissance.

The definitive study here is John Irwin's *American Hieroglyphics: The Symbol of the Egyptian Hieroglyphics in the American Renaissance*.[2] Irwin centers on Poe, and in particular on *The Narrative of Arthur Gordon Pym*, but much that Irwin says about Melville's *Pierre* is as relevant to *Ancient Evenings* as is Irwin's brilliant commentary on *Pym*. Irwin argues that Emerson and those he stimulated—Thoreau and Whitman positively; Poe, Hawthorne, and Melville negatively—found in ancient Egypt a vision of resurrection through reincarnation or reappearance that they could oppose to the Hebraic vision of the resurrection of the body. Certainly the attitudes toward death of the Pharisees, and of mythological Egypt, could not be more antithetical than they were, and perhaps American writers inevitably prefer the Egyptian account of personal survival, as Yeats did also. Irwin, commenting on *Pym* and on *Pierre*, sees in the Egyptian resurrection a kind of Freudian displacement of the writer's body into the writer's book, of blood into ink. As the great Western version of the *Abendland*, nineteenth-and twentieth-century American literature perhaps takes on an almost Egyptian sublimity, an exaltation of cultural belatedness as the second chance of a literal life beyond death. Mailer's *Ancient Evenings* yet may seem a work in *Pierre's* sad class, if not quite that of *Pym's*, an American vision of final sunset.

I call the American literary vision of death "belated" in contrast to the ideas of death first in normative Judaism and then in early Christianity. Post-Biblical Judaism associated the salvation of each Jew with that of all Jewry, and the third century CE sage Rab said of the world to come that in it "there is no eating and drinking, no begetting of children, no bargaining, no jealousy and hatred, and no strife." This is akin to the quite Pharisaic reply of Jesus to the Sadducees that "when they rise from the dead they neither marry nor are married, but are like angels in heaven." Irwin, in his *American Hieroglyphics*, contrasts the Jewish and Christian versions of personal immortality to the Egyptian notion of personal survival:

> As the empty tomb and the vanished body evoke the Judeo-Christian concept of an immortal self that is independent enough of the body to have dispensed with even a bodily image, so the monumental pyramid and the mummified corpse express the Egyptian sense that the immortality of the personal self is constitutively linked to the preservation of such an image....

Irwin reads Poe's *Pym* and to a lesser extent Melville's *Pierre* and *Mardi* as a kind of Egyptian reversal of the Jewish and Christian understanding of death as God's revenge for our original sin against the Father. Like Poe and Melville, Pynchon and the Mailer of *Ancient Evenings* participate in this reversal which, as Irwin says, "refers not to death as revenge, but to a revenge against death, the revenge that man attempts to take, through art, against time, change, and mortality, against the things that threaten to obliterate all trace of his individual existence." Thus Melville said of his Pierre's Maileresque attempt to write a book of "unfathomable cravings" that: "He is learning how to live, by rehearsing the part of death."

Mailer too wishes us to learn how to live, in an America where he sees our bodies and spirits as becoming increasingly artificial, even "plastic" as he has often remarked. If our current realities, corporeal and psychic, manifest only lost connections, then Mailer's swarming, sex-and-death-ridden ancient Egyptian evenings are intended at once to mirror our desperation, and to contrast our evasions with the Egyptian rehearsal of the part of death. Myself, I vote neither for the sage Rab nor for the vitalistic magus Mailer, but I acknowledge the strength of his crude forces and fierce thoughts.

Mailer concludes his book with an enigmatic rhapsody, in which the Ka or double of Meni the First expires, and the power of the dying heart enters the Ka of Meni the Second. That combined Ka sails toward rebirth, while Mailer-Meni declares somberly: "I do not know if I will labor in greed forever among the demonic or serve some noble purpose I cannot name." That may be a touch grandiose, but it is thoroughly American, and perfectly Gnostic also in its aspiration to join itself to an alien God. Mailer, until now, has seemed to lack invention, and so after all to resemble Dreiser more than Hemingway, a judgment that *The Executioner's Song*, an undoubted achievement, would sustain. *Ancient Evenings* is an achievement of a more mixed kind but it is also an extravagant invention, another warning that Mailer is at home on Emerson's stairway of surprise.

NOTES

1. *The Egyptian Book of the Dead: The Papyrus of Ani in the British Museum* (Dover, 1967).
2. Yale University Press, 1980.

RICHARD POIRIER

In Pyramid and Palace

Until its final revision, *Ancient Evenings* carried the subtitle "The Egyptian Novel". It was a helpful hint that what was to follow was meant to be quite unlike the so-called "American novel" or the English, French, German or Russian novel. *Ancient Evenings* is indeed the strangest of Norman Mailer's books, and its oddity does not in any important way have to do either with its Egyptian setting or with the exotic career—exotic even by ancient Egyptian standards—of Menenhetet, its protagonist-narrator whose four lives, including three reincarnations, span 180 years (1290 to 1100 BC) of the nineteenth and twentieth dynasties (1320 to 1121 BC). What is remarkable here is the degree to which Mailer has naturalized himself as an ancient Egyptian, so that he writes as if saturated with the mentality and the governing assumptions, some of which he revises rather freely, of a culture in which the idea of the human is markedly different from what it has been in the West for the last 1,500 years or so. Mailer has never before tried anything so perilous, and the prodigious demands he makes on the reader are a clue to his ambitions. This is at once his most accomplished and his most problematic work.

Of the twenty-three books Mailer has written so far, only *Ancient Evenings* achieves the magnitude which can give a retrospective order and enhancement to everything else. Up to now it has been possible to think of

From *The Times Literary Supplement* 184, no. 4 (June 10, 1983): 591-92. © 1983 by Times Newspapers Limited.

him as perhaps a great writer, but one who had yet to write his major book. Many commentators have mistakenly credited him here, and in his last novel *The Executioner's Song*, with a new degree of self-effacement. Looking back from the new book one can see even more clearly than before that the central condition of nearly all his writing depends not on some prior sense of self, the famous Mailer ego, but rather on self-fragmentation and dispersal. Even when, as is so often the case, Mailer is his own subject, he cannot be said to exist simply in the narrative that tells his story, but is to be found instead within a larger, expressive structure of which his voice is only one part looking for other parts. Just as it radically reduces his literary, let alone his personal identity, to assume that the voice in *Armies of the Night* refers us directly to the "real" Mailer, so it is equally mistaken to assume that because that voice is absent from *Ancient Evenings* he has thereby and suddenly become invisible.

Quite the reverse. The book comes into focus only when we are able to recognize the complicated way in which it is the most self-revealing of his works. Menenhetet, for example, carries out the implications of Mailer's more directly autobiographical writings because even as he tells stories about himself he is by that very process trying to put himself together from several different, remembered versions. This is also the case when Mailer writes about a march on the Pentagon or a championship fight. He treats the earlier Mailer who participated in those events as if he were already a soul or a spirit. The Mailer of the later time not only records but contends with earlier versions of himself, until the work is a record of the abrasions out of which will emerge, or so he hopes, a form he can call himself or his work or his career. The form his narratives achieve is what has survived of "Mailer" from the past, but the achievement is conditioned by a recognition that some of the many selves who make up a single person have been sacrificed to the making of form. Any form, especially for a believer in karmic roots, creates a longing for some possibly larger and more inclusive one. "Karma tends to make more sense than a world conceived without it", he remarks in a recent interview, "because when you think of the incredible elaborations that go into any one human being, it does seem wasteful of the cosmos to send us out just once to learn all those things, and then molder forever in the weeds.... There is some sort of divine collaboration going on."

Books of sustained visionary ambition—and this is true even of *Paradise Lost* or *Moby-Dick*—are bound to have stretches of tiresome exposition, phrasings that are ludicrous, whole scenes that, as Johnson remarked, should have been not only difficult but impossible. *Ancient Evenings* has Honey-Ball's scenes of spellbinding in "The Book of Queens". Nearly anything can happen here, and does, and what is remarkable is not that the American reviewers found things to make fun of, but that the risks usually pay off: moments of subliminal ecstasy, visionary descriptions of royal personages, of pools at sunrise and gardens which bring on a kind of sexual swooning, of floatings down the Nile. Mailer seems more at home in the writing than in any of his books except for *Why Are We In Vietnam?* He luxuriates, sometimes to the limits of patience and beyond, in accounts of Egyptian low life, in the power put into play during a royal dinner party, in details of costume and what must have been at best a truly awful cuisine. Near the beginning Meni calmly tells us what it feels like, moment by moment, to be eviscerated and embalmed, and there are equally confident accounts of the practice of magic and of the wholly chaotic polytheism of the Eygptians.

Mailer has imagined a culture that gives formal, and not merely anthropological sanction to what in his other works often seems eccentric or plaintively metaphysical, like his obsessions with "psychic darts" and mind-reading, with immortality, with battles of the gods (Liston and Patterson, it now seems, were later versions of the Egyptian gods Horus and Set), with villainous homosexuality, with magic and sorcery, and with excrement as an encoding of psychic failure or success. Having so often written as if the self had several versions, he is completely at ease with Egyptian names for the seven spirits of the self that continue to exist in different degrees of intensity after death.

Two spirit-forms that figure importantly in this book are the Ka and the Khaibit. The Ka, for which the term Double is a useful but inadequate substitute, is born with a person to whom it belongs and bears his exact resemblance; even after death it is that part of a person that requires the food and drink left for it in the tomb. It also requires sensual gratification. Thus, the Ka of, say, a third incarnation could encounter the Ka of the first and have sexual commerce with him—which means with himself—just as could a Ka with his own Khaibit, or Memory. In fact, Meni, who died mysteriously at twenty or twenty-one and thinks that he may have been one of the reincarnations of Menenhetet, finds himself, soon after the novel begins, kneeling on the floor of the Pyramid of Khufu with the elder Menenhetet's member in his mouth, and while it is an abhorrent experience he realizes that he may be coping, as it were, with himself and that the unpleasantness is a kind of preparation for his passage from the Land of the Dead through the horrors of the Duad to either the upper or the lower world. It is possible to assume that the two forms remain fixed in this position—the time, we can with difficulty work out, is roughly 100 BC—while they visualize the immensely long night of story-telling, the Night of the Pig, when any truth can be told without the fear of retaliation, a millennium back at the palace of Rameses IX.

Whether at the palace or at the pyramid, the scene of the novel is a scene of telling, of narration, of recollection. At the palace, where the reader mostly finds himself, Menenhetet and Meni are more decorously positioned than they are in the pyramid. The elder is telling the stories of his lives to the Pharaoh, who hopes by listening and interrogation to become more closely identified with his great ancestor Rameses II, while the younger, his great-grandson then aged six, nestles between his mother, Hathfertiti (who is Menenhetet's granddaughter and, for many years, his lover) and the Pharaoh (whom little Meni, using his powers of clairvoyance, knows to be his real father) while his reputed father (Hathfertiti's brother as well as her husband and Overseer of the Cosmetic Box) sulks to one side before eventually absenting himself.

The novel does not yield to summary or to any clear sorting out of family trees, and depends instead on the blurring of distinctions between persons or between historical events and visionary ones. Divided into seven books, possibly in obedience to the seven spirits or lights of the dead, it begins with the awakening of a Ka: "Crude thoughts and fierce forces are my state. I do not know who I am. Nor what I was. I cannot hear a sound. Pain is near that will be like no pain felt before." Some central themes are immediately announced: birth and rebirth, mystifications of identity and of genealogy, elemental dread. Once it has slithered out of the pyramid, the Ka walks through the avenues of the Necropolis in a vague search for the tomb of a friend named Menenhetet II. He finds the tomb, after some suitably macabre incidents, in one of the cheaper neighbourhoods and gradually realizes that he is himself the Ka of Meni II and that next to his partly exposed and deteriorating remains are those of the renowned Menenhetet I, moved from its own much grander resting place by the spiteful Hathfertiti.

After getting acquainted and finding their way into the great Pyramid of Khufu, they begin their recollection, which is also their attempted recollection of themselves. Even at the outset, and with only two figures in question, the effort to distinguish between them takes us into a thicket. And that is where we are meant to be. We are meant to understand that multiple identities, identities that in their passage through time come to blend with one another, are common among the fantastic array of Egyptian gods and therefore among those humans for whom the gods are a paradigm of mortal existence. Any Egyptian of high birth, for example, can consider himself an Osiris, the greatest of the gods (but not always), and can find a pattern for his own past life, or anyone else's past life, in the pains and indignities that were visited upon Him. It is therefore appropriate that Meni, in his bewilderment about himself, should ask Menenhetet to tell the stories that make up the long second book, "The Book of the Gods". The story of Osiris, Isis, and of the bitter, buggery-ridden battles between their son Horus and his uncle Set is a phantasmagoric version of much that happens to Menenhetet as his story unfolds in subsequent books.

Menenhetet, born the son of a whore, has an innovative skill as a charioteer which brings him to the attention of the extraordinarily beautiful and imposing Rameses II or, as he is called, Unsermare. At his side, and assisted by the Pharaoh's pet lion, Hera-Ra, Menenhetet helps turn disaster into victory against the Hittites at the battle of Kadesh. But he is then held responsible for the death of Hera-Ra, who sickened from eating too many amputated Hittite hands, and is exiled for fifteen years as a supervisor of a remote gold mine in the desert. It is there that he learns from a dying friend that a man may be born again by dying during the consummation of sexual intercourse. Bribing his way back into the court of Unsermare, he becomes the commander of troops and then Governor of the Secluded—which means that he supervises the Pharaoh's "little queens" while being forbidden their sexual favours.

He breaks this interdiction with Honey-Ball in retaliation against Unsermare for having taken him by "both mouths" before Kadesh. And when Unsermare repeats this violation, this time in the company of some of the "little queens", Menenhetet is driven to the still more dangerous revenge of embarking on an affair with the most exalted of the queens, Nefertiri, who turns out to be one of Mailer's most engaging characterizations. Even as he is stabbed to death by the Crown Prince, he manages to leave within Nefertiri the seed of his first reincarnation. He thereby becomes his own father, though his and, above all, Nefertiri's parentage must be hidden from Unsermare, who is persuaded by Honey-Ball that he has begotten the child with her. And so it goes. The urgent, exploratory stories told by Menenhetet and the others are accompanied throughout by an attendant detail so exasperatingly complete as to suggest now and then that Mailer, like Pynchon, cannot resist displays of his encyclopedic researches—said to have included a total absorption of the Egyptian funerary literature called the Book of the Dead.

Mailer has convinced himself that the book must be dense if it is also to be authentic. Thus Meni needs to be told the intricate story of the gods, the Pharaoh needs to be told exhaustively about his ancestors, Menenhetet needs to rehearse his lives because each of them is convinced that only a person who can remember and explain his deeds when alive, or when he somehow partook of the life of another, can pass out of the Land of the Dead. And because of the endless mirroring of one life in another and in the lives of the gods, there is, for the anxious spirit, no limit to recollection, no ascertainable boundary.

While over the course of the seven books the various tales do manage to achieve some degree of narrative sequence and development—as they would have to do when all the characters are in search of some kind of teleology—each book also spirals out of and back into the scene of telling, and even that scene is set in a time when events have already become encrusted with centuries of re-telling and interpretation. No American reviewer of the novel has yet noticed the crucial admission by Menenhetet to Meni in the last chapter: that what might be called the Egyptian "gospels" in "The Book of the Gods" constitute an interpretation rather than an authentication of what they report. "If you think of the story of our Gods at the beginning of our travels, I will now confess that I imparted it to you in the way that these Romans and Greeks tell it to each other. That is why my tale was familiar yet different from what you know. For our Land of the Dead now belongs to them, and the Greeks think no more of it than a picture that is seen on the wall of a cave."

Ancient Evenings to some extent resembles Faulkner's *Absalom, Absalom!* or those novels of Conrad such as *Nostromo*, where, as Edward Said describes them, there is "evidence of a felt need to justify in some way the telling of a story". Faulkner and Conrad are more successful than Mailer in creating suspense and expectation within the stories, and among characters vividly differentiated; though *Ancient Evenings* is not lacking in suspense of this kind—it is there in the stunning account of the battle of Kadesh, or the intrigues between the rival Queens. Nefertiri and Rama-Nefru—the design of the book as a whole refers us finally to motives which are as vague as Mailer's or any novelist's motives for writing. Mailer offers none of the illusions so brilliantly sustained by Conrad, that there is something we want to know and that we will eventually know it, that a centre will be located in a wilderness of possibility, that the true shape of a person's life will emerge out of the mysteries that have shrouded it. The disaffection or impatience which many will feel with *Ancient Evenings* is likely to result from the fact that telling and listening have less to do with a desire to get somewhere (unless the reader is satisfied with being told that it has something to do with the saving of souls, and is meant to help Meni and Menenhetet pass through the Duad) but rather to get away from the loneliness, darkness, waste and dissolution which are, interestingly enough, the conditions Mailer has worried about since the mid-1950s as peculiar to the fate of the writer, especially the American writer, in the last half of this century.

It is in this context that one should consider his obsession with buggery. The obsession has in the past carried Mailer into a metaphysics of human biological creativity as a compensation for meaninglessness (the forty-six chromosomes in each cell of the body are, he tells us in *The Prisoner of Sex*, "a nest of hieroglyphics") and from there to a religion of artistic creativity (he had already observed in *The Armies of the Night* that these hieroglyphics are "so much like primitive writing"). Like the building of Hell in the nether regions by Milton's Satan, buggery for Mailer is a perverse response to God's invitation that we join him in the creation. For some centuries—long before Rojack in *An American Dream* refers to an evil girlfriend's backside as "der Teufel"—buggery has been associated with the Devil's terrain. In nearly all his work Mailer at some point contemplates the significance of a juxtaposition concisely described by Lawrence when in "Pornography and Obscenity" he observed that "The sex functions and the excrementary functions ... work so close together, yet they are, so to speak, so utterly different in direction. Sex is a creative flow, the excrementary flow is towards dissolution, decreation ...".

Though Menenhetet, like the Mailer of "The Metaphysics of the Belly" (*The Presidential Papers*), offers positive theories of scatology, the anus is mostly imagined as the site of evil. But there is also for Mailer a kind of art which is a trope for buggery. Writing about Genet he has referred to those aesthetic acts which "shift from the creation of meaning to the destruction of it", offering as further examples "the therapy of the surrealist artist, of Dada, of Beat". And he continues, speaking now of his own involvement in this dilemma: "jaded, deadened, severed from our roots, dulled in leaden rage, inhabiting the centre of illness of the age, it becomes more excruciating each year for us to perform the civilizing act of contributing to a collective meaning." *Ancient Evenings* represents such an attempt, haunted by failure, to discover "collective meaning", to create spiritual (and literary) genealogies that are as strong and mysterious as biological ones.

Questions of origin soon become, for Mailer, questions also about originality and authorship. It is impossible to claim either of these, so the book will tell us, without first accepting one's incalculable obligations to a marvellous but murky antecedence. Mailer's (and our) debts to the past, it is suggested, are enormous; they are also mysteriously entangled and untraceable. It is therefore a mistake to suggest, as some reviewers have done, that because Menenhetet is given "that look of character supported by triumph which comes to powerful men when they are sixty and still strong" he is meant to represent Mailer, or that he is Hemingway, Mailer's precursor. Mailer partakes both of Meni and Menenhetet, who at the end are transformed into yet another dual figure: a triumphant Icarus-Daedalus. In the final scene Menenhetet embraces and dissolves into the young man's Ka as it tries to escape the destructive force of "the abominable onslaught of offal" and to ascend the ladder of lights, knowing it will take not goodness to get to the top, but strength.

The joining has been made possible because Meni comes at last to accept all the stories he has been listening to, and, along with these, all the burdens of the past. "The tales he has told our Pharaoh, had been told for me as well. It was I whom he wanted to trust him." He cannot disown any of it because he cannot even know for sure that he did not somehow father himself or father his own father, whoever that might be, as did Ra in Egyptian mythology. Way back in the book we were told that "The God begets the God who will be his father. For the Gods live in the time that has passed, and time that is to come."

Genealogies confound one another to create a future that can call on the assembled strengths of Menenhetet, Meni, all the characters they have loved, the Egyptian gods, along with their latest manifestations in Christian mythology, and, not least, the now enriched figures of Mailer's earlier writings and earlier selves. The "I" in the last paragraphs is a composite of all these but it is also the creative spirit with whom Mailer associates himself in an apocalyptic vision that could anticipate either the coming of, in Yeats's phrase, "the fabulous, formless darkness" of Christianity, or the last phase of our own civilization:

A pain is coming that will be like no pain felt before. I hear the scream of earth exploding. In this terror, vast as the abyss, I still know more than fear. Here at the centre of pain is radiance. May my hope of heaven now prove equal to my ignorance of where I go. Whether I am the Second or the First Menenhetet, or the creature of our twice seven separate souls and lights, I would hardly declare, and so I do not know if I will labor in greed forever among the demonic or serve some noble purpose I cannot name. By this I am told that I must enter into the power of the word. For the first sound to come out of the will had to traverse the fundament of pain. So I cry out in the voice of the newly born at the mystery of my first breath, and enter the Boat of Ra.

This is, then, Mailer's "portrait of the artist as a young man", but it does not allow, as Joyce's does, for much distinction between that "artist" and the author of the book. If we are reminded of Joyce it is certainly not for the ironic reservations about Stephen implied in the last chapter of *A Portrait* and the first section of *Ulysses*, or even for the moment on the sea shore when Stephen imagines that "his soul had arisen from the grave of boyhood, spurning her graveclothes. Yes! Yes! Yes! He would create proudly out of the freedom and power of his soul, as the great artificer whose name he bore, a living thing, new and soaring and beautiful, impalpable, imperishable." This is a beautiful but forever embarrassing moment in the long history of the artist *exalté*, and Joyce meant to bring into question the prospects of anyone in the twentieth century who chooses to "enter into the power of the word". Mailer has always been frighteningly naive about this "power" and especially—as was revealed by his involvement with Jack Abbott—the privileges that should be accorded it, and he fully endorses Meni's grandiloquence. This is his most audacious book largely because behind it all is the desire, once and for all, to claim some ultimate spiritual and cultural status for the teller of stories, the Writer. Which is yet another ancient and perhaps pernicious story, though Mailer will always need to believe every word of it.

STACEY OLSTER

Norman Mailer After Forty Years

"I want to serve God," declares one of the players caught up in the intrigue of *Tough Guys Don't Dance*, Norman Mailer's most recent work of fiction. "What people don't comprehend is that if you want to serve, you have to grow balls big enough to take on His attributes" (149). The same might be said of the desire that has fueled Mailer's own career, if not from the publication of his first novel in 1948, then certainly since his first statements about the nature of God, Man, and the Devil appeared in *Advertisements for Myself* eleven years later. The recent surge of Mailer scholarship shows just how united critics have become in estimating the value of that 1959 "watershed book," as Mailer himself calls it (*Pontifications* 145), in which the duty of aiding an embattled God was presented as the doctrinal basis of Hip. Yet the divisions among critics as to the ethics of fulfilling such an intention attest to the continuing vexation that Mailer's ambition—or, depending upon the reader, arrogance—still inspires.

That the issue at hand is nothing short of ethical is clear from the passage in *Tough Guys*. When defined by Mailer's speaker to include "the heavy responsibility of exercising vengeance" (149), serving God means attributing to oneself a divine sanction in the allocation of judgment—a dangerous matter when the person who assumes such powers is morally compromised himself, in this case, a police chief who has chopped off the

From *Michigan Quarterly Review* 28, no. 3 (Summer 1989): 400-16. © 1989 by The University of Michigan.

head of a woman in his quest for moral arbitration. In contrast, Mailer's assumption of divine responsibility definitely involves less risk to others. Having early described the need of art "to intensify, even, if necessary, to exacerbate, the moral consciousness of people," and having proposed the novel as "the most moral of art forms" (*Advertisements* 343), Mailer restricts his deistic endeavors to what can fit between the covers of a book. At the same time, in expanding his purview within those intermediate pages to the creation of a personal world view, a personal cosmology that can be "better than a reality," his conception of his role is, in its own way, no less audacious than that which inspires Police Chief Regency. As Mailer says, "I mean there's something so beautiful about one mind being able to come up with a vision that's not Godlike but close enough to the Godlike to give us a vision of how marvelous the Lord's mind might be" (*Conversations* 260–61).

That vision is by now familiar to any reader of Mailer's work. God and the Devil are engaged in a war whose progress can be read over the course of human history. Because the outcome of that war is as yet undetermined, and because the God of Mailer's scenario is not the omnipotent being of Judeo-Christian religions, any person can influence the shape of the future by the kind of actions he chooses to perform. With each person given a task commensurate with his capacities, "one of us to create, another to be brave, a third to love, a fourth to work, a fifth to be bold, a sixth to be all of these" (*Presidential Papers* 159), readings can be taken from the degree to which people fulfill their promises. Even more idiosyncratically, with the phenomena of the natural world invested with both life-supplying and life-denying properties, any element acquires importance from the degree to which it advances or retards creation, whether it be as obviously relevant as cancer, as universally found as excrement, or as banal in its form as driftwood.

The audacity of the vision, of course, springs from the very idio-syncracy that defines it, suggesting a creator who refuses to acknowledge any outside referents or submit his theories to the test of hard evidence. As Mailer explained:

> I want my brain to live. I want to adventure out on a few thoughts. The fact that I can never demonstrate them is not nearly so important to me as the fact that I may come up with an hypothesis so simple, so central, that I may be able to apply it in thousands of situations. If it begins to give me some inner coherence, if I begin to think I know more as a result of this philosophy, why not?
>
> (*Conversations* 213)

For a number of reasons. As more sympathetic critics have charged, such intellectual solipsizing may only mask intellectual sloth. Robert Gorham Davis, Mailer's sophomore-year English teacher at Harvard, recalled Mailer's knowledge of "the major figures of the past" as "pretty slight or superficial, a lot taken from secondary sources," his "spottiness" and "habit of not reading deeply or systematically when he got interested in something" to have been "obvious back then" (Manso, *Mailer* 48). Jean Malaquais, Mailer's mentor in the next decade, attributed his hypothesizing in the 1950s to a similar predilection: "lacking a proper philosophical background, he aims at building a system of his own" (Manso, *Mailer* 255). Furthermore, such theoretical deliberations may mask artistic reservations, in that having constructed such a personal system in his writing, out of the most bizarre set of images, metaphors, and subjects, Mailer removes the risk of having his work compared to that of other authors, in which case he who proclaims the necessity of taking risks in writing—"How dignify it if large risks aren't being taken?" (*Conversations* 325)—exempts (or, more to the point, pre-empts) himself from his own admonition.

As the interviews recently collected by J. Michael Lennon attest, throughout the course of his career, Mailer's public pronouncements have provided proof to sustain both charges. "Intellectuality delivers the writer to self-questioning and to despair at his own limitations," he remarked in 1951 when describing to Harvey Breit the difficulty of creating a comprehensive world view in a novel, "it vitiates the attempt at large, serious works because you are unable to suspend the critical faculties even at the times when you should" (16). Commenting to Barry Leeds, "I don't want to write about anything unless I can do something with it that hasn't quite been done before" (372), he also confirmed, in 1987, the impulse toward deliberate restriction of subject matter that has helped him to carve his own literary niche from the very beginning: to choose to write about the Pacific instead of Europe in World War II "because it was and is easier to write a war novel about the Pacific" (*Advertisements* 10); to make "murder, suicide, incest, orgy, orgasm, and Time" his frontier after *Barbary Shore*, knowing "I was never going to be a greater poet than James Joyce or a greater mystic than Yeats or a greater sociologist than John Dos Passos or a greater stylist than Hemingway" and thus was never "going to get near any one of them on their terms" (*Advertisements* 85; Manso, *Mailer* 254); in short, always to have "taken a field—I'm a bully—where there's no competition" as a way of insuring certain victory (*Conversations* 326).

And yet, I would argue, it is not the need to fashion "an hypothesis so simple, so central," and so personal that should spark controversy over

Mailer's work. When one sets the historical milieu in which he began writing
against the philosophical systematizers who had shaped his youth—a task
whose ramifications Joseph Wenke has explored admirably in the first parts
of *Mailer's America*—Mailer's refusal "to become a flunky for some other
thinker" becomes understandable (*Conversations* 192); with Marxism replaced
by Stalinism and Freud displaced by doctoral devotees, it is no wonder that
Mailer would conclude, in 1962, "It's better to work alone, trusting no one,
just working, working, working ..." (*Presidential Papers* 136). Nor should his
denial of outside authorities be confused with a denial of outside events;
while retaining a war between God and the Devil as the root of his
constructed history, he has remained attentive all along to the dictates of the
history that surrounds him and has adjusted his vision accordingly. The
election of John F. Kennedy brings forth God's blessings; his assassination
lets loose the Devil's forces. A 1967 March on the Pentagon is too ambiguous
to judge for one or two decades; the 1968 riots in Chicago confirm a war we
will be fighting for forty years. It is not, then, the *fact* of a systematizing
world view that should evoke controversy over Mailer's work. Rather, it is
Mailer's need "to apply it in thousands of situations" that demands scrutiny,
for the condition he is constantly drawn to examine with it is the state of
American society specifically, but the situations on which he imposes his
schema are not equally appropriate for his needs.

Mailer's love affair with America is disturbing on a number of counts,
not the least of which are the contradictions at its base. Holding to the belief
that America was "destined by history if you will, to be the greatest country
that ever existed," Mailer subscribes to what is essentially a Puritan sense of
mission, fully aware that the nation has not "come near it" (*Conversations* 68),
conscious, in fact, that the imperialist tendencies to which that mission gives
rise answer the question of *Why Are We In Vietnam?* completely. Drawn, as
those first settlers were, to those "people at the summit" to whom God and
the Devil are most attentive (*American Dream* 230), and bored, if not
repulsed, by those "slobs" who remain in the middle (*Deer Park* 129), he ends
up drawn—almost against his will—to the force of those people whose
actions his work most condemns: Croft in *The Naked and the Dead*, Kelly in
An American Dream. More problematic than his *ambivalence* about America,
however, is Mailer's *representation* of America in his writing. Although he has
expressed the desire to create the kind of panoramic social novel of Tolstoy
or Stendhal, he also has acknowledged the way the rapidity of change in
America precludes the ability of artists to render it comprehensively:

> The realistic literature had never caught up with the rate of
> change in American life, indeed it had fallen further and further

behind, and the novel gave up any desire to be a creation equal to the phenomenon of the country itself; it settled for being a metaphor. Which is to say that each separate author made a separate peace. He would no longer try to capture America, he would merely try to give life to some microcosm in American life, some metaphor—in the sense that a drop of water is a metaphor of the seas, or a hair of the beast is for some a metaphor of the beast—and in that manner he might—if he were very lucky— have it all, rich and poor, strategy and tactics, insight and manner, detail, authority, the works. (*Cannibals* 99)

Until *The Executioner's Song*, Mailer was no exception to the rule here, finding America encapsulated in figures as diverse as John F. Kennedy, Marilyn Monroe, even his own wives, and places as different as Hollywood, Alaska, and Washington, D.C. But the qualities that endow a microcosm with macrocosmic reverberations have not always been inherent in his choices. Indeed, the expansion of significance in one way has often entailed a reduction of complexity in others. This has been especially true when Mailer has sought to embody America in actual figures. To describe Cherry in *An American Dream* as looking "like Grace Kelly," "a little of Monroe," and "a dozen lovely blondes" to justify the "clean tough little American boy in her look" (94–95) is to give more texture to a character that is weakly defined in a piece of *fiction*—the most weakly defined character in the book, as Mailer himself has admitted. To describe Marilyn Monroe herself as "every man's love affair with America" (*Marilyn* 15) is to reduce to formula a woman of *fact* whose multiple dimensions his work is trying to capture. Even worse, to describe his love for his own wife as "damnably parallel" to his love for America (*Armies* 193) is to turn a real-life person into a freeze-dried image, force a changeable human being to fit a preconceived artistic mold, and, in so doing, subordinate the actual to the artificial.

Yet Mailer's problems with macrocosmic reverberation have been no less apparent in his choice of setting. Although professing, "I don't believe a metaphorical novel has any right to exist until it exists on its ground floor" (*Conversations* 210), the grounds on which he builds his works do not always provide sufficient support for his whole structures. The Pentagon in *The Armies of the Night* in which Mailer symbolizes "the military might of the Republic" (68) can sustain the weight he ascribes to it because it does house the Defense Department, which, in turn, did dispatch American soldiers to Vietnam; the 1967 March on Washington can rise to "quintessentially American" status (241) because the city in which it occurs serves as capital to the American Republic; and soldiers dressed like Rogers and Clark, Wyatt Earp, Kit Carson, and Daniel Boone can evoke successive rites of passage, from the first Thanksgiving through the Alamo to the battles of Normandy and Pusan, because the clothing they literally wear on their backs attests to a historical continuum.

In contrast, Chicago during the Democratic Convention of 1968 holds little ready-made mythical import. The "Massacre of Michigan Avenue" cannot bring to mind "the old Indian raids" of the past, much less serve as a "murderous paradigm of Vietnam" when Mailer is forced to concede, "yet no one was killed. Of course, a great many people were hurt" (*Miami* 159, 172). Aware that "symbol had the power to push him into actions more heroic than himself"—as both writer and participant, I would add—and conscious that in Chicago "there was no symbol for him" and that the "justifications of the March on the Pentagon were not here" (144), Mailer must resort to rhetorical gamesmanship, the sense of "craft" he likens to a "St. Bernard dog with that little bottle of brandy under his neck" (*Conversations* 94), to help gain his desired effect—which he does not even get in the end. With the "forcing style" that Richard Foster has noted, which "seeks to force reality into the matrix of an idiosyncratic vision," the prose that Tony Tanner finds "simmering at a high degree of excitability just short of hysteria" (Lennon, *Essays* 22–23, 56), Mailer inflates the slaughter in Chicago's stockyards at the beginning of the piece to try to compensate for the resonance its final scenes are unable to convey. But the device yields only a barrage of sensory overload: a sweat of "hell-leather," a stench "not so simple as the collective diarrhetics of an hysterical army of beasts," excrement of "pure vomitous shit," and smoke of "burnt blood and burnt bone and burnt hair to add their properties of specific stench to fresh blood, fresh entrails, fresh fecalities already all over the air" (88–89). Seeking to enhance the poverty of his own imagery, Mailer yokes it to one rich with familiar connotations. But describing the televised violence at the convention as breaking the "Democratic Party in two before the eyes of a nation like Melville's whale charging right out of the sea" (172) leads him into just the sort of comparisons he has always sought to avoid, for the lesser authority of one voice is only highlighted by reminders of the greater authority of the other.

What is refreshing about the recent works of criticism on Mailer, notably Harold Bloom's and J. Michael Lennon's collections of reprinted essays and Chris Anderson's chapter on Mailer in *Style as Argument*, is the alertness their authors bring to Mailer as rhetorician. Although Joan Didion may overstate the case in claiming, "It is a largely unremarked fact about Mailer that he is a great and obsessed stylist, a writer to whom the shape of the sentence is the story" (Lennon, *Essays* 79), there still remains a great deal of validity to her point, especially when one recalls how much early criticism of Mailer's work conflated the artist with the art and concerned itself with his espousal (or, depending upon the writer, lack of same) of violence and his animus (or, depending upon the writer, lack of same) against women. It may well be a sign of Mailer's changing status that the essays in the collections that are devoted to these issues, particularly the ones that deal with his alleged sexism (such as those that discuss his *Prisoner of Sex* Town Hall appearance in 1971) are among the least interesting for being the most familiar, whereas those that concern themselves with Mailer's rhetoric are among the most provocative. In this latter regard, Tony Tanner's essays (one of which appears in each collection) may be cited as having taken the lead, as evidenced by his 1967 review of *Cannibals and Christians*, in which Mailer's search for new metaphors is related to the growth of the modern city (Lennon, *Essays* 54–59).

Indeed, so far has the appreciation of Mailer's style come that later essays move from summarizing its attributes to scrutinizing its degree of success. Whereas Richard Poirier commended sentences that "allow the most supple possible movement back and forth between minutely observed 'journalistic' details and a panorama that includes the forces that impinge upon and transform those details, perhaps to inconsequentiality" (Bloom, *Mailer* 104), and Robert Solotaroff praised efforts "to ground the intuitive in the factual, the mystical in the phenomenal, the psychic in the biological and the apocalyptic in the historical" (Lennon, *Essays* 124), Bloom's collection opens with its editor's introductory assertion that Mailer's "formidable literary energies have not found their inevitable mode" (2). In its inclusion of Alvin B. Kernan's discussion of *Fire on the Moon* as one of its final pieces, an essay that beautifully explores the failure of Mailer's imagination to find suitable images to convey the moon shot, it closes on a similar note. And in its unifying claim that the "rhetorical dilemma" of contemporary nonfiction is the limits of language to express in words "the inexplicable energies, intensities, and contradictions of American experience" (5), Anderson's study extends the difficulty facing Mailer into the primary obstacle of all nonfiction writers.

It is not merely a growth of sophistication in Mailer scholarship that has led to this later elegiac tone, to the concentration on stylistic failure more than success. It is also, quite simply, a response to the fact that much of Mailer's later work, from *Armies* through *The Fight* roughly, *does* suffer from imagistic deprivation. In 1966, Mailer was demanding "metaphors to fit the vaults of modern experience" and "forms of an intensity which will capture the complexity of modern experience and dignify it, illumine—if you will—its danger" (*Cannibals* 310–11); by 1970, he was ready to admit that "Events were developing a style and structure which made them almost impossible to write about" (*Fire* 82). And so despite a stated belief in an "aesthetic economy to symbolic gestures—you must not repeat yourself" (*Armies* 183), we find in the works that followed *Armies* more and more recycling of earlier symbolic scenes. Stephen Rojack's walk around the parapet in *An American Dream* reappears as Norman Mailer's balcony balancing act in *The Fight*, a daring of heights that originates as far back as the I and R patrol's climb of Mount Anaka's narrowing ledge in *The Naked and the Dead* and is projected as far forward as Tim Madden's attempt to climb the Provincetown Monument in *Tough Guys Don't Dance*. Mailer released from jail in *Armies*, feeling "closer to that freedom from dread" than when he first came to Washington and "happy" with "this clean sense of himself" (238) returns as Mailer facing the police in *The Siege of Chicago*, feeling "close to some presence with a beatific grace" and "happier than he had been at any moment" since hearing of Bobby Kennedy's shooting (220–21). Likewise, we get, in those works of the same period, more and more piggy-backing on the imagery of earlier authors: not just in singular scenes, like the reclamation of Melville's whale to show the split in the Democratic Party, but in depictions of central figures that form the basis of entire works—Melville's Leviathan for *Fire on the Moon's* spaceship and Ahab's monomania for the "Iron of [its] Astronauts" (54, 92, 293).

Much of this decline can be attributed to the cumulative effect of rather obvious historical factors: the deaths of all those people, from Hemingway to the Kennedys to Monroe, in whom Mailer had invested so much symbolic import; the feeling that "no revolution had arisen in the years when he was ready" (*Miami* 188); the sense that "the army he was in ... had dropped out, goofed and left the goose to their enemies" (*Fire* 386); leading to the conviction that "Everybody had been cheated so many times; everybody had cheated others so often. It was hard to remain angry that one had been defrauded. It was even hard to get angry" (*Fire* 74). I would suggest, however, that Mailer's artistic decline was also an inevitable consequence of the *form* in which he cast his vision of America. A writer who links the destiny of a nation to the fate of its artists, who finds those artists "embody[ing] the essence of what was best in the nation" and views their talents encapsulating "the dreams and the ambitions" of the country's "most imaginative part" (*Presidential Papers* 91) is *not* an author who should be working through microcosm, whatever the limitations that confront him. A novelist with such a romantic and grandiose view of the artist needs a canvas that is "commensurate to his capacity for wonder," to recall the words of an earlier American romantic. In short, he needs to attempt the Tolstoyan tapestry of macrocosm. It is the shift in Mailer's writing from one form to another that makes *The Executioner's Song* and *Ancient Evenings* stand out so prominently. The composition of these works provides ample proof that, after forty years, Mailer—though sometimes down—is never out. At the same time, looking at these two works in conjunction provides proof of his continuing need for careful choice, for in the first he picks a subject that fits his vision as tight as a glove, and in the second he picks a subject in which the seams between theme and technique strain to bursting.

Mailer has admitted that even before he wrote *The Executioner's Song*, Gary Gilmore provided "a perfect example of what I've been talking about all my life" (*Conversations* 263). Certainly, Gilmore's statements about reincarnation, risk, and karma provided a vivid illustration of some of the more idiosyncratic subjects that Mailer has tackled over the years. Gilmore's belief that "The bravest people are those who've overcome the greatest amounts of fear" (467) echoes Marion Faye's definition of courage in *The Deer Park*: "There is no pleasure greater than that obtained from a conquered repugnance" (128). His view of death as "consciousness unencumbered by body" (480) reiterates the view of death as "an existential continuation of life" that introduces the "Eleventh Presidential Paper" (214). And his wish to face death by firing squad for having killed two young men because "with death you pay all your debts" (728) recalls the need for expiation that prompts Stephen Rojack to contemplate a night in Harlem for having beaten Shago Martin and to face a night with Barney Oswald Kelly for having killed his daughter Deborah, for "That was the way to pay for it" (*American Dream* 190). Here, in the flesh, was Mailer's "White Negro"— twenty years after Mailer conceived him—in both his most and least compelling guises, the mystic who chooses death, conscious of that "depth of desperation to the condition which enables one to remain in life only by engaging death," and the cold-blooded psychopath "at his extreme" who is incapable of restraining "the rage of his frustration" from exploding (*Advertisements* 304–05).

As Mailer also admitted, no less did Gilmore provide him with a "quintessentially American" example of what he had been saying about *America* all his life (*Conversations* 270). Born on an overnight stop at the Burleson Hotel in McCamey, Texas—and moved by his parents six weeks later—here was a man whose history confirmed Mailer's charges about the rootlessness of the country, "since almost no American could lay claim to the line of a family which had not once at least severed its roots by migrating here" (*Presidential Papers* 39). Here was a man whose infantile needs for "perfection quickly" (37) Mailer had earlier embodied in the "spirit of the supermarket" and the sunsets of Los Angeles, where people go "to live or try to live in the rootless pleasure world of an adult child" (*Presidential Papers* 32). And here was a man in whose various poses—twenty-seven according to the journalist who counted them—was contained a cross-section of American society: "racist Gary and Country-and-Western Gary, poetic Gary, artist manqué Gary, macho Gary, self-destructive Gary, Karma County Gary, Texas Gary," and, last but not least, Gary "the movie star, awfully shit-kicking large-minded aw-shucks" (806).

Yet "quintessentially American" is exactly the same phrase that Mailer used for the 1967 March on the Pentagon, that microcosmic event in which he portrayed the nation's schisms. And "quintessentially American" sounds too much like "A Peculiarly American Statement," the title of the *Naked and the Dead's* "Time Machine" section for General Cummings, the man in whose drive for power Mailer found that of the country contained. *The Executioner's Song*, in fact, opens with an incident that suggests that America's story will be personified in that of Gary Gilmore: a literal fall from a forbidden apple tree is ripe with intimations of lapsed grace and lost Eden. So, too, is the book's opening ripe with extended *historical* connotations. The trip from prison to Salt Lake that Gilmore makes after his release is "practically the same route" his great-grandfather took "when he jumped off from Missouri with a handcart near to a hundred years ago, and pushed west with all he owned over the prairies, and the passes of the Rockies" (22), a frontier journey toward that "new Zion in the Kingdom of Deseret" (315) whose prospects Brigham Young had proclaimed to his flock as much as John Cotton had promoted "Gods Promise To His Plantations."

The difference, however, between Mailer's portrait here and his portraits elsewhere can be measured by the difference between what he portrays for his readers himself and what he calls on his readers to imagine. Unlike New York City in *An American Dream*, in which he had "the diseases of America settle, fester, and finally begin to burn" (*Existential Errands* 302), and unlike Brooks Range in *Why Are We in Vietnam?*, which served as "crystal receiver of the continent" (183), Utah in *The Executioner's Song* both *suggests* the theocratic principles upon which the nation was founded and *serves*, quite literally, as an illustration of those principles in practice. "The Church and the State were deeply entangled," ACLU lawyer Julie Jacoby realizes. "The Church *was* the State" (755). And in a state in which this same Church "owned the land, ran the banks, and controlled the politicians" (893), the origins of the land where Edward Winslow saw "religion and profit jump together" (1624) are constantly reenacted. "Those angels, Mormon and Moroni, meant More Money," concludes free-lance lawyer Dennis Boaz. "No wonder the Mormons were getting to be the richest church in America. All that sanction to make More and More Money" (521). At the same time, in a state in which coffee and tea are forbidden, it also is no wonder that those who fail to live up to that sanction feel trapped within the walls of a prison. "Prison was wanting to breathe when somebody else had a finger up your nose," as Gilmore's girlfriend Nicole well knows. "Prison was being married too young and having kids" (100). Should this welfare mother ever forget the fact, she need only look at the landscape that surrounds her, in which the desert "was at the end of every street" (40).

As the Western voices of the book's first half are joined by the Eastern voices of its second, and their sounds swell to form a symphony, we see that the schism that Mailer portrays here is not a split between regions. Almost all the characters in Mailer's social tapestry are shown to be migrants in one way or another—and not just the more obviously unstable candidates like Nicole Baker, who drifts from place to place (Utah to California to Oregon) as much as she does from marriage to marriage (three before her nineteenth birthday and "more guys than you wanted to count" [82]). Assistant Attorney General Earl Dorius moves from Virginia to Los Angeles to Salt Lake as a child and finds that "the roots he had always craved" in the past can only be found in the job that he holds in the present (662). Max Jensen, Gilmore's first victim, and his wife decide they need more space in which to live and solve their problem with a twelve by fifty-four foot trailer. The few exceptions, like Gilmore's mother Bessie, who *do* grow "root straight down" (332) are dispossessed over the course of the novel: the mountain that has symbolized her claim to the state of Utah she renounces on the last pages— but not before she loses the house she has lived in because the Church will not pick up its deed. Similarly, it is not only Gilmore, in jail for half his life, who seeks a life of perpetual youth. Managing the Busy Bee Day-Care Center as well as the City Center Motel, and viewing marriage as "a constant goal of making each other happy," Ben Bushnell, Gilmore's second victim, and his wife both literally and figuratively inhabit "a world of two-year-olds and four-year-olds" (242–43).

Most important, it is not only the social misfit Gilmore whose anger erupts as violence when he cannot obtain his wishes. "Since the First World War Americans have been leading a double life," Mailer wrote in 1960, "and our history has moved on two rivers, one visible, the other underground ..." (*Presidential Papers* 38). It is this same tension between manners and mayhem that forms the schism that is portrayed in *The Executioner's Song* again and again. Joe Bob Sears, the husband Nicole meets at church, calls her "Poopsie" and "Baby Doll" and "Honey"; he also sits on her, chokes her, and smacks her "when he felt like it" (124). Pete Galovan answers a hot line for addicts in Hawaii, works with the Jesus Movement in Seattle, and throws one of his wife's children across the room when back in Utah. Nearly everyone in the book seems to own a weapon. When Gilmore offers a Derringer to Nicole's mother for protection, she replies, "I've already got a gun" (187). She does—her husband's Magnum. Nearly everyone seems to treat domestic violence as a casual and commonplace occurrence. When Nicole's neighbor, Kathy Maynard, tells an interviewer about her first husband shooting himself in the foot and stabbing himself with a knife, she remains more attentive to her child getting into a jar of peanut butter (564–65). The nonchalant mention of these private incidents lulls the reader into treating the more publicized ones cited, such as Claudine Longet killing her lover and the hi-fi killers pouring Drano down their victims' throats, with a similar degree of aplomb. Viewed within the panoramic context of so *many* acts of violence, Gilmore is *reduced* in stature, from an *exemplar* of American tendencies at the beginning of the book to one more *example*—albeit an extreme one—of those tendencies by the end. We do not wonder why *he* acted as he did, but why so many others did not. We are reminded that it was not his *acts* that made him distinctive—one need look at any newspaper if one has doubts—but rather his willingness to be held accountable for them that did.

To the extent that this willingness to accept execution sprang from a belief in karma, Mailer saw Gilmore as ahead of his time, "the stalking horse or the vanguard" of the West's "going around a tremendous bend" in its approach to Eastern concepts of reincarnation (*Conversations* 258). According to Michael Cowan, Mailer's own movement toward such concepts sprang from an inability to find Western images weighty enough to sustain his vision any longer: "It may be partly this worry that has prompted him in the last decade to begin exploring ways in which non-American roots—the African sensibility charted in *The Faith of Graffiti* (1974) and *The Fight* and the Egyptian ethos of *Ancient Evenings*—can renew American imaginative life" (Lennon, *Essays* 158). If this is true, however, somewhere between inception and publication the opposite seems to have occurred. When Mailer finally encounters African sensibility in *The Fight*, Bantu philosophy is turned into American theology, "the Calvinism of the chosen" (39), and Mobutu is transformed into a Puritan statesman, "the chosen of God and *le roi soleil* all in one" (108). Similarly, for all his pains to divorce *Ancient Evenings* from modern America, and to develop within it a consciousness "that's so different from our own that we read it in wonder as if we were reading about

Martians" (*Conversations* 296), the Egypt his book revives looks all too much like the America he has always reviewed. Unable to break free of the hold that it has on his own consciousness, he projects America onto every foreign culture that he encounters, and, in succumbing to this compulsion, the source of his greatest virtue becomes the source of his greatest vice.

In many ways, the connection between America and Egypt in particular should have come as no surprise, for reaching to the latter to portray the former had been evident in Mailer's works of the past. A drive for all-out fallout-shelters is described as having "left us Egyptians as a nation: a million underground one-room crypts stocked to the barrel top" (*Presidential Papers* 115). A room in the Waldorf Towers exudes a presence "like the command of a dead pharoah" (*American Dream* 220). Columns of the Pentagon recall columns of Egyptian architecture, the "abstract ubiquitous mud" of the Nile that built one equaled only by the "abstract ubiquitous money, filthy lucre" that boosts the other (*Armies* 175, 179). What *is* surprising about the reversal in *Ancient Evenings*, however, is how *thoroughly* Mailer reaches for American traditions in order to depict those of Egypt. As in *The Executioner's Song*, geography tells much. A drive down Utah's Interstate goes from "one newly built town to another" (629); a walk down Egypt's Western Bank shows "so much space that you could see a number of new towns, built in regular rows between the great boulevards, and climbing into the foothills" (323). A split by Nile waters that creates a literal nation of Two-Lands also yields customs—Double-Throne, Double-Crown, Twice-Royal Seat (575)—that make Egypt a testament to inherent schism. As in Mailer's earlier works, leaders tell even more. Depicted as the man closest to the gods, and revealing divinity "by even the smallest of His moves" (421), the pharoah becomes an ancient Egyptian type. And much like the most promising of types, the statesman who, like Kennedy, bridges the country's fissures as he does his own, and, in so doing, "takes our national anxiety so long buried and releases it to the surface—where it belongs" (*Cannibals* 170), Mailer's pharoah assumes the burden of his land's reconciliation. Horus and Set, the warring gods of Egypt's mythology, do not fight each other when embodied in the pharoah: "The Pharoah is so powerful that He makes Them live in peace" (683).

The problem is not only that the declining state of affairs in Mailer's Egypt so closely resembles the declining state of affairs he earlier found in America, that the ancient land that "only the Temple of Amon could hold together" by the time of Ramses the Ninth (806) recalls the modern one whose "fissure in the national psyche" had "widened to the danger point" by 1960 (*Presidential Papers* 40). It is that the language with which Mailer portrays those affairs is so unequivocally American in its idiom. When characters announce that metalworkers and carpenters of the Necropolis of Thebes have gone on strike (238), we have visions of Jimmy Hoffa risen from the grave (or wherever) and Albert Shanker entrenched in arbitration. When blacks are described as knowing "how to speak with their drums, and very well" (229), we hear, again, all those claims about rhythm that were rightly put to rest. And when satisfying sex is commended with "May I say it was my first great fuck" (380), we remain without any sensory analogue. True, we *don't* know how ancient Egyptians sounded, but we *do* know for certain that they did not sound like that—in which case, what's good for Rojack's goose is not suitable for Menenhetet's gander. Because he stays so glued to American dialect, Mailer cannot realize the potential for invention that his audience's ignorance about ancient Egypt offered. Like a cookie cutter, he keeps forcing its idiomatic imprint over his material, to the extent that when, on occasion, he *can* break free of its influence and let his imagination run free, the pent-up forces that are unleashed overcompensate in a language that is nothing less than ludicrous, leaving us to contemplate "Fekh-futi" for "Shit-Collector" (166), "rep" for "ca-ca" (214), and "Nak-nak" for copulation (381).

In a novel that constantly draws attention to the sounds of language, a novel narrated by a character whose name means "Foundation-of-speech" (297) and who recognizes "that I could only learn what I knew as my voice passed into the air" (184–85), this failure to fashion a sound appropriate to its context is devastating. Even worse, in a novel that asserts "the power of the word" in one of its final sentences (844), and seeks an immortality of art as analogous to the immortality of the soul, the failure to find a powerful language raises doubts about the future of its own author's career.

When, at one point in the novel, Menenhetet One recalls one of the pharoah's queens copying passages from the temple's library onto her own rolls of papyrus, he alludes to the reasons for the power of the written word:

> Watching her write, I would think of all the little scribes I had known who engaged in such tasks, and I would brood on the power of this act, and ask myself why such puny men were able to appeal so greatly to the Gods even though, when they spoke, they were never true-of-voice, but frail as reeds, scratchy voices most of them. Yet the words they painted onto the papyrus were able to bring forth the power that rests in silence. So they could call on forces the true-of-voice would never reach. (515–16)

As Mailer moves into his fifth decade as a writer, the voice of the performer that antagonized by its arrogance *has* been silenced more and more. "I think as you get older you make peace with who and what you are," he said in 1986. "It doesn't help my day to see a good photograph of myself in the paper, because there *are* no good photographs any longer." Unfortunately, when he turns his attention to activities like filmmaking, the scribe who attracted so many admirers is silenced as well. "Something had gone out of the writing," he conceded a year later, "maybe the belief that it makes a difference" (*Conversations* 358, 375). "Turning professional" is what Ron Rosenbaum called it. "It means learning to choose good works over profligate grace. It means accepting the idea that he may be the historian of our time, but not its hero" (*Conversations* 177–78).

Yet if "turning professional" also means replacing the ambitiousness of a planned trilogy with the two-month alacrity of *Tough Guys Don't Dance*, "an example," as Mailer put it, "of what happens when you have to do what is necessary" (*Conversations* 365), I'd rather have the lapsed hero than the lauded historian. The "difference" that Mailer's work has made should never be determined by ordinary standards of critical or commercial success, the warfare of the literary marketplace. The "difference" that his work makes needs to be measured by other criteria of combat, as he himself realized: "A commando raid is not measured by its aesthetic perfection. It's measured by the amount of life it generates, by the amount of stimulation it gives in military history and the amount of time professional soldiers will spend in discussing it afterwards" (*Conversations* 174). The words ring as true today as they did when spoken in 1970. If, after forty years, discussion still continues, how great were the territories its guerrilla leader conquered—and how great remain the lands to be commanded by his presence still.

WORKS CITED

Anderson, Chris. *Style as Argument: Contemporary American Nonfiction.* Carbondale: Southern Illinois UP, 1987.

Bloom, Harold, ed. *Norman Mailer.* Modern Critical Views. New York: Chelsea House, 1986.

Lennon, J. Michael, ed. *Conversations with Norman Mailer.* Jackson: UP of Mississippi, 1988.

———, ed. *Critical Essays on Norman Mailer.* Critical Essays on American Literature. Boston: G. K. Hall, 1986.

Mailer, Norman. *The Naked and the Dead.* New York: Signet-NAL, 1948.

———. *Barbary Shore.* New York: Signet-NAL, 1951.

———. *The Deer Park.* 1955. New York: Berkley Windhover, 1976.

———. *Advertisements for Myself.* 1959. New York: Berkley Medallion-Putnam, 1966.

———. *The Presidential Papers.* 1963. New York: Berkley Medallion, 1970.

———. *An American Dream.* 1965. New York: Dell, 1970.

———. *Cannibals and Christians.* 1966. New York: Dell, 1967.

———. *Why Are We in Vietnam?* 1967. New York: Berkley Medallion-Putnam, 1968.

———. *The Armies of the Night: History as a Novel / The Novel as History.* New York: Signet-NAL, 1968.

———. *Miami and the Siege of Chicago: An Informal History of the Republican and Democratic Conventions of 1968.* New York: Signet-NAL, 1968.

———. *Of a Fire on the Moon.* 1970. New York: Signet-NAL, 1971.

———. *The Prisoner of Sex.* New York: Signet-NAL, 1971.

———. *Existential Errands.* Boston: Little, Brown, 1972.

———. *Marilyn.* 1973. Great Britain: Coronet-Hodder, 1974.

———. *The Fight.* Boston: Little, Brown, 1975.

———. *The Executioner's Song.* 1979. New York: Warner, 1980.

———. *Pieces.* Boston: Little, Brown, 1982.

———. *Pontifications.* Ed. J. Michael Lennon. Boston: Little, Brown, 1982.

———. *Ancient Evenings.* 1983. New York: Warner, 1984.

———. *Tough Guys Don't Dance.* 1984. New York: Ballantine, 1985.

Manso, Peter. *Mailer: His Life and Times.* New York: Simon & Schuster, 1985.

Mills, Hilary. *Mailer: A Biography.* 1982. New York: McGraw-Hill, 1984.

Wenke, Joseph. *Mailer's America.* Hanover: UP of New England, 1987.

GABRIEL MILLER

A Small Trumpet of Defiance: Politics and the Buried Life in Norman Mailer's Early Fiction

In one of the *Presidential Papers* Mailer wrote, "Our history has moved on two rivers, one visible, the other underground; there has been the history of politics which is concrete, practical, and unbelievably dull ... and there is the subterranean river of untapped, ferocious, lonely and romantic desires, that concentration of ecstasy and violence which is the dream life of the nation" (46). Much of Mailer's writing, like much of the American writing from which he consciously borrows, is concerned with such dualities. As he declared in "The White Negro," Mailer finds the twentieth century, for all its horror, an exciting time to live because of "its tendency to reduce all of life to its ultimate alternatives" (33). This fascination with dynamic polarities is reflected in Mailer's style as well, as he has struggled in his modeling of language and form to fuse the real, political/social world with the world of dream and myth. In reading his novels chronologically, one can trace Mailer's process of borrowing and merging different styles, then discarding them, and experimenting with others in quest of a voice that will be most compatible with his own recurrent themes and emerging vision. Mailer's central subject is the relationship between the individual will and a world that attempts to overwhelm and extinguish it. Intimately connected with this spiritual warfare is the subject of power, particularly political power, and the individual's need to resist the encroaching forces of totalitarianism. Mailer's

From *Politics And The Muse: Studies in the Politics of Recent American Literature*, edited by Adam J. Sorkin. © 1989 by Bowling Green State University Popular Press.

early fiction clearly warns that modern man is in danger of losing his dignity, his freedom, and his sense of self before the enormous power of politics and society.

These concerns are already apparent in his first novel, *The Naked and the Dead* (1948), which despite its brilliant, evocative scenes of men at war, is ultimately a political novel. Mailer describes his attitude about the Second World War in "The White Negro":

> The Second World War presented a mirror to the human condition which blinded anyone who looked into it ... one was then obliged also to see that no matter how crippled and perverted an image of man was the society he had created, it was nonetheless his creation, his collective creation ... and if society was so murderous, then who could ignore the most hideous of questions about his own nature? (312)

The Naked and the Dead elaborates this harrowing perception of the individual who exemplifies and perpetuates what is wrong with the society he inhabits. In this first novel Mailer equates the army with society and thereby explores the fragmented nature of that society, which has militated against social development, revolutionary or otherwise. In so doing, Mailer demonstrates his own loss of faith in the individual's ability to impose himself creatively, perhaps redemptively, on the oppressive condition of the post-war world.

The novel exhibits a hodgepodge of styles and influences: the works of James Farrell, John Steinbeck, and John Dos Passos inform its structure and form. Herein the thirties novel, with its emphasis on social engagement and reform, collides with a pessimistic, even despairing world view, as Mailer blends naturalism with symbolism, realistic reportage with nightmare images and hallucinatory dream landscapes, documentary portraits with political allegory. The dramatic thrust of the novel, however, springs from Mailer's fascination with his three central figures: General Cummings, Sergeant Croft, and Lieutenant Hearn.

Cummings is presented as a despotic fascist, wholly preoccupied with the power he wields over the island which his troops occupy. When Hearn accuses him of being reactionary he dismisses the charge, claiming that the war is not being fought for ideals but for "power concentration" (140). His plan to send a patrol to the rear of the Japanese position to determine the validity of a new strategic theory is prompted by raw opportunism, and it results in the death of three men. Croft, on the other hand, is a brave but illiterate soldier who embraces the war cause to satisfy his lust for killing and conquest. He is Cummings' collaborator, carrying out the general's orders without question. It is Croft who leads the men through jungles and swamps to pit them and himself against Mt. Anaka, even after the Japanese have surrendered (though the patrol does not know it), to further his own ambitions.

Hearn is the character who bridges the gap between the soldiers and command. Although he represents the liberal voice in the novel and so seems ideally positioned to embody the moral center in this desperate society, he emerges as a rather vague and empty character, even less sympathetic than most in Mailer's vast array of characters. This surprising deficiency in Hearn is surely intentional, as Mailer introduces an intelligent and sometimes outspoken man only to emphasize how ineffective he is. Resented both by the commanders and by the soldiers, he is eventually killed for no purpose; such is the fate of liberalism in Mailer's universe.

The political argument develops primarily in dialogues between Cummings and Hearn, whom Cummings is trying to convert to his autocratic views. This overt confrontation of ideologies, a staple of the political novel and a device Mailer would repeat less successfully in his next novel, provides an abstract gloss on the narrative, while the use of the "Time Machine" episodes to delineate the lives of the men more subtly equates the structure of society with the army. America is thus portrayed as a place of social privilege and racial discrimination, as exploitive and destructive as the military organization that represents it. Mailer presents the individual as either submitting to these repressive forces or attempting to maintain some spiritual independence. The fates of Hearn and, to some degree, Red Valsen, a Steinbeckian hobo and laborer who struggles to preserve his private vision, indicate that defiance is fruitless. Both men are destroyed, while Cummings and Croft, in their ruthless drive to power, prevail and triumph.

However, this schematic simplification does not reflect the complexity of Mailer's view, conveyed in some aspects of the novel that undercut the apparent political formula, most notably his narrative style. Mailer recounts his tale in a tone of complete objectivity, his authorial voice remaining detached and disinterested. Considering the moral dimensions of his story, this lack of anger or indignation is disorienting, and the effect is strengthened by Mailer's unsympathetic treatment of Hearn and the vibrant images of Cummings and Croft, who seem to fascinate him. Clearly Cummings' egoism repels Mailer, but it also attracts him, for in this island tyrant he perceives also the individualistic impulse to reshape and recreate an environment and in so doing, to form a new reality.[1] Cummings thus possesses a kind of romantic aura as a dreamlike projection—which Mailer will recast in different forms in his subsequent fiction—of the active response to life which Mailer advocates in principle, if not on Cummings' specific terms. Croft, too, seeks a channel in which to funnel his powerful drives. Both men see evil as a vital force and their apprehension of it (not only in people, but in nature as well) provides them an energy and a decisive manner that the weaker, idealistic characters lack.

Still, at this point in his career Mailer did not want to exalt Cummings and Croft at the expense of Hearn. Therefore, in his climb up Mt. Anaka, Croft is left finally with feelings of despair: "Croft kept looking at the mountain. He had lost it, had missed some tantalizing revelation of himself. Of himself and much more, of life. Everything" (552). At another point Mailer sums up Croft thus: "He hated weakness and he loved practically nothing. There was a crude unformed vision in his soul but he was rarely conscious of it" (124). This man has energy but no form. Mailer the novelist is himself searching for the kind of form necessary to shape his vision. The liberal philosophy of a Hearn is rejected as insufficient to the challenges of modern history. It lacks the energy and daring of Croft and Cummings, but they still frighten Mailer, and he refuses to align himself with their authoritarian methods. Concluding the novel with Major Dalleson, a mediocre bureaucrat, enjoying the monotony of office details, Mailer instead pulls back from taking a definite position on the struggle he has chronicled. As Richard Poirier points out, he "has not yet imagined a hero with whose violence he can unabashedly identify himself" (26).

After completing *The Naked and the Dead*, Mailer went to Paris, where he met Jean Malaquais, an anti-Stalinist Marxist philosopher and novelist. They spent countless hours discussing politics and philosophy, during which Malaquais laid the groundwork for Mailer's broader understanding and thinking about politics. By the time Mailer returned to America he had come to believe in collective political action and the necessity of the artist's direct engagement in the political sphere. He put this new creed into practice by working vigorously in the 1948 presidential campaign of Henry Wallace, who was running on the Progressive Party ticket against the incumbent Harry Truman and Republican Thomas Dewey. Wallace's campaign was marked by much controversy and dissent, as many leftist intellectuals felt that Wallace was deceived by the Communists and so refused to vote for him. Mailer, however, remained loyal to Wallace, whose candidacy was effectively repudiated by the electorate, with only 2.37 percent of the vote. This overwhelming defeat ended Mailer's involvement in collective political action; in bitter disillusionment he later dismissed the whole affair, commenting, "The Progressive Party, as an organization, was almost as stupid as the army" (qtd. in Mills 111).[2]

Mailer's political orientation is presented in a very direct way in his second novel, *Barbary Shore* (1951). Making plain his disenchantment with Stalinism, he also reasserts his view that liberalism is dead, the proletariat in despair, and the right in control. Not only is the liberal dream dead, but so is the the Marxist vision, which the novel maintains was mankind's last hope, now blasted by the Stalinist subversion of socialist ideals. Russian communism and American capitalism are both seen as reactionary and repressive; privilege and oppression are now ascendant.

In his second novel Mailer is attempting to cut himself off from the past and forge his own personal vision, and although he will not succeed here, *Barbary Shore* nevertheless heralds a bold departure. In structuring this work Mailer abandons the omniscient narrative technique of *The Naked and the Dead*, adopting in its place the first-person narrator, a device to be retained in his subsequent fiction. Mickey Lovett is an amnesiac, a psychic casualty of war who becomes part of a nightmarish present. He has no real past—though he manages to recollect bits and pieces as the novel progresses—and so must make a commitment to the present. The novel's action takes place in a rooming house in Brooklyn Heights, where Lovett's relationships with its various inhabitants form the story, which is told partly in realistic and partly in symbolic/allegorical terms.

This narrator's amnesia opens the way for a significant stylistic ambivalence, as Lovett's probing of self and memory infuses his story with numerous surreal, dreamlike moments. It is clearly implied in the book's first half that the world cannot be fully understood by rational means; the "subterranean river" is always winding its way through consciousness, undercutting any reliance on reason alone. In these sections Mailer achieves his best writing, for his obsessions with individual psychology and motivation seems to interest him more than the political novel he obviously wants to write. When the action switches from Lovett's relationships to the confrontation between Hollingsworth, a government agent, and McLeod, a former revolutionary Socialist, the novel becomes didactic, much of it devoted to arguments about politics and history. Ultimately *Barbary Shore* becomes more a polemic than a novel as Mailer loses his grip on his fictional voice and his book's design.

As a novelist Mailer does not fully break free from the past, for this book owes much to Hawthorne's *The Blithedale Romance*, which is also concerned with a failed attempt to create a new and better world.[3] Mailer's skepticism about the viability of social progress and the allegorical structure of his work parallel Hawthorne's, as does his choice of the name Hollingsworth for his villain. In *Blithedale*, Hollingsworth, a reformer of criminals, is revealed to be an egoist who is blind to the complexity of human nature and incapable of real love. Mailer's Hollingsworth is a government undercover agent who is in the building to investigate McLeod and to recover from him a mysterious "little object" which disappeared from the State Department some years ago. This Hollingsworth also likes to present himself as a humanitarian, but he is exposed as a fascist, equally incapable of love. Another strong echo is provided in Mailer's use of the symbolically and ironically named Guinevere, a temptress who draws Hollingsworth, McLeod and Lovett into her orbit, much like Hawthorne's Zenobia.

Furthermore, Mailer's narrative method recalls Coverdale, the narrator of *Blithedale* (which is Hawthorne's only novel narrated in the first person). Hawthorne has Coverdale fashion his material, as Hawthorne writes in the preface, like a play, "where the creatures of his brain may play their phantasmagorical antics, without exposing them to too close a comparison with the actual events of real lives" (27). Lovett/Mailer attempts to organize and shape his material in a similar way. In *Barbary Shore* Mailer has deliberately narrowed his canvas from the expanse of his first novel to a small cast whose actions are situated almost exclusively in the small boardinghouse. Here they are carefully manipulated as they come and go, performing their allegorical and political functions as they act out their various parts in the story. It is also a convenient device for Lovett, who has lost his past, to try to structure and so control his present as he structures the novel he is writing.

The novel's political expression centers around McLeod, whose career represents in microcosm the recent history of Russian socialism. Affiliated with the Russian Communist Party for nineteen years, he embodies the altruistic ideal of Trotskyism now degenerated into Stalinism and incriminated in the Nazi-Soviet pact, the purges, and the labor camps. McLeod, who had come to be known as the "hangman of the Left Opposition" (130), abandoned the Party and came to America where he worked for the State Department. His leftist sympathies causing him to leave that job, he has assumed a new identity and married Guinevere, and he is now hiding out in the Brooklyn boardinghouse, where he spends time studying history and striving to understand through rigorous Marxist analysis why the revolution went wrong.

Guinevere, unlike her husband, remains ignorant of politics. Sexually vital and self-indulgent, she attracts all the men in the novel. In the novel's allegorical scheme her union with McLeod emphasizes the degeneration of the intellectual Marxist ideal as it merges either with materialism or, more broadly, with the lack of social engagement that she represents.

McLeod's antagonist is Leroy—Mailer puns ironically on the French word for king—Hollingsworth, a reactionary who seems more sinister than General Cummings because he disguises his fascist views behind a friendly manner. Like Hawthorne's Hollingsworth, however, he is a cold, vapid, robot-like functionary whose power Mailer sees as signalling the approach of Barbary. McLeod connects Hollingsworth with an advancing "state capitalism" which conjoins "state profit and state surveillance" and in which "the aim of society is no longer to keep its members alive, but quite the contrary, ... how to dispose of them" (200), and indeed, Mailer's Hollingsworth displays no moral comprehension nor intellectual depth. Greedy and sadistic, he merely serves the system that empowers him, and his elopement with Guinevere at the novel's end constitutes the author's ultimate comment on the fate of America, merging the fascist with the materialist.

The other central player in Lovett's vision is Lannie Madison, a young woman spiritually formed by the ideals of the Russian Revolution. A Trotskyite, she has been decimated psychologically by the war and its aftermath, and she is now a pathological remnant of her former self. Like Guinevere, she casts a spell over Lovett, reminding him of his own radical days, when he, too, was fired by a vision of human progress and betterment. Now bitterly reproaching herself for being foolish enough to hope for a better world, Lannie views the post-war society as a larger version of the concentration camps, similarly dedicated to the eradication of individualism and emotion. She blames McLeod for the betrayal of the ideals of the revolution.

Lovett, too, is a former Trotskyite, and he describes his early devotion in terms at once realistic and dreamlike:

> I was young then, and no dedication could match mine. The revolution was tomorrow, and the inevitable crises of capitalism ticked away in my mind with the certainty of a time bomb, and even then could never begin to match the ticking of my pulse ... For a winter and a spring I lived more intensely in the past than I could ever in the present, until the sight of a policeman on his mount became the Petrograd proletariat crawling to fame between the legs of a Cossack's horse.... There was never a revolution to equal it, and never a city more glorious than Petrograd....(91)

The passage is haunting and suggestive, like the feeling it describes, because it vividly characterizes the spiritual fervor of the youthful idealist, while its images convey the elusive intensity of the ideal itself. This Petrograd is an eternal city, a symbol of human perfectibility, yet beyond human reach. Lovett's amnesia, the novel suggests, results not only from the war but also from the death of his ideals and his devotion to an ennobling cause, which has cut him off both from his sense of self and from his past.

Barbary Shore concludes with McLeod's suicide, as Hollingsworth and Guinevere run off together and Lannie is arrested by the police. McLeod has, however, willed the "little object," the subject of Hollingsworth's search and the emblem of his own endangered Marxist ideals, to Lovett. Thus it is left to Lovett to keep the socialist dream alive while awaiting the apocalyptic war to come. The novel ends on a note of pessimism as Mailer echoes Fitzgerald:

> But for the present the storm approaches its thunderhead, and it is apparent that the boat drifts ever closer to shore. So the blind will lead the blind, and the deaf about warnings to one another until their voices are lost. (223)

The final line also concludes Chapter One, and the resulting suggestion of cyclical movement underscores Mailer's cynical view of human possibilities.

That pessimistic perspective is most prevalent in the dream-like sequences which evoke the narrator's personal sense of loss, but it is also supported by the political collapse narrated in realistic, historical terms. Again, Mailer portrays the human race as spiritually bankrupt, unable to grow or evolve beyond the state of Barbary. The spiritual malaise of the modern world colors much of the novel's prose, ultimately picturing a dark and barren landscape where no dreams may take root. In the face of this enveloping gloom, McLeod's legacy to Lovett seems weak and ultimately, as Mailer never specifically defines it, merely symbolic. Probably Mailer's belief in politics is only symbolic as well: at this point in his career he surely seems to be saying that political solutions have no practical value. If McLeod leaves anything to Lovett, it is a renewal of feeling, a rejuvenation of the psyche, but the effect of this endowment on Lovett's troubled spirit remains unexplored. In Mailer's later work, on the other hand, the individual's spiritual/psychological vitality will become paramount, and it will be linked not to political urges but to existential ones.

Like *Barbary Shore* Mailer's next novel, *The Deer Park* (1955), is a first-person narrative by a spiritually dislocated would-be novelist. Serguis O'Shaugnessy is both an orphan and a victim of historical disaster: a wartime bomber pilot, he became sickened by the recognition of his role as a killer.

Revolting against the horror of this "real world" (47), he suffered a nervous breakdown and then retreated to the fictitious community of Desert D'Or, a Palm Springs-like enclave situated near the cinema capital of Southern California and on the edge of the western desert. There Sergius drifts in search of some meaning to compensate for the emptiness of his world. Creatively and sexually impotent—Mailer's emphasis on sex in this novel signals an important shift in his thematic concerns—Sergius finds a perfect haven in Desert D'Or, which is full of aimless people like himself. Most prominent among these lost souls are Charles Francis Eitel, once a powerful Hollywood director, and Marion Faye, a drug dealer and pimp.

Eitel occupies the political center of the novel. Once recognized as a gifted artist who made socially responsible films in the thirties and as a committed radical who fought for democracy in Spain, he refused to cooperate with the House Committee on Un-American Activities in its Hollywood witch-hunts in the 1940s and 50s. There-upon blacklisted by the industry, he forfeited his power and his identity, and when Sergius meets him, he is hiding out in Desert D'Or, ignored by its more prosperous citizens. Eitel's loss of artistic and sexual potency represents for Sergius the betrayal of past values, which he feels he has lost as well, and so Eitel's future becomes a matter of personal significance to him.

The destructive power of the congressional committee makes it an obvious example of the totalitarian nature of American life, but the energy of evil permeates the novel's setting in another way, for Desert D'Or is a place of extraordinary sexual license. The title of the novel refers to Louis XV's infamous Deer Park, a description of which is used as an epigraph which reads in part: "Apart from the evil which this dreadful place did to the morals of the people, it is horrible to calculate the immense sums of money it cost the state." The carnal atmosphere of the isolated desert community is not for Mailer representative of America, a sexually repressed society; instead he implies that the libertine life enjoyed by the inhabitants of Desert D'Or is their reward for supplying the American public with movie myths about its democratic ideals. Charles Eitel once measured himself in rebellion against such a world.

In his exile Eitel is given a chance to recover his sense of self through his relationship with Elena Esposito, a failed dancer and actress who remains, nonetheless, a natural and courageous woman. With her his sexual potency is restored, and he begins work on an ambitious script which he hopes will reclaim his integrity as an artist. However, this burst of personal and artistic fortune does not last, as Eitel, becoming fearful of the risks his renewed vitality exposes him to, finally capitulates to the pressure of Hollywood. He confesses before the committee, recanting his youthful ideals, and is allowed to make a watered-down version of his original script. This apostasy blights his relationship with Elena, and she leaves him for a time.

Interestingly, the autocrat-figures in *The Deer Park*, the studio heads and producers, while formidable in power and prestige, are represented in a generally comic fashion. Their despotic control of the creative community seems neither frightening nor appalling, as was the grim dedication of Hollingsworth. Eitel well knows how to handle Herman Teppis (a studio head) and Collie Munshin (a producer and Teppis' son-in-law), although he fails to challenge their authority in any meaningful way. By undercutting the Hollywood power structure with such deliberate ridicule, Mailer seems to be opening the door for a character to defeat the oppressive system, but Eitel is a broken man, no longer possessed of the stamina needed for sustained rebellion. His capitulation before the committee signals an end to Mailer's preoccupation with politics as a solution.

Mailer's prescribed alternative to Eitel is Marion Faye. As Richard Poirier perceptively points out, "Faye is the secret center of *The Deer Park*.... The truth was simply that perversity and power interested [Mailer] far more than those efforts at health which led to limpness or defeat" (30). This partiality for vigor in preference to virtue, apparent in the subtexts of Mailer's first two novels but suppressed because it discomfited him, here rises to the surface for the first time: Eitel is defeated because he has lost his passion and his courage. Of little worth now are his refining powers of intelligence, a certain amount of compassion, and a large residue of guilt; according to Faye, these "vices" (159) only weaken men and turn them into "slobs" (147). In a deceptive world of compromise and illusion, more forceful modes seem called for, and Marion Faye believes in pushing himself to the limits of experience, seeking the "experience beyond experience" (332) that will empower him to overcome all obstacles to his existential freedom. He cultivates this mystical bravado by leaving his doors unlocked, thus exposing himself to the metaphoric threads of the desert and the very real threats of his local enemies; in fact, he hopes to open a door to some authentic experience at the precipice of reality. He enjoys driving at great speed to a mountain top where he looks out over the desert, the gambling city, and the atomic testing grounds. This last sight fills him with loathing for the military and the political leaders who justify its destructive power. At the same time, Faye yearns for the cataclysm it promises, for he recognizes in Desert D'Or a prime locus of the rationalized immorality of modern society, and he dreams of its violent destruction. Anticipating the perverse attitude Mailer would formulate two years later in "The White Negro," Faye is, in fact, a deliberate psychopath, regarding irrational violence as a means to exercise some control under repressive conditions. Perceiving that a violent act committed without regret or regard for social restraints can give him unlimited power and authority, he replaces the guilt that infuses Eitel's life with a numbing apathy. Faye, however, is too wholly a nihilist, repudiating all feeling, to represent an acceptable alternative to the defeated idealism of Eitel.

The central intelligence who strives to make sense of these psychosociopolitical phenomena is, again, the narrator, Sergius O'Shaugnessy. Like Mailer, Sergius views the world as a divided landscape:

> I had the idea that there were two worlds. There was a real world as I called it, ... and this real world was a world where orphans burned orphans. It was better not even to think of this. I liked the other world in which almost everybody lived. The imaginary world. (47)

The escapist, "imaginary" world of Desert D'Or teaches him, however, that this, too, can be a painful and destructive place. At the end of the novel Sergius imagines Eitel sending him a message to confess that he has lost his artistic drive, his belief that the created world is "more real to us, more real to others, than the mummery of what happens, passes and is gone." He then urges Sergius,

> So ... try for that other world, the real world, where orphans burn orphans and nothing is more difficult to discover than a simple fact. And with the pride of an artist, you must blow against the walls of every power that exists, the small trumpet of your defiance. (374)

From the voice of an exhausted generation of idealists, the young man thus receives the charge to persevere in the artist's quest for individual truth and validity against the oppressive forces of delusion and distortion.

After much tribulation, Sergius finally leaves Desert D'Or, to travel in Mexico and then settle in New York. At last he has cut himself off from politics—"I was still an anarchist, and an anarchist I would always be" (355)—and devotes himself instead to sex. Concluding with the injunction, "Rather think of Sex as Time, and Time as the connection of new circuits" (375), he (and Mailer) have clearly rejected engagement in the fortunes of a larger society in favor of the pursuit of personal relationships. In this novel

Mailer seems to be moving in new directions, seeking to refocus his attention to the individual rebellion against repression rather than the society-wide political activism that has yielded him no solutions in the past. Unfortunately, the central voices here remain weak, perhaps because he is still struggling for definition and real commitment to his new ideas. Faye, while provocative, is too extreme a character to command sympathy, and even Sergius is not a very compelling personality. Passive and unresponsive, he projects no convincing sense of the emotional consequences of his experience.

In examining Mailer's early fiction it is important to consider his masterful short story, "The Man Who Studied Yoga" (1952), written after the disillusionment expressed in *Barbary Shore* but before *The Deer Park*. Here Mailer writes for the only time about "normal" middle-class characters, Sam and Eleanor Slovoda, who are presented as a mature, well-adjusted couple. Sam is an ex-radical and aspiring novelist who makes his living writing continuities for the comics; Eleanor thinks of herself as a painter, but is also a housewife and mother. The story's central event occurs when they host a dinner for some friends, one of whom brings along a pornographic film, which they all watch and discuss. After the guests leave, the Slovodas run the film again and make love as they watch it. Then, his wife having fallen asleep, Sam thinks about his unrealized life as a writer and as a man. The film has reminded him of longings which are never to be satisfied, of the frustrations which underlie his comfortable life. In contrast to the sedate existence of these characters is one guest's tale of Cassius O'Shaugnessy, the man who studied yoga. A world-traveler who has spent his life testing himself against a variety of experiences, he occupies the moral center of the story. His example of self-realization highlights by comparison Sam's own inability to express or extend himself or to relieve his anxieties. Apparently he is doomed to live out his life in conformity to social convention and to be forever secretly despairing and frustrated.

Sam is clearly a more prosaic middle-class model for Eitel, and the story of Cassius a preparation for the extremist alternative of Marion Faye. However, Mailer would specifically elaborate on the response to life he was working toward in his early fiction in his famous essay, "The White Negro" (1957). Therein he declares that it is the fate of modern man to live with death, which is the heritage of the Second World War. The only response to such a situation is "to accept the terms of death, to live with death as immediate danger, to divorce oneself from society, to exist without roots, to set out on that unchartered journey with the rebellious imperatives of the self" (313). The exemplar of this condition of instinctual consciousness is the urban American Negro: by replacing the imperatives of society with the more vital and life-affirming imperatives of the self, the Negro makes it impossible for social institutions to account for him in their own terms. This form of rebellion is for Mailer the essence of "hip":

> So there was a new breed of adventurers, urban adventurers who drifted out at night looking for action with a black man's code to fit their facts. The hipster had absorbed the existentialist synapses of the Negro, and for practical purposes could be considered a white Negro. (315)

The hipster, then, defies "the collective murders of the State" (328) by becoming a psychopath. The strength of the psychopath is that he knows what is good or bad for him and knows that he can change "a negative and empty fear with an outward action" (320). He is an existentialist in that his values are determined by his inner psychological needs. His energy derives from the orgasm: "Orgasm is his therapy—he knows at the seed of his being that good orgasm opens his possibilities and bad orgasm imprisons him" (321). Thus Mailer finds sources for energy and being in the self, and so he turns away from society towards an inner world which contains the seeds of his well-being. Poirier explains: "The 'Negro' is the child in all of us, but the child after Freud, and the essay is a call to us to become 'children' not that we might escape from time but that we might re-engage ourselves with it" (79).

Mailer's first attempt to explore this inner, subconscious world in his fiction was *An American Dream* (1965), an extraordinary tour de force in which his language and style attain a new level of poetic suggestiveness, bridging the two worlds of external and internal reality. It is, again, a first-person narrative, told by Stephen Richards Rojack, a war hero, former congressman and professor of psychology, who recounts a thirty-two-hour psychic journey in which his old self is destroyed as he struggles toward spiritual and psychological rebirth. His odyssey begins with the murder of his estranged wife, Deborah, who represents for him an anti-life force. To be reborn involves immersing oneself in the destructive element, so Rojack must court death and so gain a heightened awareness of life. In order to free himself of the shackles of societal conformity, he must push himself to the limits of experience. Symbolically Rojack realizes this self-liberation when he visits his father-in-law, Barney Kelly, high atop the Waldorf Towers, where Kelly has summoned him to discuss his daughter's death. In order to free himself of Kelly, a man of enormous wealth and power, Rojack realizes that he must go to the terrace and walk the parapet: the performance of this act symbolizes his self-renewal.

Rojack thus makes of himself the kind of primitive being who is in contact with his non-rational self, and Mailer apparently envisions him as a prototype of the heroic new individualist who will emerge in modern America to assault the repressive state. The subconscious being a state outside time and civilization, Rojack arrives there in classic American literary fashion when he "lights out" for the prehistoric jungles of the Yucatan and Guatemala at the end of the novel.

Since *An American Dream* Mailer has written only three novels—*Why Are We in Vietnam?* (1967), *Ancient Evenings* (1983), and *Tough Guys Don't Dance* (1984)—reaffirming in each case his devotion to individual consciousness as the rightful sphere of aesthetic concern. In his early work the social world retained sufficient importance that Mailer felt obligated to serve the demands of mimesis even while moving away from it; in the later fiction that ambiguity is resolved in favor of a subjectivity that supersedes realism. It seems clear that the Norman Mailer of the past twenty years is more comfortable in the realm of non-fiction, where the demands of social and political reality force him to keep a tighter rein on the extravagant energies of his imagination. In works such as *The Armies of the Night* (1968), *Of a Fire on the Moon* (1971), and *The Executioner's Song* (1979), Mailer's narrative talents and his prodigious capacities as an observer of American social and political life merge into a fluent and compelling whole. Perhaps he realizes that the "big book" about America that he has longed to write will have to unite the two voices, the realistic and the romantic, in a coherent and sustained vision. So far the ability to do so seems to have eluded him.

NOTES

1. Mailer's attraction to Cummings and Croft is also discussed by Norman Podhoretz in "Norman Mailer: The Embattled Vision."

2. Another excellent source for biographical information is Peter Manso, *Mailer: His Life and Times.*

3. The relationship between *Barbary Shore and Blithedale Romance* is discussed by Laura Adams, *Existential Battles: The Growth of Norman Mailer* (41-42), and John Stark, *"Barbary Shore:* The Basis of Mailer's Best Work."

Works Cited

Adams, Laura. *Existential Battles: The Growth of Norman Mailer*. Athens: Ohio University Press, 1976.

Hawthorne, Nathaniel. *The Blithedale Romance*. New York: Norton, 1958.

Mailer, Norman. *An American Dream*. New York: Dell, 1971.

——— *Barbary Shore*. New York: Signet, 1953.

——— *The Deer Park*. New York: G.P. Putnam's Sons, 1955.

——— "The Man Who Studied Yoga." *Advertisements for Myself*. New York: Berkeley, 1966. 145-173.

——— *The Naked and the Dead*. New York: Signet, 1951.

——— *The Presidential Papers*. New York: Berkeley, 1976.

——— "The White Negro." *Advertisements for Myself*. New York: Berkeley, 1966. 311-331.

Manso, Peter. *Mailer: His Life and Times*. New York: Simon and Schuster, 1985.

Mills, Hilary. *Mailer: A Biography*. New York: Empire Books, 1982.

Podhoretz, Norman. "Norman Mailer: The Embattled Vision." *Partisan Review* 26 (1959): 371-391.

Poirier, Richard. *Norman Mailer*. New York: Viking, 1972.

Stark, John. "*Barbary Shore*: The Basis of Mailer's Best Work." *Modern Fiction Studies* 17 (1971): 403-408.

NIGEL LEIGH

Marxisms on Trial:
Barbary Shore

If there are large formal differences between *The Naked and the Dead* and Mailer's second novel, *Barbary Shore*,[1] there is nevertheless a close political kinship between the two books. The Marxist influence in *The Naked and the Dead* is translated in *Barbary Shore* into Marxist perspective. The only actual Marxists in the first novel—if Hearn is excluded as a left liberal or proto-Marxist—are an anonymous hobo in a time-machine section and the members of Havard's John Reed Club who expel Hearn from their group. In *Barbary Shore* Marxism is centralized. As Stanley Gutman points out, the novel is nothing less than 'an inquiry into the political, social, and historical meaning of Marxism in the twentieth century'.[2] The discourse on power is established again, this time on terms that are openly political and unencumbered by generic imperatives. Whereas Mailer had, like Hearn, only 'played around' with Marxism in *The Naked and the Dead*, here he is concerned to fulfil Walter B. Rideout's definition of the radical writer's intention to 'work out in his fiction a Marxist analysis of society'.[3] The firmness of Mailer's grip on ideological matters is reflected in the narrowness and depth of the material, his extended excursions into the left, the right, twentieth-century political history and human nature. Dense, abstract and formalized expository material confined to the shorthand form of dialogue in *The Naked and the Dead* makes up the core of *Barbary Shore*.

From *Radical Fictions and the Novels of Norman Mailer*. © 1990 by Nigel Leigh.

Mailer's precise position with regard to the ideological perspectives evoked in the novel remains unclear, unstable and changing. At certain points in the text he is broadly Marxist in sympathy; at other points a narrow Trotskyist viewpoint is endorsed; and towards the end it is strongly implied through symbols that he favours a post-Marxist radical position. However, the absence of a definitive politics in the novel does not affect its basic commitment to a radical social philosophy, and it presents us with answers to a number of important questions. When did the Russian Revolution begin to fail? Is Marxism a spent force? Ought we to be left-wing? The speculative, unsettled nature of the arguments unleashed show Mailer's mind to be no more fixed or certain than it was in his factitiously coherent first novel, but the ambiguity in the exposition of *Barbary Shore* represents an intellectual and political improvement on *The Naked and the Dead* because it is more honest. No attempt is made to subjugate ideas that threaten the overall moral and aesthetic programme of the book. In fact there is an almost complete absence of those elements of planning which safely guided the 'construction' of *The Naked and the Dead*. For better or worse, Mailer thinks thematically rather than aesthetically, without the insurance policy of sound structure. This makes the novel an invaluable source for an understanding of the details of Mailer's political development on the left (which was virtually forgotten in the 1960s and 1970s), and it demonstrates the degree to which the theme of power can intrude upon the texture of his fiction.

In 1955 Mailer said, with reference to the writing of *The Naked and the Dead*,

> I was an anarchist then, and I'm an anarchist today. In between I belonged to the Progressive Party during the Wallace campaign, and then broke off rather abruptly at the time of the Waldorf Peace Conference in 1949. What followed was a period of political wandering in the small circle of libertarian socialism. I was at the same time very radical and half-hearted about it.[4]

Reflecting again in 1963, he pointed out that he 'started *Barbary Shore* as some sort of fellow traveller and finished with a political position which was a far-flung mutation of Trotskyism'.[5] Between the writing of *The Naked and the Dead* and *Barbary Shore* Mailer became fully radicalized. Many potential radical influences had been avoided in the first novel as a result of their association with something he actively avoided in his work: 'it was and is easier to write a war novel about the Pacific—you don't have to have a feeling for the culture of Europe and the collision of America upon it. To try a novel about the last war in Europe without a sense of the past is to fail in the worst way.'[6] Only after *The Naked and the Dead* is Mailer able to cultivate the feeling for the culture of Europe and the sense of the past, and with these things comes a mandate to produce radical fictions.

The origins of this process lie in Mailer's relationship with Jean Malaquais, to whom *Barbary Shore* is dedicated. Malaquais is the prevailing influence on the novel, the source of its main ideas, its presiding consciousness and the model for one of its most important characters. Mailer met Malaquais, an anti-Stalinist Marxist philosopher-novelist, in Paris shortly after the publication of *The Naked and the Dead* (which he translated into French), and he rapidly assumed the role of Mailer's political teacher.[7] To Malaquais, Mailer seemed to be a 'boy scout, both intellectually and mentally',[8] politically ignorant and naïve:

> Norman had a classical petit-bourgeois middle class concept of elections. You elect a representative, a civil servant, as president, and if you don't like them, you vote them out of office. I told him this was nonsense, that crooks get reelected. On that score we had differences because for him an election meant democracy. But he didn't even know the difference between direct democracy and elective democracy.[9]

In Malaquais's view, Mailer possessed no significant political orientation. He knew nothing of the Russian Revolution, very little about the Moscow Trials, and at a time when many intellectuals in the United States were anti-Stalinist he was unfamiliar with their argument. As a result of these enormous gaps, Mailer, a radical manqué, became engrossed in Malaquais's foreign perspectives. Despite Malaquais's belief that there remained in his protégé a vestigial 'lingering inclination towards a pseudohumanism or liberalism',[10] Mailer publicly expressed leftist opinions on the post-war international situation in Europe.[11] The influence of Malaquais, combined with the ignominious collapse of the Wallace campaign, consolidated Mailer's radical development. If the Wallace campaign ended for a long time Mailer's attraction to collective political action, it served to open him up to a much more extreme conception of political power. Once he became a resident of New York, Malaquais assumed responsibility for Mailer's continuing education, guiding him through studies of the French and Russian Revolutions and the American working class. Significantly Malaquais did not emphasize Marx, on the grounds that Mailer was too ignorant of political theory for it to be of any value. In discussions Malaquais concentrated on his own negative concept of state capitalism (Soviet communism), which percolated through to *Barbary Shore*.

Malaquais argued that most available versions of communism were counter-revolutionary, distortions of Marx's vision. By 1949 there is strong evidence that Mailer had absorbed Malaquais's specific brand of ideology. During the Conference for World Peace at the Waldorf Hotel, Mailer made a speech which hinged on the idea of state capitalism: 'I am afraid both the United States and the Soviet Union are moving towards State Capitalism. There is no future in that. The two systems approach each other more clearly. All a writer can do is tell the truth as he sees it, and to keep on writing.'[12] Critical of socialism, Mailer nevertheless spoke from a socialist point of view, and through this critical dialectic created a niche for himself on the independent revolutionary left. What Malaquais was instrumental in doing was in guiding Mailer away from a more conventional brand of leftism or from Stalinism. As a consequence, Mailer did not come under the historical imperative to renounce or retreat from socialism. Immune from the forces which demoralized and disillusioned the conventional American left, he was free to occupy an advanced position, albeit on his own idiosyncratic terms. The fiction of *Barbary Shore* centres on this notion of socialism's 'inheritance', and the plot to which Marxist dialectics are affixed is a reworking of Mailer's own induction into the mysteries of historical materialism. The narrative is one which, according to Walter B. Rideout, the radical novel employs most frequently: the education of a central character in a social philosophy that shakes him loose from unthinking acceptance of the *status quo*. Upon learning the true nature of class society, the character experiences a conversion to political radicalism.[13] Thus *Barbary Shore* exploits both Mailer's own experience of conversion and the sacred story of initiation told and retold in the literature of radicalism.

Barbary Shore uses Malaquais in several ways. He provides the novel with a central figure in the character of the charismatic European Marxist intellectual William McLeod (the Irish name is a pseudonym which conceals East European origins).[14] Equipped with Malaquais's intellectual instruction, Mailer can approach the theme he avoided in *The Naked and the Dead* and present doctrinal issues with uninhibited relish. In addition, Malaquais can be used to rework on new terms the relationship which obtained between Cummings and Hearn. He can provide for *Barbary Shore* what *The Naked and the Dead* lacked: a model for the relationships in charismatic induction. The feeling for culture is equally a culture of feeling, and the epistemological thrill which comes from personal transmissions of knowledge drives the novel. Thus, for Mailer, the book is inseparably associated with the vision 'formed osmotically by the powerful intellectual influence of ... Jean Malaquais'.[15]

II

There are two forms of bureaucratic power in *Barbary Shore* which are the focus of Mailer's political concern. The first is American and embodied by Leroy Hollingsworth, a representative of secret government agencies; the second is European and associated with William McLeod (or his past behaviour) and the period of Russian history from the 1917 Revolution to Trotsky's assassination and the signing of the Nazi-Soviet Pact. The first is a development of *The Naked and the Dead's* anti-fascist and anti-bureaucratic themes. The second is largely the inheritance of Malaquais.

The Naked and the Dead ends with a time machine projected prophetically towards a post-war future in which Major Dalleson will be the prototype, the coming man. Mailer's attitude towards Dalleson is derisive: 'A more imaginative man would have loathed the assignment, for it consisted essentially of composing long lists of men and equipment and creating a timetable. It demanded the same kind of patience that is needed to construct a crossword puzzle.'[16] Dull, conventional, the opposite of the charismatics, Dalleson is a stock figure: the bureaucrat.[17] Mailer sides with Cummings, who treats him with unconcealed scorn: 'Dalleson's got a mind like a switchboard he told himself. If your plug will fill one of his mental holes, he can furnish you with the necessary answer, but otherwise he is very lost.'[18] The congeries of images the Major attracts—timetables, crosswords, switchboards—evokes his closed mechanical mind. Reading reality through these restrictive cognitive maps, Dalleson never experiences the world directly. His world is uninhabited by the arcane forces which animate and obsess Cummings and Croft. Consequently he is protected against the opening-up of human vision to the degree that it will involve, as it does for Cummings and Croft, exposure to a reality that is perilously unpredictable (both men are frustrated by chance), unscheduled and unschematic.

Dalleson represents a post-war future that is essentially bureaucratic and authoritarian: rule by the officer class. Reinforcing this insight, *Barbary Shore* heralds the emergence of an American version of the police state. The historical context is again the conservative revival, during which American communism became the focus of State Department and governmental agencies' interest in national security. Written immediately prior to the Korean War and rise of McCarthyism, the novel anticipates both developments. (Ruth Prigozy's view that *Barbary Shore* is 'the most serious novel to emerge from the McCarthy period'[19] underestimates the degree to which Mailer predicts the worst excesses of McCarthyism between 1953 and 1955.) The prophetic Dalleson-figure is Leroy Hollingsworth, an undercover government agent sent to investigate the political mentor (McLeod) of the novel's narrator, the writer-manqué Michael Lovett. He also intends to secure the return of an unnamed 'little object' (p. 196) which has been appropriated by McLeod from the US Government, to whom he has defected from an American communist organization. Commentators do not agree which governmental agency employs Hoollingsworth. For Barry Leeds he is simply a 'secret policeman'.[20] Andrew Gordon also sees him as an ambiguous 'government agent'.[21] Jean Radford goes further and describes him as 'an agent for the national security organization closely resembling the FBI'.[22] In Robert Solotaroff's view, he is certainly an FBI agent,[23] and both Jennifer Bailey and Robert Begiebing agree.[24] But Philip Bufithis is less certain: he works for 'possibly the FBI or the CIA'.[25] And Stanley Gutman prefers ttto see him as 'an agent of something like the CIA'.[26]

Evidence drawn from the whole of Mailer's work suggests strongly that Hollingsworth is the first example of an obsession with the powers and activities of the CIA (formed in 1947) which is a distinctive theme of Mailer's until the 1970s. In an open letter to President Kennedy, Mailer warned against the CIA's view of Cuba.[27] In his film *Maidstone* Mailer creates a secret service, based on the CIA, which threatens the autobiographical hero played by Mailer.[28] In *St George and the Godfather* conspiracy theories are returned to: 'Aquarius [Mailer] sometimes thought it was his life's ambition to come up with evidence that the CIA was tripping on American elections.'[29] And in 1973 Mailer went so far as to create an organization called the Fifth Estate, reflecting his view that the CIA and FBI were constantly manipulating the American public:

> I want a people's FBI and a people's CIA to investigate these two.... If we have a democratic secret police keeping tabs on Washington's secret police, which is not democratic but bureaucratic, we will see how far paranoia is justified.... What happened in Dallas? What about Martin Luther King? The real story behind Watergate? How many plots are there in America? Two? Three? None?[30]

Although Mailer's counterintelligence plan did not develop, it finally emerged in Washington, first as the Committee for Action Research and then as the Organizing Committee for the Fifth Estate, and Mailer refers to it as 'the best political idea of my entire life'.[31] He also argued that there had been secret government involvement in the death of Marilyn Monroe.[32] But the crowning achievement of Mailer's longstanding preoccupation with the

CIA is undoubtedly his 1976 essay 'A Harlot High and Low', which contains an epigraph from Malaquais: 'There are no answers. There are only questions.'[33] Here Mailer searches—in vain again—for a 'model' for the 'penetration of Central Intelligence'.[34]

The seeds of this obsession with the CIA and secret government stretch back to the beginnings of Mailer's work. In *Barbary Shore* Hollingsworth's character is Mailer's first attempt to penetrate the epistemology of Central Intelligence. Jean Radford's assertion that Hollingsworth 'embodies some of the qualities of Croft and Cummings'[35] misses his real affinity with Major Dalleson, and the degree to which both characters are essentially portraits of depersonalization. Hollingsworth is a jumble of contradictions: bland on the surface, bestial beneath; untidy but obsessed with order; shy yet aggressive; humble and vain; gracious and sadistic. His excessive formality ('his politeness was irritating'— p. 38) masks his true feelings, which are, to use the novel's primary image, barbaric. Without naturalness or spontaneity, Hollingsworth's overcivilized behaviour indicates its opposite, a complete absence of genuine manners. Guinevere's daughter, Monina, penetrates through to Hollingsworth when she bites his hand:

> Hollingsworth was caught by surprise. Unguarded, a moan escaped from his mouth, his eyes opened in fright. What nightmares were resurrected? He sat helpless upon the chair, his head thrown back, his limbs rigid, a convict in the death-room, his body violated in the spasms of the current.
>   'I'm innocent,' he screamed. (p. 125)

The repressed, compartmentalized personality structure of the bureaucrat is neurotic. Guilt, fears of persecution and sexual chaos are concealed from public view. Beneath Hollingsworth's attempts at sexual charm lies the puerile, predatory mind of a rapist (p. 97). Beyond that there are moments when he seems 'womanish' (p. 225), and his approaches to McLeod sometimes hint at sexual attraction (something similar was implied in the Cummings–Hearn relationship in *The Naked and the Dead*). The spectrum of sexual feeling attributed to Hollingsworth argues for a lack of harmony in his nature. The elements in him do not add up; there is no integration of the different aspects of self. His mind, like Dalleson's, is a switchboard, a bureaucratized circuit of connections. Looking out through 'opaque and lifeless' (p. 40) eyes, he perceives only what he is programmed to see. As McLeod says, 'I tell myself he's got a policeman's brain, and it's only the murders he can understand' (p. 202). He cannot deal with the cryptic. He is like Kennedy's CIA, who turn 'nuances into facts, and lose other nuances, and mangle facts into falsities'.[36] In Mailer's view, Central Intelligence can only possess the zero and the one, and 'theoretical incapacities' (p. 161) prevent Hollingsworth from understanding much of what McLeod confesses with regard to the matters under investigation.

His personal culture (boondock simplicity, a taste for Westerns, pornography and ballroom dancing), hostility to metropolitan values, philistinism, and cover job as a Wall Street clerk locate him in the context of the conservative revival. To McLeod, the focus of wisdom in *Barbary Shore*, Hollingsworth is a 'madman' (p. 36); the rigid categories he operates with are the essence of 'state information' (p. 153). The confession McLeod is required to make must therefore conform to a reductive pattern:

> Admits to being a Bolshevist.
> Admits to being a Communist.
> Admits to being an Atheist.
> Admits to blowing up Churches.
> Admits to being against free enterprise.
> Admits to encouraging violence.
> Advocates murder of President and Congress.
> Advocates destruction of the South.
> Advocates use of poison.
> Admits allegiance to a foreign power.
> Is against Wall Street. (p. 72)

Thought and behaviour are made to comply with an already-existing stencilled model. As in Dalleson's map-reading exercises on the final page of *The Naked and the Dead*, 'state information' overlays a grid on reality. McLeod's resistance to this process, given his willingness to confess, is a refusal to package the complexities of his political culture in accordance with these requirements: 'I resent Leroy for my judge and the fact that he makes a smudge on the paper and is indifferent to what I have endured I find intolerable' (p. 202). With his own intimate knowledge of bureaucratic power, he will not acknowledge its maddened rationality. Hollingsworth's 'political education' (p. 148) is thus kept on charismatic non-bureaucratic terms that are alien to his most basic procedures and taxonomies.

Hollingsworth's bland depersonalized self derives from a subservience to the structural power he represents. He is banally evil. The vacancy of self, the absence of distinguishing personal qualities, is a functional component of the model of power in which he is a vector. Through him Mailer argues that the American state, particularly in its secret aspects, is dangerous to its subjects; and in the final pages of the novel, when the rooming house in which most of the action takes place is invaded by 'agents from the country we live in' (p. 248) there is an image of internal state terror which compares with the practices of Stalin's secret police. Despite national and ideological differences, capitalism and communism are shown to exist on the same plane. Thus, at a certain point, Hollingsworth and McLeod, who has worked for both Stalin and the CIA, are interchangeable. As McLeod observes, 'the truth is that there are deep compacts between Leroy and myself, you might almost say we are sympathetic to each other' (p. 199). Hollingsworth's emergence at the end of *Barbary Shore* with the 'inheritance' of McLeod's confession (though not the sought-after 'little object') repeats the conclusion of *The Naked and the Dead* and is central to the bleak political signal Mailer is transmitting. In symbolic terms, the unreconstructed bureaucrat, immune to the influence of McLeod's confession, finds favour with both the capitalist proletariat (represented by the sexual favours of Guinevere) and its subsequent generation (represented by Guinevere's daughter). Even the mentally disturbed Trotskyist, Lannie Madison, is prepared to support Hollingsworth: 'if there is a future, it is with him' (p. 179). Only McLeod is capable of recognizing the political pattern of ascending bureaucracy and exact value of Hollingsworth's 'inheritance': '"So you come soon to power," McLeod said quietly, "but you have merely inherited a crisis, and yours is the profit of cancer"' (p. 233). Hollingsworth's emergence only extends the political bureaucracy which took hold of the century after the Russian Revolution; it simply adds to the process of political retardation.

However, the specific theme introduced by Hollingsworth is not pursued in great detail. This is partly because it repeats what has already been said about Dalleson, but primarily Hollingsworth is neglected because of Mailer's almost total preoccupation with McLeod's charismatic personality and the Marxist material only he can introduce and handle in the fiction. Thus in the second half of *Barbary Shore* Hollingsworth is used mainly to sustain a dramatic situation in which McLeod can speak at inordinate length on issues relating to the history of socialism, a role he shares with Michael Lovett, the true recipient of McLeod's inheritance. The issues evoked by Hollingsworth are either abandoned or absorbed into the larger theme of bureaucracy associated with McLeod alone. If Hollingsworth is the rising bureaucrat of the capitalist state, McLeod is an ex-bureaucrat from the communist state. Politically they are moving in opposite directions. McLeod is the novel's 'great reader' (p. 25) and 'thinking man' (p. 104), the intellectual epicentre from which the text derives. His vast amount of political experience, knowledge of Europe and feeling for culture permit him to 'understand finally the gory unremitting task of history' (p. 200). He is the only character with an overview of the world situation. The reverence in the text for McLeod's powerful intellect ('his intelligence was acute'—p. 34) and his assumption of the role of 'pedagogue' (p. 68) is Mailer's acknowledgement of his own political mentor. But the patina of sophistication McLeod has is not composed solely of knowledge or personal culture; it is also the guilt and pessimism of accumulated experience (the realm Cummings is about to be thrust into at the end of *The Naked and the Dead*), and what fascinates Mailer here is the complex fate of the radical mind.

McLeod naturally assumes the role of mentor towards the tyro Lovett: 'In everything he did there were elements of such order, demanding, monastic. He was unyielding and sometimes forbidding' (p. 35). (In similar terms, Cummings refers to himself as a 'chief monk, the Lord of my little abbey.'[37]) But Lovett resists the destabilizing effect of the charismatic personality and admits only to a 'left-handed fascination' (p. 25) with the older man. The conversations between the two men are intense, abstruse and, for Lovett, demanding. McLeod is teasingly gnomic, oblique and mysterious. Overstretched by these encounters, Lovett sometimes 'shunned his company' (p. 28). McLeod's ability as an interrogator ('He had a facility for wearing one down'—p. 26) is shown in the way he inspires involuntary admissions and spontaneous confessions: 'I discovered myself telling him one day about the peculiar infirmity I was at such pains to conceal from everyone else' (p. 34); 'in his presence I could find enthusiasm for the balm of confession' (p. 66). The crucial difference between McLeod and Hollingsworth as interrogators is that McLeod's scrutiny is 'so dispassionate, so balanced'. McLeod does not abuse his personal authority.

However, McLeod's political record is as evil as General Cummings'. What makes him morally superior to Cummings is his repentance, charted in a vein of religious imagery beneath the novel's ideological surface. Lovett's accusation that McLeod is a bureaucrat touches a raw spiritual nerve:

> Once I told him, 'You sound like a hack,' and McLeod reacted with a rueful frown. 'An exceptional expression for you to employ, Lovett,' he told me softly. 'I take it you mean by "hack" a representative of the people's state across the sea, but I'm wondering where you picked up the word, for it indicates a reasonable amount of political experience on your part' (p. 35).

An enormous reservoir of guilt is contained within McLeod's personality. Joining the 'movement' when he was twenty-one and leaving when he was forty (he is forty-four in the novel's present) is described as 'nineteen years with the wrong woman' (p. 105). It is revealed that he has played an obscure but active role in Stalin's purges as a 'hangman of the Left Opposition' (p. 153). In the words of Lannie, the deranged Trotskyist, he has been 'the undertaker of the revolution' (p. 158). In fact the details of McLeod's assassinations elicit Hollingsworth's professional respect: 'one has to admire his efficiency' (p. 191). McLeod's defence of his actions hinges on the denial of self implicit in bureaucratic power; he was 'the product of a system', an instrument or extension of the state. His crimes were therefore selflessly motivated. A personal moral-political crisis only occurs on the death of Trotsky (ambiguously described in the text) and the Nazi-Soviet Pact. Defecting to the US Government, he worked in yet another bureaucratic capacity as a 'statistician' (p. 151). But this attempt to reverse his actions for the communist state 'merely succeeded in doubling it' (p. 202). Thus McLeod has been the consummate hack, operating for both ideological systems; a 'true reactionary' (p. 158), as he refers to himself. It is even implied that he was partly responsible ('just a cog'—p. 203) for Trotsky's assassination. As a bureaucrat he despised the very idea of Trotsky since it inspired guilt and self-hatred: 'the thought of him was unbearable.'

At the time of the novel's present McLeod is not politically active and no longer a 'joiner' (p. 35). Socialist experience has amounted to personal tragedy; being a state functionary has left him 'destroyed as a person' (p. 185). As an independent leftist, a 'Marxist-at-liberty' (p. 36), he searches for a non-bureaucratic alternative in writing and study. This recontemplation of the basic aims of socialism is a way of continuing to affirm Marxist politics. Precisely what sort of politics is left vague, but the gesture is hopeful: 'Thus notice the admirable path I have taken from the bureaucrat to the theoretician' (p. 202). As a writer he redeems himself, preparing articles and pamphlets for the radical conventicle. He may be a broken political spirit, a 'poor retired bureaucrat' (p. 108) who is 'completely adrift' (p. 205), but he has transcended the authoritarian influence of the state in both its communist and capitalist forms. He is no longer 'a servant of any power' (p. 195).

The radical analysis advanced by McLeod, which underlies the whole novel, is composed of two elements. It is a *retrospective* overview of the failure of socialism in the Soviet Union after 1917 and a *prophetic* assessment of the growing similarities between the Russian and American states and their effect on the world situation. Although Mailer is critical of developments in socialism since the revolution, he does not go as far as Wilhelm Reich and argue that all socialist revolutions are bound to fail. He adopts the position ultimately attributable to Trotsky: 'when the events of 1917 failed to induce similar proletarian uprisings in the countries of the West, the revolution was doomed' (p. 228). After initial success the revolution began to collapse in the midst of an internal ideological debate about world revolution *versus* revolution in one country. Through McLeod's expositions Mailer argues that the central irony of the revolution is that its energies became directed against the very principles it helped to liberate. The state's legitimization of violence and terror during the purges of those labelled counterrevolutionary marks the point at which the abuse of power began. To avoid the formation of opposition (Mailer's 'Left Opposition'), members and officials were liquidated. Stalin, though he is never mentioned in *Barbary Shore*, is the embodiment of this bureaucratization of socialism, and terror is understood wholly as a phenomenon associated with Stalinism rather than as an instrument used throughout the revolution to consolidate its aims. In other words, Mailer remains sentimental about the revolution itself and isolates it from the negative critique of socialist power. Thus he is not prepared to trace the philosophy of mass terror to its theoretical source in Marx's concept of the dictatorship of the proletariat, the necessary though (ideally) transitional phase of authoritarian hegemony. Instead he prefers the view, derived from Malaquais, that Stalin's dictatorship is an aberration and not a development of Lenin's systematic application of Marxist theory.

Yet the pattern of Mailer's version of the failure of socialism arguably owes as much to Max Weber as it does to Marx. McLeod's description is of the routinization or bureaucratization of charisma: 'It is the fate of charisma, whenever it comes into the permanent institutions of a community, to give way to a process of tradition or of rational socialization.'[38] In Weber's model this routinization process in inevitable: 'In its purest form charismatic authority may be said to exist only in the process of originating. It cannot remain stable, but becomes either traditionalized or rationalized, or a combination of both.'[39] Thus only in the beginning can a revolution be genuinely revolutionary. As the cultural historian Bernard de Jouvenal puts it, 'The beginnings of a revolution are of an indescribable charm. The event, while it is still in suspense, seems to open up every possibility.'[40] Mailer uses Stalin to reclaim the revolution, celebrate the purity of its origins. No matter how faulty its practices might be, its theory remains sound. In this way Mailer can be both a socialist and an ardent critic of socialism. As a result of holding this dialectical view, and because of the historical lateness of his arrival at Marxism (he was never a member of the Communist Party), Mailer is effectively spared the kind of destructive inner struggle experienced by older writers such as Arthur Koestler (the influence of whose *Darkness at Noon* on *Barbary Shore* is evident), André Gide (to whom Malaquais was amanuensis) and Richard Wright. These writers were forced to retreat from communism as a belief system, while the routinization of the revolution's charisma implies no such personal tragedy for Mailer.

The second part of McLeod's analysis is more apocalyptic than the first. In the wake of the failure of socialism, 'state capitalism' (p. 226) has emerged. Both the Soviet Union and the United States (monopoly capitalism) are in a condition of near-crisis. Monopoly capitalism requires the steady expansion of markets and is committed to a programme of imperialism and colonialism, while the Third World (which is the object of this programme) is moving rapidly towards forms of state capitalism.[41] The crisis of state capitalism hinges on its 'inability to raise the standard of living' (p. 228). Socialism, 'lost in the necessity for survival' (p. 229), has created the conditions of slave labour. The economy has deteriorated and has no internal capacity to improve productivity. The separate condition of each ideological system makes war an inevitable outcome: 'I think it is reasonable to assert that if either of the two powers is unable to solve the economic problems without going to war, it must follow that war will come. But what if both the Colossi suffer such contradictions? A fortiori the inevitability receives its double guarantee' (p. 228). Each bloc prepares for war from its own imperative to survive. But it will be a war between two systems that have grown alike, between 'virtually identical forms of exploitation' (p. 230). From that moment

> the rate of production is never again capable of steady increase. The search begins for methods to stimulate it. State competition becomes substituted, and artificial campaigns between state corporations, accompanied by all the machinery of propaganda, make exhaustive efforts to match the requirements of armament. Piecework reappears. Such a process is narcotic. The injection must become progressively more intense, until the price for losing a competition becomes the neck of a bureaucrat. The first stage of cannibalism has been reached, and the bureaucracy finds itself obliged to dispose of the same personnel it needs so desperately. They are a class which comes to power at the very moment they are in the act of destroying themselves. (p. 231)

The process is the long road to the 'concentration camp' (p. 232) inside the state and war outside it. War becomes the permanent condition ('the police are everywhere'—p. 230) and the deterioration continues 'until we are faced with mankind in barbary' (p. 233).

McLeod's analysis is an extension of the thesis put forward by Cummings in *The Naked and the Dead* that 'this is going to be the reactionary's century, perhaps their thousand year reign'.[42] *Barbary Shore* continues to worry this insight. Cummings and McLeod are both theorists of forces of reaction (fascism, Stalinism) and participants in the phenomena they describe, insiders. Although this kind of writing against the power of the state lies within a distinguished tradition stretching back in American literature to Thoreau and Tom Paine, in *Barbary Shore* the critique of bureaucratic state power is problematic, not only because it is crudely incorporated into the novel's fiction but primarily because Mailer's presentation of the material overvalues its significance. Jean Radford is prepared to dismiss the Mailer-McLeod critique on the grounds that it is 'couched in fairly orthodox Trotskyist terms',[43] and readers of any persuasion will encounter difficulties. For the anti-Stalinist left, Mailer's intellectual pyrotechnics are much too commonplace to be engaging. Beyond the thrill of radical recognition lies only leftist *Weltschmerz*. (Malaquais found the book basically unsatisfying.) For the popular readership, though, the theoretical hardware which clearly intoxicates Mailer is far too formidable, sectarian and obscurely handled to be compelling. As McLeod himself points out, he speaks 'in the most abstract and general terms' (p. 234). In centralizing the critique of state power and making *Barbary Shore* rest on it, the novel becomes simultaneously banal and obscure. It is difficult to see for whom this material was intended. However, Mailer luxuriates in the climate of dialectics and rigorous analysis, and from the point of view of the theme of power the novel is particularly revealing. It demonstrates the degree to which Mailer is capable of being absorbed by theoretical questions about power and how politically motivated his writing can be. In the sophistication of its politics, considerably more advanced than the vocabulary of *The Naked and the Dead*, it highlights Mailer's capacity for development and provides ample evidence of his attempt to root himself in a leftist tradition. Above all, it clarifies Mailer's urge to be a writer of didactic intentions, whose mission is to spread ideas, in this case the political ideas of McLeod's analysis.

III

McLeod's pivotal analysis is largely a negative gloss on Marxist power: socialism is man's only hope but it has been corrupted. The pessimism of this overview leaves little room for a viable conception of Marxism, although the purpose of the discourse in *Barbary Shore* is to further the aims of socialist thought. Mailer's achievement is to arrive at a critical if not a full-blown Marxist position within a fictional context and the conducive atmosphere of internal debate, and a controlling form of radical politics does emerge in the final pages of the novel. The focus of this is Lovett's politicization, the abandoning of his political neutrality and belief that the radical cause is 'hopeless' (p. 107). He divests himself of the self-image of a non-political writer 'There was my typewriter, and somehow I did not want to leave it there. Why I took it with me I hardly knew, but within the hour I had dropped it in a pawnshop and followed my impulse to the end, the name I gave was not my own and the address I wrote was a street which did not exist' (p. 240). Relinquishing his manuscript propels him from amnesia, pastlessness, into time and transforms him into a historical agent. He moves from the cultivation of sentiment to action. Through McLeod the amnesiac has made a literal recovery of consciousness. Laying the groundwork, McLeod has prepared Lovett for study (p. 251) and the continuation of his own return to theory. The fundamental purpose of his confession has therefore been for Lovett to bear witness. The apparent interlocutor, Hollingsworth, is incapable of understanding and bored by the discourse. The other symbolic witness, Lannie, is too deranged to benefit from its information.

In addition to this programme of political re-education, McLeod's will leaves to Lovett the 'remnants' of his 'socialist culture' (p. 256). This symbolic transference, which echoes Mailer's relationship to Malaquais, attests to the power of charismatic transaction. At first sight this image of individual power seems to conflict with the preoccupation with historical materialism. As Mailer himself points out, 'men enter into social and economic relations independent of their wills' (p. 138). But in the context of such proliferating bureaucracy (communist and capitalist) the idea of intense personal relations gains radical credibility and becomes associated with the style of Marxism which the novel ultimately endorses: the 'heritage' of fundamental revolutionary values connected with Trotsky and the charismatic doctrine of permanent revolution. Here Mailer manages to locate a political optimism which anticipates the 'rising of the Phoenix' (p. 256).

Although the independent radicalism of *Barbary Shore* is expressed poetically, it falls a long way short of providing any basis for collective action. The suggestion is that there will be a long period of abeyance during which the radical tradition will persist as an underground. Lovett moves towards a personal non-collective activism in the interstices of American society, a secret exile which resembles that experienced by the counterforce of Thomas Pynchon's *The Crying of Lot 49* ('How many shared Tristero's secret, as well as its exile? What would the probate judge have to say about spreading some kind of legacy among them all, all those nameless, maybe as a first instalment'[44]). Pynchon blends the same ambiguous images of inheritance and exile to describe the structure of America's adversarial culture. The critic Frank D. McConnell argues that Pynchon's version of the underground network is 'more serious and more compelling than Mailer's, precisely as his own commitment (political and metaphysical) to the necessity of the underground is more intense. He recognizes, as only a member of a revolutionary class can, the inherent sorrow and danger of revolution.'[45] But the real difference between the two conceptions of the underground is that Mailer's is seriously ideological whereas Pynchon's is non-ideological, a regulatory counterforce which maintains the reality of the *status quo* and is not part of a revolutionary dialectic. (In fact recent information indicates that Pynchon's notion of an underground is, at least in part, inherited from Mailer.[46]) The suggestion that Pynchon is a member of a revolutionary *class* is an ideological absurdity. Lovett's exile and inheritance are ambivalent because they connect a disillusion with socialism with an initiation into its mysteries. Finally, it is only possible to arrive at a version of Marxism that is tentative, personalized, marginal and quixotic. Lovett is the 'poor hope' (p. 256) of the left.

In the absence of a clearly defined radical politics of immediate practical relevance, *Barbary Shore* becomes an essay in powerlessness to effect social change, individual helplessness and depersonalization. As Stanley Gutman says, the novel 'hides its small hope behind a vast dream of despair'.[47] McLeod's discourse takes up the theme of alienation at the social level and is based on Marx's early economic and philosophical manuscripts (the so-called 1844 Manuscripts), which were not published until 1932. In these writings alienation is the key concept for the analysis of capitalism. (Later Marx focused on class relations and the cluster of terms used for alienations disappeared from his work.) For Robert Solotaroff the novel's 'obsessive concern with just how bad both capitalisms [American and Russian] are seems primarily to have been the product of fairly intensive readings of Marxist literature from 1948 to 1950, particularly *Das Kapital*, Trotsky's *History of the Russian Revolution*, and the latter's polemics against the Soviet state'.[48] But this indiscriminate impression fails to catch the precise radical inflections in *Barbary Shore*. Malaquais restricted Mailer's encounters with Marx's own writings, and his own radicalism followed the fashionable early Marx in its emphasis on the worker's loss of control over the process of work, the product of his labour and his eventual reification:

> A man is capable of participating efficiently in the modern industrial process, with all its demands for skill, intelligence, and intense labour, only if there is a reward possible, to wit an adequate scale of living and a promise of an improved future. Deprived of the minimum of comfort and hope, workmanship must degenerate. Little balm for the labourer if factories swallow the earth, when they fail to provide him with creature comfort, and less balm for the bureaucrat when the failure to produce becomes increasingly more serious. (p. 299)

Marx distinguishes three types of alienation: reification, the sale of oneself as a commodity, and the experience of estrangement.[49] In McLeod's discourse Mailer elaborates on the first two senses of alienation, but the primary feeling of alienation in *Barbary Shore* generates from Lovett himself, whose experience is one of estrangement. Like Robert Hearn, who tries to 'get by on style', Lovett is passive, blank and lacking in personal distinction (since there is no physical description of him, he is impossible to visualize). His emptiness is symbolized by his amnesia: 'The details of my own history were lost in the other, common to us all. I could never judge whether something had happened to me or I imagined it so' (p. 11). Until halfway through the second chapter he remains an unnamed, unidentified voice, and, as controller of the narrative, its registering consciousness, he is anxious and disturbed. A war wound facilitates his perception of himself as a 'cripple' (p. 63). The injury is not romantic but part of a severe erosion of self: 'At times I am certain I used to lie on the bunk and stare at a photo of myself taken in England or was it in Africa? I would examine the face which the doctors assured me would be almost duplicated' (p. 64). Pastless, faceless, he has experienced a literal depersonalization and estrangement.

The half-hearted attempts made by Lovett to become a writer are symptomatic of his damaged condition. The novel he works on but never completes is, like *Barbary Shore*, a bleak exploration of bureaucracy and alienation: 'I intended a large ambitious work about an immense institution never defined more exactly than that, and about the people who wandered through it' (p. 54). Towards the end the novel is forgotten, no more significant than Guinevere's banal script ideas (pp. 56–9) or Lannie's crazed experimental poems (pp. 132–3), a symptom of the malaise of non-connection rather than a critical tool for dealing with it. Mailer associates

Lovett with Narcissus, and his fragments of literary self-reflection suggest alienation without transcendence. His name alludes to this narcissistic love of one's own image: 'Her mouth curled again. "You can't love anybody Mikey, for you're Narcissus, and the closer you come to the water the more you adore yourself until your nose touches, and then you're alone again"' (p. 131). Lovett's personal emancipation comes only with the selling of his typewriter, the abandonment of his novel and the dissipation of literary ambitions. True recovery comes with political rearmament, which projects him into an underground existence (he is last seen fleeing into an alley) where he will be immune from the kind of harmful exposure to history which has caused his amnesia (alienation).

Alienation is not only present in McLeod's discourse or individual characters: it is also inscribed in the formal construction of the novel. Just as *The Naked and the Dead* begins and ends with a code image (a map of Anopopei and Dalleson's absurd map-reading classes using pin-ups), *Barbary Shore* opens and closes with a dream trope of collective estrangement:

> I am a traveller. He is most certainly not myself. A plump middle-aged man, and I have the idea he has just finished a long trip. He has landed at an airfield or his train has pulled into a depot. It hardly matters which.
>
> He is in a hurry to return home. With impatience he suffers the necessary delays in collecting his baggage, and when the task is finally done, he hails a taxi, installs his luggage, bawls out his instructions, and settles back comfortably in the rear seat. Everything is so peaceful. Indolently he turns his head to watch children playing a game upon the street.
>
> He is weary, he discovers, and his breath comes heavy. Unfolding his newspaper he attempts to study it, but the print blurs and he lays the sheet down. Suddenly and unaccountably he is quite depressed. It has been a long trip he reassures himself. He looks out of the window.
>
> The cab is taking the wrong route!
>
> What shall he do? It seems so simple to raise his hand and tap upon the glass, but he feels he dare not disturb the driver. Instead he looks through the window once more.
>
> The man lives in this city, but he has never seen these streets. The architecture is strange and the people are dressed in unfamiliar clothing.
>
> He looks at a sign, but it is printed in an alphabet he cannot read. (pp. 12–13)

In the dream Lovett shouts at the man, 'You are wrong, I say, although he does not hear me; this city is the real city, the material city, and your vehicle is history.' The image is of anomie, confusion and future shock in an indecipherable reality.[50] On the final page of the novel, in a mood of spiralling hysteria, the image returns: 'Meanwhile vast armies mount themselves, the world revolves, the traveller clutches his breast' (p. 256). That no real progress has occurred in the course of the novel is reinforced by the pessimistic repetition of the closing incantatory words of chapter 1 at the end of the novel: 'So the blind lead the blind, and the deaf shout warnings to one another until their voices are lost' (p. 13). Both the traveller image and the incantations sustain an unrelievedly gloomy view of recent history.

Alienation is the political note the novel sounds most stridently. But this ought not to be understood only in terms of Mailer's idiosyncratic position. Rather there are distinct similarities between *Barbary Shore* and a number of other novels of the same period, notably Saul Bellow's *Dangling Man* and Ralph Ellison's *Invisible Man*. Each of these books, written as notes from an underground, charts the effects of a moral-political collapse of perspective on a marginalized hero. Mailer's *amnesia*, Bellow's *dangling* and Ellison's *iinvisibility* are tropes for the inner vacuities of cultural or political estrangement. Bellow presents a central character, Joseph, who finds himself bereft of all political certainties as he awaits military induction. His reaction to this is to turn inward in an attempt at self-recovery. Like Lovett, he does little but sit in his room, worry, think and attempt to write. He 'dangles' passively because no rationale can be constructed to justify action. Bellow's expository material is structured as interior monologues with an imaginary dialectical character, 'The Spirit of Alternatives', that are no more graceful than Mailer's discourse-making. However, rather than agonizing over Marxism, Joseph wrestles with his own, and Bellow's, political background in liberalism and the Enlightenment philosophers. His writings, which are left as incomplete as Lovett's novel, are a desperate examination of the promises of freedom and self-fulfilment offered by the rationalist thinkers (including Marx). 'The Spirit of Alternatives', playing the same role as McLeod, pessimistically contradicts Joseph, forcing him to accept the absurdity of his claim to a separate, distinct identity. By the end of *Dangling Man* Joseph cannot bear the weight of doubt, and his programme of self-recovery founders. Unlike Lovett, he surrenders with relief to a bureaucratic life:

> Hurray for regular hours!
> And for the supervision of the spirit.
> Long live regimentation.[51]

Ralph Ellison's invisible man begins in and returns to the same claustrophobic, marginal 'border area'[52] inhabited by Lovett and Joseph, and his room is literally rather than figuratively chthonic. *Invisible Man* emerges out of Ellison's complete disillusion with Marxism (the Brotherhood of the novel) and all other political discourses, and his hero's 'residence underground'[53] is perceived in more sanguine terms than either Mailer's or Bellow's; it is a hibernation, 'a covert preparation for a more overt action'.[54] But, like Lovett and Joseph, the invisible man has not formulated the precise action he should take: 'The next step I couldn't make, so I've remained in the hole.'[55] Unclear whether he is 'in the rear or the *avant-garde*',[56] he has followed the advice given to Lovett and returned to theory: 'Here, at least, I could try to think things out in peace.'[57] He has neither capitulated like Joseph or activated himself like Lovett. A cultural middle way, flirted with but ultimately rejected by Lovett and Joseph, is found in writing. As a writer, the invisible man can deal with alienation. Something an old schoolteacher has said to him about Joyce's *Portrait of the Artist as a Young Man* is the key to his development: 'Stephen's problem, like ours, was not actually one of creating the uncreated conscience of his race, but of creating the *uncreated features of his face*.'[58] The creation of self, solving the problems of one's own identity, is the prerequisite of more socially responsible styles of behaviour. Face comes before race. Writing permits Ellison's hero to make music out of invisibility (alienation), but the song of self is no romantic indulgence; it is a hard-headed preparation for a programme of action: 'Without the possibility of action, all knowledge comes to one labelled "file and forget", and I can neither file nor forget.'[59]

Mailer's underground man undergoes a recovery of self which is less dramatic than the invisible man's. He has yet to create the features of his face: 'When I stare into the mirror I am returned a face doubtless more handsome than the original, but the straight nose, the modelled chin, and the smooth cheeks are evidence of a stranger's art' (p. 11). Despite his valued inheritance, he has 'much to learn' (p. 250), and he remains, in Chester Eisinger's words, 'the victim of nameless terrors and alienation, who cannot make a vital relationship between his ideas and the society he lives in'.[60] That this feeling comes out of Mailer's own experience has been made clearer in a recent comment on the overwhelming sense of deracination in this period:

> I was having a form of twentieth century experience which would become more and more prevalent: I was utterly separated from my roots. I was successful and alienated and that was a twentieth century condition. This went into all my work after that in one

way or another and will go on forever because by now I suppose
I can say that kind of personality interests me more than someone
who is rooted.[61]

Ultimately *Barbary Shore* is not only a study in alienation but an alienating
novel for the reader to deal with. The close attention paid to politics and
power is at the expense of formal and aesthetic considerations. Although it
develops, according to Mailer, 'without any plan',[62] it becomes even more
arch and artificially coded than its exposition with the half-hearted
introduction of Hawthornian allegorical elements which clash with the
historical preoccupations.[63] No novelistic synthesis of these elements is
achieved. At the bottom of this failure lies Mailer's inability to find a fictional
correlative for the ideas he is working out. In his study of left-wing fiction
Walter B. Rideout warns of the dangers involved for the radical novelist
'when schematized thinking of any kind is inorganically imposed on the
creative process';[64] and Irving Howe has pointed out that the question of
what determines the success or failure of a political novel is linked to the
larger question of what art is, in the sense that no novel, finally, can succeed
simply on the basis of an idea itself.[65] In the case of *Barbary Shore* it is not
simply that the dialogue is artificial (as in a romance); there is an overall
failure to establish links between the highly developed exposition and the
sketchy story of human relationships. A gap exists between the political
discussion, which is presented in the form of long, dense interior (Lovett)
and exterior (McLeod) monologues, and the fictive elements of character,
description, setting and plot. Mailer's preference for the former over the
latter leads him to neglect the dramatic core of the novel. Thus what Rideout
calls the tricky problem of 'how to combine the unburdening of capitalist fact
with a convincing statement in fictional terms'[66] is never properly addressed,
and the reader of whatever political persuasion balks at the formal and
technical inelegance. If, as Howe argues, the novelist's task is always to show
'the relationship between theory and experience, between that ideology that
has been preconceived and the tangle of feelings and relationships he is
trying to present',[67] *Barbary Shore*'s inertia derives from its overemphasis on
its preconceived theory.

    The formal dissatisfactions of *The Naked and the Dead* arise from its
'sturdy' structure; the themes it pursues are choked by Mailer's extensive
planning. *Barbary Shore*'s problem is almost the reverse: the theme
overwhelms the flimsy fictional structure erected to support the book. The
writing refuses to obey any imperatives of form because Mailer is totally
preoccupied with the novel as a vehicle for political wisdom or, in

epistemological terms, what the novelist, philosopher and critic William Gass calls the 'truth function'[68] of literature. Gass provides an eloquent caution against the novel's suitability for this kind of work:

> Fiction is not a form of meaning, nor a means of attaining wisdom. As a philosopher, to put on the other hat, I have a very dim view of the ability of literature to give us knowledge. But fortunately, it seems to me, we can read literature without taking it seriously in that direction while seriously taking it in another direction. As long as you can keep the work on the plane of making statements about the world, then the question becomes 'Are these statements wise statements, deep statements, true statements?' But in my view the integrity of the work is all that matters aesthetically. I mean, my books are made up. They're not about the world. I don't have any wisdom and I have never met a writer yet who had.[69]

The American post-modern writer Gilbert Sorrentino has expressed a similar view: 'For some reason, incomprehensible to me [the] mimetic concept has all but defined the "important" novel in this country. We love our novelists to be seers, to have Important ideas.'[70] Clearly *Barbary Shore* is committed to the truth function and Important ideas to the extent that almost everything else is forgotten, and as a designed artefact with internal consistencies it is deficient. But despite this indisputable criticism *Barbary Shore* has a fascination. As Richard Poirier, alone among critics, realizes, it is 'especially appealing to those ... who look into the structures of a book hoping to find a clue to the author's sense of analogous social, economic, or political structures'[71]—in other words, those of us who are interested in examining the operations in the truth function of Mailer's fiction.

NOTES

1. Norman Mailer, *Barbary Shore* (London: Panther, 1972). Page references are given parenthetically in the text.

2. Gutman, *Mankind in Barbary*, p. 34.

3. Walter B. Rideout, *The Radical Novel in the United States* (London: Oxford University Press, 1956) p. 166.

4. Mailer, *Advertisements for Myself*, p. 26.

5. Kazin, *Writers at Work*, p. 262.

6. Mailer, *Advertisements for Myself*, p. 26.

7. See Mailer's tribute, 'My Friend Jean Malaquais', in *Pieces and Pontifications* (London: New English Library, 1983) pp. 97-105.

8. Quoted in Mills, *Mailer: A Biography*, p. 97.

9. Ibid., pp. 97-8.

10. Ibid., p. 99.

11. Ibid., p. 103.

12. Ibid., p. 101.

13. See plots of novels discussed in Rideout, *The Radical Novel in the United States*

14. The name McLeod seems to be important to Mailer: a Major McLeod appears in *The Naked and the Dead*; one of Mailer's sons is called Stephen McLeod Mailer.

15. Mailer, *Advertisements for Myself*, p.87.

16. Mailer, *The Naked and the Dead*, p. 327.

17. Dalleson's emergence brings *The Naked and the Dead* remarkably close in its feeling for the banal absurdity of military organization to Joseph Heller's *Catch 22* (London, Jonathon Cape, 1962), without Mailer being as bitterly funny as Heller. Dalleson is a prototype for Scheisskopf, the character who achieves the greatest power in *Catch 22*.

18. Mailer, *The Naked and the Dead*, p. 327.

19. Ruth Prigozy, 'The Liberal Novelist in the McCarthy Era', *Twentieth Century Literature* 25, no. 3 (Oct 1975) p. 260.

20. Leeds, *The Structured Vision of Norman Mailer*, p. 61.

21. Andrew Gordon, *An American Dreamer* (Toronto: Associated University Press, 1980) p. 80.

22. Radford, *Mailer: A Critical Study*, p. 51.

23. Solotaroff, *Down Mailer's Way*, p. 49.

24. Bailey, *Mailer: Quick-Change Artist*, p. 25; Robert J. Begiebing, Acts of Regeneration (Columbia: University of Missouri Press, 1980) p. 24.

25. Bufithis, *Norman Mailer*, p. 72.

26. Gutman, *Mankind in Barbary*, p. 30.

27. See Norman Mailer, *The Presidential Papers* (London: Panther, 1976) pp. 76-94.

28. For a discussion of paranoia and the making of *Maidstone*, see James Toback, 'At Play in the Fields of the Bored', *Esquire*, Dec 1968, pp. 151-4.

29. Norman Mailer, *St. George and the Godfather* (New York: New American Library, 1972) p. 307.

30. Mills, *Mailer: A Biography*, p. 391.

31. Ibid., p. 394.

32. Norman Mailer, *Marilyn* (London: Hodder and Stoughton, 1974) p. 242.

33. Mailer, 'A Harolt High and Low', in *Pieces and Pontifications* pp. 159-205.

34. Ibid., p. 160.

35. Radford, *Mailer: A Critical Study*, p. 16.

36. Mailer, *The Presidential Papers*, p. 80.

37. Mailer, *The Naked and the Dead*, p. 75.

38. Gerth and the Mills, *From Max Weber: Essays in Sociology*, p. 235.

39. Ibid., p. 155.

40. Bernard de Jouvenal, *On Power* (Boston, Mass: Beacon Press, 1962) p. 4.

41. For a full discussion of the process Mailer describes, see Harry Magdoff, *The Age of Imperialism* (New York: Monthly Review Press, 1969) pp. 27-66.

42. Mailer, *The Naked and the Dead*, p. 74.

43. Radford, *Mailer: A Critical Study*, p. 53.

44. Thomas Pynchon, *The Crying of Lot 49* (London: Picador, 1979) pp. 124-5.

45. Frank D. McConnel, *Four Postwar American Novelists* (Chicago: University of Chicago Press, 1977) p. 174.

46. Thomas Pynchon, *Slow Learner* (Boston, Mass: Little, Brown, 1984) p. 7.

47. Gutman, *Mankind in Barbary*, p. 29.

48. Solotaroff, *Down Mailer's Way*, p. 40.

49. For a discussion of these terms, see Bertell Ollman, *Alienation: Marx's Concept of Man in Capitalists Society* (Cambridge: Cambridge University Press, 1971).

50. For an absurd overinterpretation of the traveler image, see Leeds, *The Structured Vision of Norman Mailer*, pp. 70-1.

51. Saul Bellow, *Dangling Man* (New York: New American Library, 1972) p. 191.

52. Ralph Ellison, *Invisible Man* (Harmondsworth: Penguin, 1965) p. 466.

53. Ibid., p. 7.

54. Ibid., p. 8.

55. Ibid., p. 7.

56. Ibid., p. 467.

57. Ibid., p. 468.

58. Ibid., p. 467.

59. Ibid., p. 466.

60. Chester Eisinger, *Fiction of the Forties*, (Chicago: University of Chicago Press, 1963) p. 93.

61. Mailer, *Pieces and Pontifications*, p. 147.

62. Kazin, *Writers at Work*, p. 263.

63. For a comparison between *Barbary Shore* and Hawthorne's *The Blithedale Romance*, see Laura Adams, *Existential Battles: The Growth of Norman Mailer* (Athens, Ohio: Ohio State University Press, 1976) p. 41.

64. Rideout, *The Radical Novel in the United States*, p. 287.

65. See Irving Howe, *Politics and the Novel, passim.*

66. Rideout, *The Radical Novel in the United States*, p. 230.

67. Howe, *Politics and the Novel*, p. 22.

68. William Gass, *Fiction and the Figures of Life* (New York: Alfred A. Knopf, 1970) p. 38.

69. Quoted in Larry McCaffery, The Metafictional Muse (Pittsburgh: University of Pittsburgh Press, 1982) p. 175.

70. Quoted in *Washington Book World*, 13 Feb 1980, p. 9.

71. Poirier, *Mailer*, p. 71.

PETER BALBERT

From Lady Chatterley's Lover *to* The Deer Park: *Lawrence, Mailer, and the Dialectic of Erotic Risk*

"Poor memory is so indispensable to passionate lovers."
—*The Deer Park*

"A man has to fend and fettle for the best,
and then trust in something beyond himself."
—*Lady Chatterley's Lover*

I

The incisiveness and passion of Norman Mailer's defense in *The Prisoner of Sex* (1971) of D. H. Lawrence's life, art, and vision should come as no surprise to those who follow the open book of Mailer's intellectual history. In several essays and interviews previous to that underrated work of catharsis, prophesy, and criticism, Mailer generously acknowledges the seminal influence of Lawrence on both himself and the dialectical climate of the twentieth-century. Indeed, Mailer's intensely manichean novels—through their familiar litany of concern with love, sex, inhibitive society, and modern mechanization—appear like a karmic reformulation of Lawrence's own most prominent preoccupations. But as Mailer acknowledges in *The Prisoner of*

From *Studies in the Novel* 22, no. 1 (Spring 1990): 67-81. © 1990 by the University of North Texas.

Sex, it is a frighteningly transformed world since 1930—"technologized and technologized twice again ... since [Lawrence's] death"[1]—and such a radical transformation of society is reflected in the different tapestries of art in Mailer and Lawrence. For instance, the sprawling urban environments and political agendas of Mailer's fiction contrast with that integration of biblical intensity and pastoral serenity so evident in Lawrence's work. Mailer's modern hell and Lawrence's lost utopia suggest the disparity between Mailer's often journalistic coverage of a debacle and Lawrence's angry, religious indictment of a people's apostasy and a flock's misguided motives.

It is the genre of the novel, however, which they both fervently believe is most conducive to the depiction of those sexual doctrines that invariably infiltrate their work. Mailer's outspoken praise of the power of fiction insists—in recognizably Lawrencian language—on an intimate relation between the metaphysics of a novel and a novelist's obligation to urge that philosophy even at the risk of over-insistence. In this regard Mailer argues that "the novel at its best is the most moral of art forms because it is the most immediate, the most overbearing, if you will."[2] Such a declaration about fiction combines notions of an ethical imperative ("most moral"), uncensored honesty ("overbearing"), and the primacy of instinctual judgement ("most immediate"). Mailer's comment recapitulates the tone and imagery of Lawrence's more celebrated statement of genre preference in "Why The Novel Matters" and in Chapter Nine of *Lady Chatterley's Lover*. In the essay Lawrence maintains that the novel "can make the whole man tremble" as it tells "the whole hog" of "man alive,"[3] and in the novel Lawrence notes the revelatory potential of such a function: "the novel, properly handled, can reveal the most secret places of life."[4] In effect, his explanation not only highlights the intimate sexual focus in *Lady Chatterley's Lover*, but it also suggests Lawrence's abiding erotic preoccupation in all his work: his central goal to eliminate what he calls in "Pornography and Obscenity" "the dirty little secret" of sex[5]—that is, to eliminate the extremes both of Victorian prudery and modern mechanization and decadence. Similarly, Mailer describes sex as "the last remaining frontier of the novel which has not been exhausted by the 19th and early 20th century novelists";[6] his praise of the novel and his Lawrencian belief in the doctrinal responsibility of art come together in the statement that "the final purpose of art is to intensify, even if necessary, to exacerbate, the moral consciousness of people."[7] Such emphatic phrasing also recalls the conviction of Lawrence's assertions that all "art is utterly dependent on philosophy,"[8] and "every work of art adheres to some system of morality."[9]

From early in his career Mailer has freely acknowledged a more precise debt to Lawrence than is evident merely in his own moral fervor and prophetic insistence. Mailer's sexual aesthetic—that existential dialectic of risk and openendedness dramatized most graphically in such works as *The Deer Park*, "The Time of Her Time," *An American Dream*, and *Tough Guys Don't Dance*—begins with his recognition that Lawrence's celebration of instinct is a bedrock faith from which all discussion of the prescient novelist from Nottingham must begin. Mailer further insists that Lawrence's religious imperative to get "beyond the self" in the act of love, begins with the mandate to stay in close touch with the very self that is to be transcended. Amid the climate of cynicism and disillusion that followed the devastations of The Great War, Lawrence is preeminent among those artists who formulate a new vision of belief, and for D. H. Lawrence it is the primacy of emotional and sexual impulse that we have come to call "blood consciousness." Mailer begins to derive his own brand of existential doctrine in *The Deer Park* (1955) and—in more formal fashion—in "The White Negro" (1957); while the latter essay flirts with credos about self-defining violence that Lawrence would not approve, the essential direction of Mailer's remarks is clearly derived from Lawrence's notions of instinct and repression. In the preliminary pages of that essay, Mailer asserts, in relation to what he approvingly describes as Hemingway's dictum of "if it feels good, it is good," a list of formative influences for his own developing philosophy, and he states that "the intellectual antecedents of this generation can be traced to such separate influences as D. H. Lawrence, Henry Miller, and Wilhelm Reich."[10]

In the years following "The White Negro," Mailer increasingly clarifies Lawrence's legacy to him, as he begins to build on notions of risk and courage that were at least implicit in Lawrence's stress a half-century earlier on sexual transcendence. For instance, in *Cannibals and Christians* (1966), Mailer reprints a 1963 interview that begins to integrate sexual doctrines with a working aesthetic: "I learned from Lawrence that the way to write about sex was not to strike poses but to be true to the logic of each moment. There's a subtle logic to love."[11] Mailer's repeated term "logic" holds an interesting clue to the paradoxical insights about passion that he derives in part from Lawrence. It is a "logic" that is emotional rather than rational, for it is tied to certainties of instinct and to confidence about the senses. Such a fiercely existential basis, always confirmed by the *experience* of the character, provides a more alive and perceptible truth than any tentative awareness suggested by the cautions of educated conditioning or by the rationalized temperance of a culture. The "logic to love" often conveys its truths inscrutably, for the direction of the depicted passion has its own unpredictable laws, and the "emotional rightness" of a scene in life or in a novel depends on the existential mood of characters rather than on the predetermined formulae of the world or of fiction. For instance, there is that memorable logic to love evident in *The Deer Park*, amid the twists and turns in the car of that initial sex scene between Lulu and Sergius. Her neurotic fears and childish restraint at first foil his adolescent aggressiveness and priapic urgency; when he is finally made exhausted and resigned by the range of her refusals, she suddenly and gently helps them both make love—as if all along she must reconnoit her own scenario of control before she would yield. Her charming logic is to discover, fresh for herself, that proper temperature and posture for love and sex as they grope between the seats. To Lulu's praise that he's a "wonderful" lover, Sergius correctly ans wers that he's "just an amateur"[12]—his acknowledgment, no doubt, of the lesson in patient, spontaneous passion he has just learned from Lulu in the sedan.

Thus Mailer's phrase about Lawrence's legacy comprises an appropriate oxymoron in which the heart supplies the knowledge and direction of love. It recalls the significance of Lawrence's own comparable formulation in *The Rainbow*, "a logic of the soul."[13] That resonant phrase occurs as Lawrence stipulates the irresistible urgings of blood knowledge in a frightened yet courageous Tom Brangwen. In the scene when the phrase appears, Tom abandons—as a Lawrencian act of faith—the usual logic of an ordered courtship; he abruptly leaves his rustic home, with virtually no preliminary doubts about his quest or its consequences, to ask an aloof, fascinating Lydia Lensky to be his wife: "There was an inner reality, a logic of the soul, which connected her with him."[14] Tom's motivation results from the same blood knowledge that urges Ursula to finish off Skrebensky under the moon, or which makes a naked Anna dance Will's annihilation, or which makes Gertrude in *Sons and Lovers* hold a baby Paul to the sun, or which makes Mellors heed the flames upon his loins as he begins his affair with Connie Chatterley. While the force of the blood is relentless in each case, the "logic of the love" affair in which the scene occurs can only develop when the character's ego is strong enough to wish to get beyond the self through some unknowable natural element (e.g., sun, moon, or flame) that is now part of the primal force of the love. Mailer, of course, is particularly sympathetic to the irrational logic of love; as he documents throughout his fiction, his characters often enact their love with a perverse abandon that their head and nerves cannot comprehend but which their heart and courage insist is the only recourse. One thinks most graphically in this regard of the walk on the parapet and the removal of Cherry's diaphragm in *An American Dream*, or— two decades later—the analogous climb up the needle in *Tough Guys Don't*

Dance. Such scenes are different in degree but not in kind from the compulsive sex in the rain by Connie and Mellors or from their ritual game of genital flower decoration. Characters do what they must, as their instincts demand satisfactions that are beyond easy rational understanding.

For a contrasting sense of the ego dominated "poses" that Mailer correctly suggests are part of Lawrence's doctrinal criticism, think of the evasive posturing of Michaelis, or of Birkin's decadent games with Hermione, or of Skrebensky's verbal affectations with Ursula, or of Paul's tired sex with Clara late in their affair: all memorable poses adopted by characters who wish to avoid the possibility of getting beyond ego to the realm of sexual transcendence. That urge to get beyond the petty limits of self, Mailer typically insists in *The Prisoner of Sex*, is the major component of a character's successful sexual self-definition in the work of Lawrence. What Mailer apparently learns from Lawrence is a socio-sexual dialectic about the workings of passion and affectation in fiction and society: Mailer sees how "poses" are so seductive and tempting because characters are willing to settle for ego-enclosed sex; they desire what Lawrence in *Lady Chatterley's Lover* calls mere "sensation," for they are unwilling or unable to leave themselves naked and without defenses. Thus the burden of Mailer's discussion of Lawrence in *The Prisoner of Sex* concerns Mailer's agreement with Lawrence that, according to Mailer's reading of him, "he believed nothing human had such significance as the tender majesties of a man and woman fucking with love"[15]—but that such majesty only results from a courageous willingness to get beyond the limitations of self. In *Lady Chatterley's Lover* Mellors confirms Mailer's earthy interpretation of Lawrencian vision with his unadorned comment, "For me, it is the core of my life: if I have a right relation with a woman" (p. 264). In addition, at one point Connie Chatterley dramatizes the fear of transcendence in love when she withholds herself from yielding to her passion for Mellors, as "she resisted it as far as she could, for it was the loss of herself to herself" (p. 185). Mailer's interpretation of real "love" in Lawrence also becomes an explanation of why sex-with-love is the elusive goal in the work of both writers:

> Lawrence's point, which he refines over and over, is that the deepest messages of sex cannot be heard by taking a stance on the side of the bank, announcing one is in love, and then proceeding to fish in the waters of love with a breadbasket full of ego. No, he is saying again and again, people can win at love only when they are ready to lose everything they bring to it of ego, position, or identity—love is more stern than war—and men and women can

survive only if they reach the depth of their own sex down within themselves. They have to deliver themselves "over to the unknown." No more existential statement of love exists, for it is a way of saying we do not know how the love will turn out.16

Mailer's existential reading of Lawrence's sexual doctrine, viewed through Mailer's consistent bias for risk and open-endedness, is evident in his criticism on Lawrence as well as in his own fiction. Even Mailer's incisive discussion of the conflict between Ursula and Birkin in *Women in Love* stresses that it is not conventional love Birkin offers Ursula, for such an easy platonic relationship is closed-ended and protected. In the end there is a species of conservatism in both writers that remains skeptical of the long-term effects of any affair that is built on sex-without-love. True, sex-without-love is often pictured as provocatively embattled and passionate in the work of Mailer and Lawrence, but unless the lust develops into the complexity of organic love, these prophetic artists withhold their admiration of the passion; the affair's depressing conclusions always appear predictable amid the egoistic exertions of its sweaty players. Ultimately Lawrence and Mailer disapprove of such sex not for puritanical reasons but because it fails to "transcend"; it fails to reach "over to the unknown" and thus it holds one or both of the lovers in an ego-enclosed competition for power. Recall here Skrebensky and Ursula in *The Rainbow* as she bypasses her lover to commune directly with the moon, or Sergius and Denise in Mailer's "The Time of Her Time," when Sergius's victory as sexual athlete is earned at the expense of a superficial confidence which his mate can puncture with her own brand of final riposte. In a recent letter Mailer articulates the dynamics of these preoccupations with sex and love, and he also provides some precise information about the issue of influence:

Lawrence's main influence for me was *Lady Chatterley's Lover*. I had the privilege of reading it back in 1941 in the unexpurgated edition. That was in the Treasure Room of Widener Library ... It changed my sex life, or rather, accelerated it into a direction it had been proceeding on nicely by itself. I accepted Lawrence's thesis about untrammeled and illimitable rights and liberties and pleasure of sexual love and the union between the two. I don't think anyone ever before, whether in literature or personal life, had stated it so forcefully for me, that one could not have sex without love, or love without sex, period. Now, as I know from the other side of 40-plus years, that is an extraordinary thesis, and can be half-right, or all-wrong, as well as absolutely so. For this reason, Lawrence's hypothesis has lived with me as my own, with all the excitement of an ongoing hypothesis that you can never quite confirm or deny (hypotheses are so much more life-giving than obsessions!). At any rate, such is my essential debt to Lawrence. His other works I admire, and I think he was a great writer, but *Lady Chatterley* changed my life.[17]

I want to build on Mailer's suggestion that *Lady Chatterley's Lover* was important to him on this issue by briefly considering that novel's relation to Mailer's first extended fiction on sex and love, *The Deer Park*.

II

The 1920's setting of the English midlands in *Lady Chatterley's Lover* bears distinct resemblance to the early 1950's Hollywood environment of Desert D'Or in *The Deer Park*. Mellors's post-World War One disillusion and anger is not unlike the depression and lack of direction that afflicts Sergius O'Shaugnessy, a traumatized veteran of the Korean War. Similarly, the decadent indolence and posturings of the wags at Wragby, presided over by Clifford Chatterley, anticipate the hypocritical and amoral court of the movie mogul, Herman Teppis. Two fictional communities in which everyone knows his place, as coal miner and starlet, housekeeper and assistant movie director, colliery superintendent and publicity man, are all subjected to the pressures of conformity and easy public righteousness. Whether it is through autocratic control of the miners or through the subjugation of Hollywood hopefuls and hangers-on, both Clifford and Teppis demonstrate how a lust for power and a yearning for sexual perversity are camouflaged through various hypocrisies and social poses. The sounds of the relentless bins of coal and the droning machinery are replaced by the more modern and invisible index of Bimmler ratings and the cost of celluloid; but there is little doubt that money and the "bitch goddess, success" (*Chatterley*, p. 102) apply to both machine cultures. Demeaning notions about sex as mere commodity are discussed with enthusiasm by the cynical coterie at Wragby, with different versions of evasion variously offered by Strangeway, Dukes, Clifford, and Michaelis. In Hollywood, Munshin, Marion O'Faye, Teppis, and others trade their lovers, pimps, and business partners in that promiscuous and alarmingly friendly manner so dreamed about a generation earlier by the futurist talkers at Clifford's country estate.

The Herman Teppis-Clifford Chatterley comparison is particularly compelling, as both characters bear a primary responsibility for a crass instrumentalizing of love and sex. For instance, Teppis's demand that Lulu Meyers marry the homosexual actor, Teddy Pope, is similar to Clifford's cold suggestion that his wife be impregnated by another man. Both the studio head and the manager of the mines feel eminently comfortable with their utter contempt for the distractions of true love, real fatherhood, or domestic monogamy. A cowardly mendacity underlies their versions of sexual prostitution, as paintings in Teppis's office glorify the beauty of innocence and marriage, while Clifford is willing for others to believe that Connie's anticipated baby is his own. Both men, in essence, employ convenient lies to conceal their own cowardice, for they lack the moral stature to deal with sex without the interference of power, ego, and control.

When characters in *Lady Chatterley's Lover* and *The Deer Park* are not involved in that manipulative sex that informs the relations between Connie and Michaelis, or Connie and her former lovers on the continent, or Munshin and Elena, or Marion and Elena, the men are often afflicted with impotence. As Mark Spilka first suggested about Lawrence's embodied organic vision in his last major novel, Clifford's literal paralysis is not meant to be cruel or gratuitously symbolic, but daringly comprehensive; his paralysis suggests that he has "no moral feet to stand on,"[18] and Lawrence himself comments on this aspect of his novel and on the symptomatic evasions of his generation when he remarks in "Apropos of *Lady Chatterley's Lover*" that "when people act in sex nowadays, they are half the time acting up ... now the act tends to be mechanical."[19] In addition, while Mellors is clearly not impotent, he has been without a woman for a long time; his experience in the war and his interval with Bertha Coutts have gradually forced him into a self-depriving isolation in the woods. In his return to sexual love with Connie he risks the return of painful memories as well as the social and legal troubles he initiates through this illicit and unorthodox affair.

In one sense *The Deer Park* can be viewed as an extended fiction about various confrontations with impotence; Martin Pelley, Sergius, and Eitel engage the trauma of their past sexual disability by searching for erotic compromises to fulfill their lives. While Pelley reaches a temporary solution through an unconventional liaison with Dorothea, Sergius's and Eitel's "tested" sexual performance is one of the persistent themes in the novel. Both men indulge in passionate, renewing affairs that temporarily come close to love. But their different responses to their affair become a reliable index to Mailer's feelings about the province of risk and courage in sex. Sergius discovers enough about himself to develop an independent strength and confidence that he lacked at the start of the novel; this achievement is most evident when he is able to end his affair on the realization that it provides him with little more than repetitive food for his ego. He becomes willing to take the mature risk, which for him is both to refuse the easy offer of fame and money, and to let Lulu go. But Eitel is seduced by a comparable offer of power and prestige, and he finally decides to abandon a relationship that might have made him whole, potent, and uncompromised. Eitel's cowardice is that he backs off from his sex with Elena when the affair becomes more complicated—that is, when it becomes more demanding to his real and vulnerable self. Eitel discovers that he is unable—in the terms of Mailer's reading of Lawrence—to win at love because he is *not* "ready to lose everything he brings to it of ego, position, or identity." On this notion of courage, it is true that Elena is equally to blame for the failure, as her resolute lack of self-confidence and her adamant fear of failure become first depressing and then wish-fulfilling. It is fair to say that by the end of the novel both Eitel and Elena lack the courage to go all the way with each other—that is, they represent those sadly "contemporary" people Mailer later describes in *Advertisements for Myself* who "cut a corner, tried to cheat the heart of life, tried not to face our uneasy sense that pleasure comes best to those who are brave."[20]

This issue of risk is crucial to the sexual dialectic enunciated in both *The Deer Park* and *Lady Chatterley's Lover*. Early in *The Deer Park*, for instance, Charles Eitel confidently remarks: "I've always thought that everything you learn is done by fighting your fear" (p. 90). It is a brave and accurate Hemingwayesque statement, and it appears as a credible reflection of that confidence Eitel gained early in his affair with Elena. Yet while there is potential for real love between them, Eitel and Elena are soon willing to settle for easy benefits and for no transaction with "the unknown." Indeed, the metaphors that Mailer uses early in their affair to describe the direction of their passion are illuminating and recognizably Lawrencian. Eitel and Elena do not get much beyond the safe enclosure of their own egos, and their characteristic failure to transcend is described in the same terms that Mailer used in *The Prisoner of Sex* (i.e., "they have to deliver themselves over to the unknown") to summarize the mandate for transcendence that always operates in Lawrence's fiction. Here there is no lapsing-out, but only satisfactions rooted in the limited lusts of the present:

> It had happened before. He had had women who gave him their
> first honest pleasure, and he had taken all the bows for his vanity,
> but he had never met so royal a flow of taste. It was remarkable

how they knew each other's nicety between love-making and extravagance. It had always been his outstanding gift, or so he felt, to be able to know a woman, and he had the certainty at little instants that he could discover every sympathetic nerve. "The onanist at heart," he had thought, and made love to a woman with care enough to have made love to himself. But Elena carried him to mark above mark. (p. 110)

It is a passionate rumination about a new love and grand sex, but the praise is mired in the self-congratulations of performance and achievement. Eitel is really the onanist in heart and soul. All he aspires to is a love that is a way station on the way to a permanence of power and prestige, not unlike the manner in which Clifford Chatterley, buoyed by the apparent possibility of a Wragby heir and embodied namesake, goes back to work at the mines with the conviction of man who has discovered a new love.

Even the predictable final failure of the Eitel-Esposito affair is conveyed by Mailer with terms derived from Lawrence. Recall Mailer's fishing metaphor that he employs to state Lawrence's antagonism to "taking a stance on the side of the bank, announcing one is in love, and then proceeding to fish in the waters of love with a breadbasket full of ego." It is relevant for the development of that affair, and particularly after Eitel contemplates his unholy bargain with Munshin. At various stages in the weeks that follow those early days of searing sex with each other, there is ample opportunity for Eitel and Elena to build on their passion and get legitimately beyond the province of lust and teacher-student fantasies. But when the bargain for the movie job beckons Eitel, that same fishing metaphor becomes sadly inverted. Eitel grotesquely fishes with his ego itself—which now becomes the hook and bait that bring Elena on land where the affair will die as the inevitable sacrifice on the altar of his career:

At the same time he did not want to end it immediately; that would be too disturbing to his work. The proper time was in a month, two months, whenever he was finished; and in the meantime, adroitly, like fighting big fish on slender tackle, he must slowly exhaust her love, depress her hope, and make the end as painless as the blow of the club on the fatigued fishbrain. "My one hundred and fourteen pound sailfish," Eitel would think, and what a match she gave him. He was as cool as any good fisherman, "I'm the coolest man I know," he would think, and with confidence, aloofness, and professional disinterest he maneuvered Elena, he brought her closer to the boat. There was always the danger she would slip the hook before he pulled her in, and so the battle was wearying. He could not let her realize how his attitude had changed; she would force a fight which would go too far; that was her pride; she would not stay a moment once she knew he did not love her, and he had to struggle with temptation not to reel in line too fast, too soon. (p. 203)

A major reason for the failure of their affair is caused by the lovers' unwillingness to undertake erotic *risk*, or more precisely, by their desire to stay the same by reaping the petty rewards of self-reflecting love. Throughout *The Deer Park* there are many passages about this need to change, this mandate to risk for the future and give oneself to the dictates of instinct and transcendence:

All the while he held Elena he felt cold as stone, but he knew that he would marry her, that he could not give her up for there was that law of life so cruel and so just which demanded that one must grow or else pay more for remaining the same. (p. 346)

Those were the laws of sex; borrow technique in place of desire, and sex life would demand the debt be paid just when one was getting too old to afford such a bill. (p. 204)

In short, in Mailer's world there are notions of a divine economy imposed on successful sexual performance and on the emotional passions of a love affair. This perspective insists that you must not protect yourself in or for the present through a merely pragmatic marriage or a repetitive sex life. Mailer insists that the unadorned pure instincts of the passion legitimately demand spontaneous growth and risk in the lovers; Eitel's stated reason "not to give her up" confirms a selfish fear in him that undercuts the motive for his anticipated wedding. Real growth for him—once he has tired of Elena— would be to suffer his loneliness alone and without sentimentality. Eitel lacks the existential courage that would make his marriage to Elena meaningful in the terms of Mailer's "law of life." Eitel will merely borrow more technique and try to effect another affectation.

III

D. H. Lawrence is also concerned throughout his work with the integrated issues of courage in modern society and an individual's willingness to suffer change in order to avoid the static routines of erotic relations. In his essay "The State of Funk," he writes prescriptive lines that anticipate Mailer's dialectic in *The Deer Park*:

> If we fall into a state of funk, impotence, and persecution, then things may be very much worse than they are now. It is up to us. It is up to men to be men. While men are courageous and willing to change, nothing terribly bad can happen. But once men fall into a state of funk, with the inevitable accompaniment of bullying and repression, then only bad things can happen.[21]

In *Lady Chatterley's Lover* it is Mellors and Connie who provide for Lawrence a dramatized standard of what is admirable erotic risk. When Connie herself memorably praises him about "the courage of your own tenderness" (p. 346), she is admiring him, in effect, for his unself-conscious willingness to put himself at risk in society in the service of an ethic he postulates with enembroidered finality: "I believe in being warm-hearted. I believe especially in being warm-hearted in love, in fucking with a warm heart" (p. 266). As I have suggested elsewhere in relation to Lawrence's fire imagery, this sexual component of warmth is both a seminal and difficult achievement in Lawrence's fictional world, for it depends on a forging process that burns off the impurities of will and ego in the act of love.[22] Connie's progressive sexual response to Mellors and her increasing ability to achieve orgasm can be charted in the novel's sex scenes through the developing prominence Lawrence gives to metaphors of flame and purging that infiltrate her response.

I suspect we do not sufficiently recognize the courage required by both lovers in *Lady Chatterley's Lover* not only to initiate their affair but also to develop their relationship beyond the requirements of easy sex in Mellors's hut. Connie's most prominent courage, of course, is in her willingness to radically oppose, through her adultery, the strict conventions of her "Ladyship" title, a step she takes when she recognizes the full dimensions of Clifford's cruel and selfish failure with her. But the extent of Mellors's courage is not often noted by commentators on the novel. Not only does the affair jeopardize his conditioned comforts in the private woods and his legal status in the community, but he must also reengage the painful memories and scars of his previous relationships with women, and particularly with his wife. He has a wound, and it is like the symbolic and literal wound of war inherited from Hemingway and Jake Barnes; it manifests itself most often as an adamant fear about the consequences and performance of his long dormant sex life: "Especially he did not want to come into contact with a woman again. He feared it; for he had a big wound from old contacts" (p. 131). Repeatedly Mellors suggests—both by his caution and through his memories—that *sex is never easy*, and that its difficulty is less in the mechanics and more in accepting the love and risk that properly emerge from the affair. A less experienced Connie is plainly unaware of the existential dimensions of risk that preoccupy Mellors. Indeed, he even asks her, "Do you care a' the risk?" (p. 173)—and he earlier announces the grounds of his wholesome concerns with a brand of Lawrencian imprimatur:

"You aren't sorry, are you?" he asked, as he went at her side.

"No! No! Are you?" she said.

"For that! No!" he said. Then after a while he added: "But there's the rest of things."

"What rest of things?" she said.

"Sir Clifford. Other folks. All the complications."

"Why complications?" she said, disappointed.

"It's always so. For you as well as for me. There's always complications."

He walked on steadily in the dark.

"And are you sorry?" she said.

"In a way!" he replied, looking up at the sky. "I thought I'd done with it all. Now I've begun again."

"Begun what?"

"Life."

"Life!" she re-echoed, with a queer thrill.

"It's life," he said. "There's no keeping clear. And if you do keep clear you might almost as well die. So if I've got to be broken open again, I have."

She did not quite see it that way, but still ...

"It's just love," she said cheerfully. (p. 165)

So an innocent Connie understandably underestimates the price that must always be paid, which is Lawrence's early statement about the iron "laws" of life and sex described by Mailer. One of the contributions of Mailer's discussion in *The Prisoner of Sex* of Lawrence's life and vision is

Mailer's compelling account of why heterosexual sex was fundamental to
Lawrence, but that its achievement could not have been easy for him:

> But he had become a man by an act of will ... he had lifted himself
> out of his natural destiny which was probably to have the sexual
> life of a woman, had diverted the virility of his brain down into
> some indispensable minimum of phallic force—no wonder he
> worshipped the phallus, he above all men knew what an
> achievement was its rise from the root, its assertion to stand
> proud on a delicate base. His mother had adored him. Since his
> first sense of himself as a male had been in the tender air of her
> total concern—now, and always, his strength would depend upon
> just such outsize admiration.[23]

It is not only Lawrence whom Mailer describes here, for I believe the passage
of psycho-biographical criticism also has relevance for Lawrence's own
depiction of Mellors, as the sensitive woodkeeper recounts with pertinent
intimacy the direction of his affection during the war:

> He thought of his life abroad, as a soldier. India, Egypt, then
> India again: the blind, thoughtless life with the horses: the
> colonel who had loved him and whom he had loved: the several
> years that he had been an officer, a lieutenant with a very fair
> chance of being a captain. Then the death of the colonel from
> pneumonia, and his own narrow escape from death: his damaged
> health: his deep restlessness: his leaving the army and coming
> back to England to be a working man again.
>
> He was temporizing with life. He had thought he would be
> safe, at least for a time, in this wood. There was no shooting as
> yet: he had to rear the pheasants. He would have no guns to serve.
> He would be alone, and apart from life, which was all he wanted.
> He had to have some sort of a background. And this was his
> native place. There was even his mother, though she had never
> meant very much to him. And he could go on in life, existing
> from day to day, without connection and without hope. For he
> did not know what to do with himself. (p. 192)

"He was temporizing with life"—that is, even amid the flash memories of his
painful past, Mellors instinctively knows that his isolation in the woods is
evasion; he knows why, in Mailer's reading of Hemingway, it doesn't "feel

good" to him. Eitel in *The Deer Park* believes that the "temporizing" has always been through his relation with Elena; for Eitel's version of "transcendence" is ultimately to rise above the complications and responsibilities of those emotional involvements that for Lawrence and Mailer make life worth living.

In a magazine piece eight years after *The Deer Park* that is later republished in *Existential Errands* (1972), Mailer lists several of his favorite passages by other writers that he collected through the years in his working notebooks; he values the passages because they produce for him "a shift in [his] memory, a clarification of the past."[24] I am interested in one passage in particular, for it has obvious relevance to the central situations in both *Lady Chatterley's Lover* and *The Deer Park*:

> The essence of spirit, he thought to himself, was to choose the thing which did not better one's position, but made it more perilous. That was why the world he knew was poor, for it insisted morality and caution were identical. He was so completely of that world, and she was not. She would stay with him until he wanted her no longer, and the thought of what would happen afterward ground his flesh with pain as real as a wound.[25]

The words could easily have been contemplated by Mellors early in his affair with Connie, as he might ponder the courage of her coming to the hut against the anxieties of his early trepidations about public disclosure. Indeed, Mailer designates the passage as "D. H. Lawrence," and although I have not found the passage in Lawrence's work, I am almost willing to take Mailer's word for it about authorship. But a more troubling issue remains, and one that suggests added complexities about my alleged notion of Lawrence's dialectical influence on Mailer and—more emphatically—on *The Deer Park*. It is not surprising that the passage calls to mind the Eitel-Elena affair, for Mailer *includes it verbatim* in *The Deer Park*, as Elena gradually gains Eitel's respect for refusing his pathetic, transparent offer of marriage:

> Finally, she had gained his respect, and he could never explain it to her. With numb fingers he touched her foot. *The essence of spirit, he thought to himself, was to choose the thing which did not better one's position but made it more perilous. That was why the world he knew was poor, for it insisted morality and caution were identical. He was so completely of that world, and she was not. She would stay with him until he wanted her no longer, and the thought of what would*

happen afterward ground his flesh with pain as real as a wound. "I'm rotten," he said aloud, and with the desire to prove his despair, he began to cry, clutching her body to him, his fists against her back, while his chest shook from the unaccustomed effort to weep. (p. 257, my emphasis)

Who can explain the intriguing mystery of the passage's appearance in Mailer's novel in 1955, or its later republication in *Esquire* magazine in 1963 and *Existential Errands* in 1972? If it likely turns out that the passage is not from Lawrence's work at all, but is a quotation from another writer forgetfully inserted by Mailer under Lawrence's name in his notebook, *Esquire* articles, and *Existential Errands*, and under his own name in *The Deer Park*, then Mailer's Lawrencian preoccupations must appear even more obsessive. Mailer's notebooks were intended to produce a clarifying shift in his memory that might produce an engaged self-perspective so useful for a writer of fiction. Is the issue of Lawrence's influence on Mailer so profound that the living writer cannot untangle his own language and vision from the enthusiasms of his acknowledged indebtedness? Have we finally uncovered a case of the amnesia of influence?

A RELEVANT POSTSCRIPT

Happily, it turns out, Mailer himself explains the mystery, both in an earlier magazine piece and in a recent letter to me. No, it was not forgetfulness nor an inexplicable tangle in those notebooks—just a playful homage by Mailer to the considerable influence of D. H. Lawrence on his own work. For I quote below the relevant text of a letter I received from him after I completed the essay as above; my letter, naturally enough, asked him to clarify his later attribution in 1963 of the lines he used in *The Deer Park* in 1955. I have since confirmed the accuracy of the explanation he provides. My reaction is both irritation that I failed to fully unravel the Nabokovian Mailer game, and pleasure that my essential point about influence receives an ever more resonant documentation. Further, that Mailer derives the masquerade precisely from *The Deer Park* makes perfect sense to me:

I have to tell you that the piece in which the "quote" from D. H. Lawrence occurs was a spoof. I was doing a column for *Esquire* back in the '60's, and at one point wrote the preface that you saw in *Existential Errands*, and then took quotes from six or seven of my books, ascribed other authors' names to them, put it in the piece, and waited to see how many people would spot the trick, which, as I recollect, was very few indeed, maybe one or two people. Then I came back to it in the following column and gave the game away. It was a humbling experience; I realized that people do not read me all that closely. I must say, however, that the authors I chose had all been influences, and the effect of their influence can be proved by the fact that no one argues with the authenticity of the quotations ... At any rate, this ought to clear up your natural confusion twenty and more years later.[26]

NOTES

1. Norman Mailer, *The Prisoner of Sex* (Boston: Little Brown, 1971), p. 151.

2. Norman Mailer, *Advertisements For Myself* (New York: Putnam's, 1959), p. 384.

3. D. H. Lawrence, *Phoenix: The Posthumous Papers of D. H. Lawrence* (New York: Viking, 1972), p. 535.

4. D. H. Lawrence, *Lady Chatterley's Lover* (New York: Grove, 1962), p. 146. All subsequent references to this edition are cited in the text.

5. *Phoenix*, p. 177.

6. *Advertisements for Myself*, p. 270.

7. *Advertisements for Myself*, p. 384.

8. D. H. Lawrence, *Fantasia of the Unconscious* (New York: Viking, 1960), p. 57.

9. *Phoenix*, p. 476.

10. *Advertisements for Myself*, p. 340.

11. Norman Mailer, *Cannibals and Christians* (New York: Dial, 1966), p. 197.

12. Norman Mailer, *The Deer Park* (New York: Putnam's, 1955), p. 95. All subsequent references to this edition are cited in the text.

13. See Chapter One in my study, *D. H. Lawrence and the Phallic Imagination: Essays on Sexual Identity and Feminist Misreading* (New York: St. Martin's, 1989) for a more comprehensive analysis both of Lawrence's reading of instinctual primacy and Mailer's interpretation of such primitive impulses in Lawrence's work.

14. D. H. Lawrence, *The Rainbow* (New York: Viking, 1961), p. 36.

15. *The Prisoner of Sex*, pp. 134-35.

16. *The Prisoner of Sex*, pp. 147-48.

17. Jeffrey Meyers, ed., *D. H. Lawrence and Tradition* (Amherst: Univ. of Massachusetts Press, 1985), p. 11.

18. Mark Spilka, *The Love Ethic of D. H. Lawrence* (Bloomington: Indiana Univ. Press, 1955), p. 183.

19. D. H. Lawrence, *Sex, Literature, and Censorship* (New York: Viking, 1959), p. 85.

20. *Advertisements for Myself*, p. 23, Robert Merrill's chapter on *The Deer Park*, in *Norman Mailer* (Boston: Twayne, 1978), is notable for its fine understanding of the more general theme of courage in Mailer and Hemingway. His use of this quotation from *Advertisements For Myself* to clarify the theme of "the tenderness of tragedy" is consistently incisive and relevant.

21. *Sex, Literature, and Censorship*, pp. 59-60.

22. I elaborate on the literal *and* symbolic significance of this forging metaphor in Lawrence's work in Chapters Two and Five of *The Phallic Imagination*, cited above.

23. *The Prisoner of Sex*, pp. 154-155.

24. Norman Mailer, *Existential Errands* (Boston: Little Brown, 1972), p. 266.

25. *Existential Errands*, p. 267.

26. Letter from Norman Mailer to Peter Balbert, Jan. 31, 1989.

MARK EDMUNDSON

Romantic Self-Creations:
Mailer and Gilmore in The Executioner's Song

Romantic writers are, for better and worse, obsessed with originality. In practice this means that each one who aspires to matter has to initiate his life as an artist with a story about what originality is, and that story must itself strike readers as being a new one. To compound the difficulty, the romantic writer is compelled, even as he recounts his version of originality, to be exemplifying it. Emerson sets out to do this much in his most celebrated essay, "Self-Reliance." The formula for originality he puts forward there is a simple one: you become original by listening to yourself. Genius derives from trusting the inner voice, abiding by one's "spontaneous impression ... then most when the whole cry of voices is on the other side" (259). Originality is not, as Wordsworth believed it to be, the product of a favored childhood, where one is "Fostered alike by beauty and by fear" (1850 *Prelude*, bk. 1, line 302). Nor is it mysteriously inborn, a celestial gift, as the German romantics tended to think. Moses and Plato and Milton became what they did—in Emerson's view—by observing the "gleam of light which flashes across [the] mind from within" and speaking "not what men but what they thought" (259).

Yet the Emersonian philosophy of self-invention is also a philosophy of self-ruin. In time, every rhetorical pearl evolves back to sand; every hard-won identity tends to "solidify and hem in the life." Romantic "self-invention"

From *Contemporary Literature* 31, no. 4 (Winter 1990): 434-47. © 1990 by the Board of Regents of the University of Wisconsin System.

frequently begins in a sort of potlatch, a ritual in which the subject is compelled to destroy his full accumulation and return to poverty, and to ignorance, that state on which, according to Thoreau, all growth depends. The American romantic faith is a faith in crisis: without ruin, no renovation. And no renovation, it's assumed, is final: always, as Emerson says, there must be abandonment.

Of all the major American writers at work now, Norman Mailer probably has come the closest to committing himself to Emerson's literary ethos of self-destroying self-invention. From early on in his career it has been Mailer's aim to baffle expectations about who he is and what he might be capable of doing. His ambition has been thoroughly Emersonian—"to dive and reappear in new places."

Mailer's style of diving and reappearing has earned him a certain notoriety, some applause, and also a good deal of vitriolic criticism, particularly about the a- or immorality of productions like "The White Negro," *An American Dream, Why Are We in Vietnam?*, and the two books on Marilyn Monroe. The charges against Mailer tend to be akin to those leveled against romantic writers as far back at least as Byron: he's violent, self-obsessed, an opportunist, a destructive opponent of what's most nourishing in humanistic culture.[1] Mailer's excesses are all the worse, to this way of thinking, in that they're amplified through the whole vulgar network of the mass media, reaching beyond the intellectuals who know how to put his clownings in context and giving the institution of Literature a bad name.

The reaction to Mailer's major book of the seventies, *The Executioner's Song,* has to be seen against the background of this kind of moralizing response to his work. For it appeared, at least from the initial reviews of the book, that Mailer had undergone a conversion. Critics noticed immediately, and usually with relief, that Mailer's commitment to a high romantic style had disappeared.[2] "Style," says Robert Frost, "is that which indicates how the writer takes himself and what he is saying" (165-66). How does the writer take himself in *The Executioner's Song?* Not at all, said most of the book's reviewers: Mailer had succeeded in refining his prodigious ego out of the book. He had achieved something like an Eliotic annulment of self, an "extinction of personality," in which he suppressed his own voice to become the medium for a variety of others. And the reason for this surrender had to do, naturally, with the failure, or at least with the obsolescence, of his former romantic project. Mailer had given up his Emersonian illusions about originality and self-reinvention. He'd replaced attempts at auto-American-biography—the creation of works in which the words "I" and "America" can at some moments (and those not always the most attractive or admirable ones) be interchanged—with social documentary. Finally Mailer was one of us. Or such was the judgment of many of those critics of Mailer who tend to think of his "talent" as a natural resource and of themselves as its board of directors. Such a judgment, given Mailer's past record, is probably worth questioning.

The Executioner's Song deals with Gary Gilmore, a figure now famous enough to have his likeness on display in Madame Tussaud's. There one may see his wax effigy executed by an invisible firing squad every three minutes or so and read the story of how Gilmore was condemned to death by the state of Utah for the murder of two young men in the summer of 1976. Gilmore refused to seek a stay of execution and demanded that the state follow through on its promise and kill him, which it eventually did. Mailer tells Gilmore's story by way of indirect discourse, from the points of view of over a hundred of the persons involved. Almost everyone, including Gilmore, submitted to extensive interviewing. Thus the book came out of careful study and reworking of tapes and transcripts.

Part of Mailer's fascination with Gilmore surely owed to his resemblance to the figure of the psychopath described in "The White Negro" twenty years before. "The White Negro," Mailer's first text with romantic aspirations, is an attempt to incarnate an authentically American voice and temper to resist the prevailing atmosphere of "conformity and depression" in which a "stench of fear ... come[s] out of every pore of American life, and we suffer from a collective failure of nerve" (300). Mailer's dilemma is Emersonian, akin to the one in which "Self-Reliance" begins. Yet his response, a mythical self-projection into a figure of rebellion whom he calls, alternately, the hipster, the White Negro, and the psychopath, owes more, I suspect, to Blake and *The Marriage of Heaven and Hell*. In his first major prophetic book, Blake transforms himself (with no little self-directed irony) into a satanic poet in order to assault the false pieties that the "Angels" who dominate the religious, political, and artistic life of late-eighteenth-century England enforce. Mailer is probably not being any more sensationalistic than Blake was when he identifies himself with the figure his orthodox contemporaries fear most. One of the many fine intuitions in "The White Negro" is that the psychopath had taken the place of Satan in contemporary morality. Mailer sees the ethic of psychoanalysis, with its endorsement of irony, stoicism, and detachment, as the repressive Anglicanism of his day, a state and corporate religion designed to quell nonconformity. The psychopath's hunger for immediacy in all things can't help but threaten a culture committed to deferred and displaced satisfactions.

Mailer's alternative is a romantic return to childhood, but a return far less tranquil and tranquilizing than the one envisioned by Wordsworth and Coleridge, or, needless to say, by the psychoanalyst. Mailer's psychopath replays the past event in the present so that he can gain back what was lost, score victories where he was, in childhood, forced to make concessions. The conception couldn't be more in the native romantic vein. When Mailer, in another context, declares that going "from gap to gain is very American" (*Armies* 44), he both evokes this design and provides a good throwaway epigraph for Emerson's collected works. Where Freud believed that the best that one could hope for would be to transform compulsive repetition into an accepting memory of the traumatic event, Mailer demands a full redemption. If the hipster "has the courage to meet the parallel situation at the moment when he is ready," Mailer writes, "then he has a chance to act as he has never acted before.... In thus giving expression to the buried infant in himself, he can lessen the tension of those infantile desires and so free himself to remake a bit of his nervous system" (308). Mailer's Gilmore comes close to exemplifying the type for whom "the decision is to encourage the psychopath in oneself, to explore that domain of experience where security is boredom and therefore sickness, and one exists in the present, in that enormous present which is without past or future, memory or planned intention, the life where a man must go until he is beat, where he must gamble with his energies through all those small or large crises of courage and unforeseen situations which beset his day" (301).

Gilmore doesn't make a cogent decision to act in this way, as Mailer's hipster does—Gilmore, at least up to a certain critical point in the book, seems incapable of making any cogent decisions. The amount of confusion he can create in a few hours' space is frequently astonishing. On one night we find him running stolen guns; fighting it out, physically, on the highway with his girlfriend, Nicole; trying (and failing) to steal a tape deck from the local shopping mall; banging into the car parked behind his when he tries to escape; eluding (cannily) a pursuing squad car; and arriving at last, in the middle of the night, at his cousin Brenda's house, where he wakes up everyone to demand fifty dollars so that he can run away to Canada.

But at other times Gilmore is more sympathetic. On the night that he gets his first paycheck, for example, he goes off to see a movie with Brenda and Johnny, her husband. The picture is Gilmore's choice, and he picks, as one might almost have predicted, *One Flew Over the Cuckoo's Nest*. It turns out that Gilmore served time in the penitentiary next to the mental hospital where *Cuckoo's Nest* was filmed and that in fact he'd been treated in the hospital itself. Gilmore is chaos throughout the film, cheering, shouting commentary, bashing on the chairs in front of him. Almost everyone gets up and moves away from him eventually, and by the end of the evening Brenda, who usually shows an exemplary patience with Gary, is completely exasperated. But Gilmore had a point to make at the film, though he made it crudely enough. He felt, one can surmise, that he had more in common with R. P. McMurphy, Kesey's pulp equivalent of Mailer's White Negro, than Jack Nicholson, who played the role, or anyone else present in the theater for that matter. So why shouldn't he be the object of attention? Exacerbating Gilmore's mood would be the fact that the crowd paying to worship McMurphy's nonconformity had rewarded Gilmore for his by keeping him in jail for nineteen out of his thirty-five years. One understands Gilmore's confusion. Mailer certainly understands it well, but he's unwilling to turn the book into an overt celebration of a latter-day hipster. There's no tendency to extend the tonal grandeur of "The White Negro" to Gary Gilmore.

But there is a point in the story where Gilmore's status changes. Up until this moment, Gilmore has been almost wholly destructive, acting on every whim as though it were divine inspiration. "He was grabbing at everything. It was as if the world was just out of reach of his fingers" (30), says a young woman of Gilmore. He wants full possession of everything glowing that comes in range.

But from the point when Gilmore decides that he is willing to die, he takes on a certain dignity. There have been no capital punishments for some time in the state of Utah, and everyone expects that Gilmore will do what every other convicted killer has done and fight for a life in jail, but he will not. The climax of the book, at least in my judgment, comes when Gilmore, having been condemned and imprisoned for the two murders, chooses to force the state of Utah to carry out his sentence and execute him. Here is Gilmore addressing the Board of Pardons to demand his own death:

> I simply accepted the sentence that was given to me. I have accepted sentences all my life. I didn't know I had a choice in the matter.
>
> When I did accept it, everybody jumped in and wanted to argue with me. It seems that the people, especially the people of Utah, want the death penalty but they don't want executions and when it became a reality they might have to carry one out, well, they started backing off on it.
>
> Well, I took them literal and serious when they sentenced me to death just as if they had sentenced me to ten years or thirty days in the county jail or something. I thought you were supposed to take them serious. I didn't know it was a joke. (675)

One may detest Gilmore for living in the world as though it were an open question whether the other people there are as real as he is, and still acknowledge his triumph of wit here. Consider the context. Gilmore has spent the balance of his life under the control of institutions. He has been told when to get up in the morning, when to sleep, when to exercise, when to eat. Society has applied enormous resources to the task of normalizing him, rendering him into a coherent, stable citizen. And if the price of subduing his antisocial instincts involves doing away with whatever imaginative potential he might possess, so be it.

Gilmore's deep joke consists in capitulating and becoming just the kind of well-disciplined subject everyone always wanted him to be, but at the wrong moment. The most imaginative act of Gilmore's life, and the costliest to himself, is to pretend to possess no imagination whatever. The result is a sudden reversal. Gilmore, in an instant, stands in relation to the institutional powers of justice as they have, for nineteen years, stood to him. He's demanding that they follow procedure, get in line, stop being so inconsiderate and whimsical. The satisfaction Gilmore derived from the deadpan "I didn't know it was a joke" had to have been great. In any event, it was dearly gotten.

It's hard not to spare a little affection for someone who was motivated, at least in part, to die for the sake of a shrewd joke. Freud, no lover of criminals, uses as his first example in the paper on humor that of the condemned man who approaches the scaffold on a Monday morning saying, "Well, the week's beginning nicely" (161). Wit entails looking down upon oneself from the position of the collective, or cultural, superego, says Freud, and seeing from that perspective how insignificant one's own life is. Gilmore's stroke modifies Freud a little: wit of his sort entails taking up the position of a superego above the cultural standard of the law, making of it a helpless child, temporarily.

Gilmore, it would seem, became capable of this sort of victory when he went to jail. As he says to his cellmate Gibbs (who turns out to be a police informer) shortly after arriving in confinement, "I am in my element now." In jail, Gilmore is a different kind of person. He draws and paints, writes some fine letters in a neo-Whitmanian mode, and develops a singular sense of humor, of which a couple of the better instances can serve as samples. Moody, one of Gilmore's lawyers, is interviewing him: "If on your passage you meet a new soul coming to take your place, what advice would you have for him?" Gilmore: "Nothing. I don't expect someone to take my place. Hi, I'm your replacement ... where's the key to the locker ... where do you keep the towels?" (888). Then there's Gilmore's proposal for a new way to make money off his death: "Oh, hey, man, I got something that'll make a mint. Get aholda John Cameron Swazey right now, and get a Timex wristwatch here. And have John Cameron Swazey out there after I fall over, he can be wearing a stethoscope, he can put it on my heart and say, 'Well, that stopped,' and then he can put the stethoscope on the Timex and say, 'She's still running, folks'" (831).

What accounts for the change in Gilmore, from Mailer's point of view presumably, is that Gilmore has developed something of a romantic faith. Gilmore's effort, from about the time that he enters prison, is to conduct himself so that he can die what he would himself credit as a "good death." And that means living the time he has left with some charity, and above all with equanimity, without signs of desperation. Gilmore's weakness lies, perhaps, in his requiring a fixed date to direct himself. But his willingness to engage death is what sets him apart from most of the other people in the book. In saying this much, I am finding a strong bias in Mailer's supposedly neutral account. But if we look at the form of *The Executioner's Song*—with form being understood in Kenneth Burke's sense as the setting up of expectations in the reader—we will see that it is far less neutral a text than most of its reviewers wished it to be.

The basic unit of *The Executioner's Song* is the short paragraph written from the perspective of one or another participant in the story. The passages work as self-contained dramatic units, a fact Mailer emphasizes by surrounding each one with a generous aura of blank space. He composes the paragraphs in the third person but injects each of them with enough of the person's idiom to convey a sense of his character. Here, for example, is Gilmore's parole officer Mont Court reflecting (with mediation by Mailer) on whether to have Gary picked up for a parole violation or let him turn himself in. "Gilmore, coming back on his own, would be fortifying the positive side of himself. He would know Court had been right to trust him. That would give a base on which to work. The idea was to get a man into some kind of positive relationship with authority. Then he might begin to change" (53). Mailer's conception of Mont Court is there to be heard in the style of these lines, and particularly in the phrase "positive relationship with authority." Here and throughout the book, Mailer works somewhat in the manner of the portrait painter who follows her subject around for a while before she begins to paint. She's waiting for him to strike a physical pose that reveals some crucial aspect of his character. Mailer combed through the relevant tapes and transcripts in search of similarly revealing moments of speech. One test of the book's integrity would be whether those represented would be willing to sign their names to their sections of the text. Most, I think, would, and in that sense the book is very much theirs.

But Mailer is alive in *The Executioner's Song* too, and not least in the rhythmical shapings that he gives to the paragraphs. The book starts, for example, with Brenda's memory of Gary catching her as she falls from the breaking branch of a forbidden apple tree. Gary then helps her drag away the branch so they won't be caught and punished. So from the beginning we're led to associate Gary with a fall, with transgression, and with—the parallels are too numerous to be discounted—the Fall. A sense that the incident might anticipate the future comes through in the passage's final line: "That was Brenda's earliest recollection of Gary" (5). The mythical echoes and the soft but perceptible drop of the last line convey a certain inevitability. Gilmore is fated, despite finer impulses, to fail. His destiny is tragic, a fact brought home to the reader by the comparable shaping of many of the passages that focus on him. Here is the end of a paragraph in which Gilmore says good-bye to his brother Mikal: "He leaned over and kissed Mikal on the mouth. 'See you in the darkness,' he said" (866). Here a priest, Father Meersman, talks to Gary about wearing a hood during the execution: "If Gary wanted to die with dignity, then he had to respect that very, very simple thing about the hood. It was there for practicality to allow the thing to run very dignified, and no movement. Gary listened in silence" (871). In this passage, Gilmore receives communion from Meersman: "Gary took the wafer on his tongue in the old style, mouth open, way back, in the way, observed Father Meersman, he had received as a child, and then he drank from the chalice. Father Meersman stood beside him while Gary consumed the bottom of the cup" (884). The kind of foreshadowing that occurs, with varying degrees of subtlety, in these passages pervades the book. One section after another about Gilmore ends with a tonal allusion to his death. The effect, over the course of a thousand or so pages, is to confer on Gary a considerable stature. Fate seems to have singled him out for sacrifice. From Mailer's point of view, it is fair to surmise, Gary earns his tragic status by saying yes to his own death.

Gilmore is not the only person in *The Executioner's Song* who is so treated. The passages devoted to his girlfriend, Nicole Baker, a figure easily as complex as Gary, finish with a dying fall at least as often as Gilmore's passages do, and perhaps more. And it is Nicole's disdain for life, evidenced by, among other things, a determined suicide attempt, *combined with* her vitality and resilience, that makes Mailer confer a tragic dignity on her as well. In fact, all of those figures in the book who live strongly in the knowledge of death receive some share of Mailer's elegiac tones. Mailer is moved by people like Brenda, her father Vern Damico, and Bessie Gilmore,

Gary's mother, and offers them the one form of authorial tribute that the book's constraints allow.

Larry Schiller, who interviewed Gilmore extensively and who eventually collaborated with Mailer on the book, is largely denied this treatment, as is Barry Farrell, a journalist who seems to share some of Mailer's private apprehensions about the workings of the world. But this is something one might have predicted: Mailer has always claimed to care more for working-class Americans than for literati and Eastern sophisticates. What is surprising, particularly in light of the reviews the book received, is the kind of shaping that Mailer gives to the paragraphs focused on Gilmore's victims and their wives. In his review of *The Executioner's Song*, Walter Karp, a tough-minded and acute political writer, praised Mailer for giving up his long-time disdain for the American squares and treating Max and Colleen Jensen and Debbie and Ben Bushnell with compassion (25—26). Here are the first two passages on the Bushnells:

> Debbie was feeling a little off one day and Ben kept wanting to take her to the doctor. She was pregnant, after all. But there were eleven kids over from the Busy Bee Day-Care Center, and Debbie didn't have the time. Ben finally raised his voice a little. At which point she told him he bugged her. That was the worst fight they ever had.
>
> They were proud that was the worst fight. They saw marriage as a constant goal of making each other happy. It was the opposite of that song "I Never Promised You a Rose Garden." They kind of promised each other. They weren't going to be like other marriages. (239)

Debbie Bushnell might own to having said everything included in these passages. But to shape the material as Mailer has, to end the passages with trite lines like "That was the worst fight they ever had" and "They weren't going to be like other marriages" makes the Bushnells seem small. They don't rate the tragic tones that Gary and Nicole get. On the next page, Mailer ends a passage of only three sentences on Debbie with the line, "She was terrific with kids and would rather mop her kitchen floor than read." This may have been true of Mrs. Bushnell, but given what passage endings mean in this book, and given that the recipient of this information is at the moment a reader, holding a thousand-page volume, it's clear that the presentation is potently biased. I have picked out some of the more extreme examples of Mailer's treatment of the victims. He's kinder to the Jensens, for example, but not very much. Mrs. Jensen's last thought of her husband leaving for work on the day he is to be killed is ominous but also, at the last moment, reduced. "He would be moving along the Interstate at just such a speed [55 m.p.h.] until he went around a slow graded turn and disappeared from sight and left her mind free to think of one and then another of the small things she must do that day" (216).

The passages on the lives that the Jensens and Bushnells led before the murders tend to begin in hope of some kind and end, also, on an upswing, an upswing that sounds hollow and naive in light of events. The couples are middle-class Americans, expectant, ambitious, unworldly, and perhaps a little smug. They live without a sense of the tragic possibilities in life, the sense that Nicole Baker seems to have from childhood and that Gilmore supposedly develops over time. *The Executioner's Song*, I would argue, is a violent polemic on behalf of the position that Gilmore (as Mailer represents him) eventually achieves. For Mailer, if I understand him correctly, attempts to write his book from a state akin to the one he attributes to Gilmore, one that acknowledges the awareness of death as the necessary condition for every just perception.

Recall that Mailer's Gilmore began to develop his sense of death as a principle of authority when he was immersed in the partial death that jail represents. Now Mailer himself has, from early in his career, been preoccupied with the experience of imprisonment. Entering prison has, in the past, meant cutting off romantic possibilities. If self-creation involves assertion and risk, then prison is the state of death-in-life because there you have to diminish yourself, draw in in order to survive. In *The Armies of the Night*, Mailer speaks of jail as a place where "a man who wished to keep his sanity must never anticipate, never expect, never hope with such high focus of hope that disappointment would be painful" (187). (The lines could serve as a compressed renunciation of Wordsworth's romantic paean to hope in book 6 of *The Prelude*.) In "The White Negro," prison is the image that comes forth most readily to figure limitation or the failure of self-reliance. "The wrong kinds of defeats," Mailer says there, "attack the body and imprison one's energy until one is jailed in the prison air of other people's habits" (300). Prison has been to Mailer what acedia was to Coleridge, what "habitual self" was to Keats, and what poverty was to Emerson, the most emphatic possible conception of imaginative death.

Correspondingly, Mailer's high romantic style, the style of *Armies* and "The White Negro," might be said to represent the mental antithesis of imprisonment. The exhilaration those texts can produce in a reader derives in part from his sense that the writing possesses boundless resources and possibilities. One feels that Mailer will never run out of metaphors. His invention will never flag, his powers of observation and analysis will persist forever. The energizing illusion is akin to the one felt in the presence of a great athlete, who seems unlimited in her ability to extemporize fresh ways of standing out in a game.

One way to think of *The Executioner's Song* is as a book in which Mailer, willingly or under some compulsion, enters the prison of a restricted style. He surrenders the freedom of Emersonian abandonment and encloses himself in the rectangular walls of the book's isolated paragraphs. He adopts a voice that is cold, flat, and spectral and makes the acquiescence to death his central principle of value. The style is terminal. Mailer's early romantic style signified an energetic denial of death. The words were supposed to seem unstoppable, a stream of invention that would never find its placid level. The culture to which Mailer addressed himself then had imposed what he saw as living death by conformity on its citizens, and the task at hand was to revitalize them. But when a culture becomes falsely vitalistic, making the denial of death the principle on which its mystifications rest, it is time to try to undermine it by the Emersonian gesture of diving to reappear in a new place.

Part of what reinforces the interpretation I've been offering thus far—in which Gilmore is understood as developing into the kind of existentialist who's in accord more or less with Mailer's literary self-image—is the degree to which the book's first readers resisted seeing these designs. A reading always appears to be more authentic when it's been wrested at the expense of some other approach that can simultaneously be revealed as self-interested, anxious, or guilty. I wouldn't be surprised if Mailer, who's played off his critics as skillfully as anyone writing today, could have predicted the eventual surfacing of the kind of "subversive" interpretation that I've offered so far. In fact, he might find this reading satisfying to a troubling degree.

I mean that we ought to be suspicious at how readily *The Executioner's Song* yields to an analysis that calls forward so many of Mailer's key preoccupations and "finds" a shape in Gilmore's career that the author of "The White Negro" might have desired for his own.[3] So it seems worth asking how we might have seen Gilmore without Mailer's subtle shapings of his story.

What's striking throughout the text—and Mailer plays on this—is the inability of all the institutional agencies and their functionaries, prison psychiatrists, social workers, wardens, and the rest, to come up with a description of Gilmore that isn't jargon-ridden and flat-minded. No one can describe to anyone else's satisfaction why Gilmore committed the murders.

And this may be true not because they haven't got access to the resources of the Novelist, but because Gilmore doesn't provide enough fixity. Perhaps one can't fairly represent his character, as Mailer habitually represents his own, in terms of some internal dynamic or dialectic. Maybe Gilmore's life doesn't lend itself to a "form"; and maybe he doesn't attempt to fashion his experience in a manner analogous to the fashioning of a literary career. From this point of view, Gilmore's only "motive" is a hunger for passionate disruption, an urge to fracture any set of social forms in which he finds himself. His profession that he wants to die made in front of the Board of Pardons may be the inception of an existential project. It may also be an act of simple, spontaneous anarchism, aiming a joke at a venerable institution, then living out the joke for the possibilities of future disruption that arise from it.

I am suggesting that a great deal of Gilmore's behavior might be best understood as parodic, as when, in prison, he begins impersonating a celebrity: signing autographs, sending T-shirts to his fans, spending hours over his mail and his clippings, using his status to try to consort on equal terms with a few others among the rich and famous. His interviews with Schiller, and with his lawyers Moody and Stanger, when read from a certain angle, offer amusing send-ups of journalistic encounters with politicians and other professional evaders. Gilmore's gross manipulations—especially of Nicole, whom he induces to attempt suicide—are the gestures of a crazed real-life film director, experimenting with a sudden unexpected power on other people's lives. Perhaps Gilmore is devoted to nothing more than a certain brutal form of "play," manifest in bitter jokes and stratagems, parody, and the creation of temporary roles, a form of play that recognizes no purpose and no standard of value other than the venting of his energies in disruptive action and passionate speech.

I'm offering the possibility, then, that the subtleties of form in *The Executioner's Song* may be employed to contain an energy inimical to cultural forms, including literary forms, even of the radical Emersonian variety. Why should Mailer exert himself in the interest of this sort of confinement? Gilmore's minority or oppositional energies are the ones that Mailer wants to identify with his own, and yet these "minority" powers, if they're going to have any real value, have to possess the potential and the inclination to enter into conflict with the triad of opposing forces that Mailer sees as threatening: chaos, evil, and waste. Gilmore's brutal "play," without end or allegiance, undermines the dialectical conception of life, life conceived of as a series of significant encounters in which one can be potentially transformed for the better, which represents Mailer's main hope for salutary development.

The vision of Gilmore against which Mailer is defending himself (and his readers) is perhaps one in tune with a contemporary tendency to give up on coherent narratives; on truth, even of the pragmatic variety; on transcendence in any form; on any unironic investment in persons, objects, or interpretations. This tendency, some have argued, is encouraged by the "postmodern" experience of life as a simulacrum, as an unguided peregrination through images and codes that bear—and admit implicitly and rather cheerfully that they bear—no relations to any possible referent. Gilmore may be a creature of this world at its worst, a product and promulgator of its values. If this is in fact the case, then Gilmore has earned the not inconsiderable distinction of being the figure who compelled America's foremost literary radical to fight culture's conserving battles for it.

Notes

1. For a representative response to Mailer along these lines, see Philip Rahv's review.

2. See the reviews of *The Executioner's Song* by John Garvey, Walter Karp, and Tim O'Brien.

3. On Mailer's self-conscious shaping of his career and his drive for interpretive priority over his own work, see Richard Poirier. My reading of Mailer is indebted to Poirier's book, as well as to Alvin Kernan's reflection on *Of a Fire on the Moon* (130–61) and to Gore Vidal's excellent review essay.

Works Cited

Emerson, Ralph Waldo. "Self-Reliance." *Essays and Lectures.* Ed. Joel Porte. New York: Library of America, 1983. 257–82.

Freud, Sigmund. "Humour." *The Standard Edition of the Complete Psychological Works of Sigmund Freud,* Ed. James Strachey. Vol. 21. London: Hogarth, 1953. 161–66. 24 vols. 1952–74.

Frost, Robert. *The Letters of Robert Frost to Louis Untermeyer.* Ed. Louis Untermeyer. New York: Holt, 1963.

Garvey, John. "*The Executioner's Song,* Mailer's Best in Years." Rev. of *The Executioner's Song,* by Norman Mailer. *Commonweal* 14 Mar. 1980: 134–35.

Karp, Walter. "Making a Killing, Norman Mailer and Gary Gilmore." Rev. of *The Executioner's Song,* by Norman Mailer. *Esquire* Dec. 1979: 25–26.

Kernan, Alvin. *The Imaginary Library: An Essay on Literature and Society*. Princeton UP, 1982.

Mailer, Norman. *The Armies of the Night: History as a Novel, the Novel as History*. New York: New American Library, 1968.

———. *The Executioner's Song*. Boston: Little, 1979.

———. "The White Negro." *Advertisements for Myself*. 1959. New York: Perigee-Putnam's, 1981. 299–320.

O'Brien, Tim. "The Ballad of Gary G." Rev. of *The Executioner's Song*, by Norman Mailer, New York 15 Oct. 1979: 67–68.

Poirier, Richard. *Norman Mailer*. New York: Viking, 1972.

Rahv, Philip. "Crime without Punishment." Rev. of *An American Dream*, by Norman Mailer. *New York Review of Books* 25 Mar. 1965: 1–4.

Vidal, Gore. "The Norman Mailer Syndrome." Rev. of *Advertisements for Myself*, by Norman Mailer. *Nation* 2 Jan. 1960: 13–16.

Wordsworth, William. *The Prelude: 1799, 1805, 1850*. Eds. Wordsworth, Abrams, and Gill. New York: Norton, 1979.

JOSEPH TABBI

Mailer's Psychology of Machines

For years Mailer has dreamed of writing a great novel of America, a "creation equal to the phenomena of the country itself" (*Cannibals* 99). For some readers, the closest he has ever come to this novel is still *The Naked and the Dead* (1948), endebted though he may have been, at the age of twenty-five, to Farrell, Steinbeck, and especially Dos Passos for the book's panoramic vision of American society. Yet it is in the strong work of the 1960s—the psychological romance of *An American Dream* (1965) and the imaginative journalism of *The Armies of the Night* (1968)—that Mailer came to see his own life as a possible embodiment of contemporary history and began, Whitman-like, to identify his personal destiny with the destiny of the nation. Here is the American author who sets himself the task of being *the* American author and who continues to engage readers despite the diminishing likelihood of his ever completing his great work.

Of a Fire on the Moon (1970) is one of Mailer's most formidable attempts to read history—the flight of *Apollo 11* to the moon—as a chapter in an ongoing fiction of his own, a "nonfiction novel" in the line of *Armies* and his 1968 convention piece, *Miami and the Siege of Chicago*. Like these precursors, the moon book is of more than journalistic value, and because Mailer dramatizes his failures no less scrupulously than he does his successes, it comes to reveal, as few traditional novels have been able to, the difficult

From *Publications of the Modern Language Association of America* 106, no. 2 (March 1991): 238-50. © 1991 by The Modern Language Association of America.

relation between technology and the private imagination. Alvin B. Kernan rightly situates Mailer's subtle attack against the rationalist world of NASA within "the entire radical wing of romanticism, the tough, revolutionary line that leads from Blake and Byron, for all their differences, through such poets as Rimbaud to Sartre and Genet" (155). Laurence Goldstein includes *Fire* in his fascinating survey of "flying machines" in modern literature, and George P. Landow concludes his ground-breaking study of nonfiction prose "from Carlyle to Mailer" with an able exposition of the most complexly technical passage in the book. But this powerful lineage cannot quite make up for a singular failing, a seeming inability on the part of Mailer to bring the temperamental force of personality to bear on what he himself, early in the book, calls "these space matters, foreign to him" (6–7). Against systems that, as Joseph McElroy was to observe on the launch of *Apollo 17*, "seemed to erase or revise the great single and possible Self at the core of our Western tradition," Mailer refused to give up "that Self's rhetoric"; thus, McElroy suggests, in *Fire* "less might have been more" (27).

Even Richard Poirier, generally among the most sympathetic of Mailer's readers, finds the book too ambitious, a work in which Mailer may have played his "standard routines" beyond the point where they still enliven perception. Poirier judges the best parts of *Fire* to be "the descriptive ones," the "masterful straight stuff" (160, 162). And whereas many readers have been bored by Mailer's intensive researches into the raw material of space technology, Poirier finds the exposition "made heavy by ambitions in excess" of them. "What to do with material so unyielding, so uniform?" Poirier imagines Mailer asking himself. And Mailer, who must have received little stimulation from the "rather flat-minded," media-insulated personalities of the astronauts, sought to make these men more interesting by delving into their unconscious psyches. "It is by such means," Poirier surmises, "that the book engages itself with the subject of dreams" (161).

Poirier is undoubtedly correct in sensing the strain with which Mailer goes after large effects—indeed, this view is supported by Mailer's own "near disclaimers" or apologies for the book's stylistic inflations (163). What Poirier may not appreciate, however, is the depth of Mailer's engagement with the psychology of the dream. This neglect is understandable, since the ideas introduced in the book's conceptually central chapter, "The Psychology of Machines," are never fully integrated into the later sections. Though these ideas do shed light on the psychology of astronauts and NASA technicians, they never amount (as if they ever could) to the promised elucidation of "some new psychological constitution to man" (*Fire* 46). Resembling Steven Rojack in *An American Dream*, Mailer proposes an existentialist theory of the dream that "would (ideally) turn Freud on his head," though it largely remains in his own head (17).

Not entirely, however. For besides the text's brilliant but unfulfilled passages on psychology, there is manuscript evidence that, at some early stage in the writing, Mailer had intended *Fire* to be the definitive statement of his dream metaphor, an integral part in his ongoing novel of America. In a discarded chapter titled "Alpha and Bravo," Mailer explicitly tried to give fictive expression to his machine psychology, although the predominantly journalistic form of *Fire* prevented him just then from realizing the draft's many imaginative possibilities. Still, the concerns of these chapters persist; *The Alpha Bravo Universe* is the working title of a massive fiction Mailer still has in mind, a three-part novel whose first part, *Ancient Evenings*, is over 700 pages long.

Fire represents more than an interesting stage in the creative development of an author, for its insights into the psychology of astronauts and machines link Mailer with other writers who, without necessarily constituting a "tradition," have had related concerns. This context suggests that the issues Mailer raises go beyond his dream of himself. In setting his private vision next to NASA's vast corporate machine and in trying to bring the two together by positing a psychology for the machine, Mailer is *testing the reality* of his obsessions. And if his initial metaphorical excursions into "the inner space of the dream" are quickly superseded by the astronauts' more prosaic journey through outer space, it is worth asking why. Given the scope of Mailer's literary ambitions, such an investigation will of necessity lead to the more general problem that has faced American writers since Henry Adams and before: that of imposing or accommodating the self and its imaginative constructions on or within a universe of impersonal force.

Origins of the Fire: The Romantic Background

From the outset, Mailer recognizes the difficulty of his project. In the book's opening chapter, "A Loss of Ego," a brief lament on the death of Hemingway serves as prologue to a "philosophical launch." While Hemingway was living, he "constituted the walls of the fort," making it possible still to believe that courage and personal style (elsewhere regarded as the insulating layers of the masculine ego[1]) might yet enable one to live with dread and to retain at least a coherent personal identity in an age that lacked any dominant principle or organizing center. The suicide of America's "greatest living romantic," happening near the start of the decade that would end in the flight of *Apollo 11*, had left a void in the culture; "[t]echnology would fill the pause" (*Fire* 4).

Thus the book begins—in despondency but with a conceit that is still powerful, even at this late hour in postindustrial America, in pitting the romantic spirit against technology's static and empty spaces. Mailer's own sentiments, it is clear, incline naturally to romanticism, or at least to the postromantic myth of the embattled ego that he himself had begun to develop more than ten years earlier in the ground-breaking essay "The White Negro" (1957). There he had made his earliest sustained attempt to elaborate a comprehensive social psychology, arguing that because our age is confronted at once with the threat of "instant death by atomic war," the memory of the concentration camps, and a stifling "slow death by conformity,"

> the only life-giving answer is to accept the terms of death, to live
> with death as immediate danger, to divorce oneself from society,
> to exist without roots, to set out on that uncharted journey into
> the rebellious imperatives of the self.

By thus insisting on the primacy of the self and, even more, by trying to preserve some private sense of his own mortality in the face of the many forms of collective death implemented by the totalitarian state, Mailer could successfully attack the "partially totalitarian," predominantly conformist society of the Eisenhower years (*Advertisements* 339). In Hemingway he had found a writer who, by the sheer strength of a personal style, had forged a similarly adversary aesthetic. Hemingway's writing could give substance to the quintessentially romantic idea that reality resides in no given objective condition but in one's immediate perception of the moment, resides, that is, in "that enormous present" where the self can act on potentiality without regard to the mores, securities, and rewards offered, or the inhibitions exacted, by society. So too might the dangerously adventurous life that illumined Hemingway's work offer a stimulating contrast to the increasingly bureaucratized existence of most Americans. Against the age's spiritual vacuums and bland psychotherapeutic insulations, Hemingway had kept a spirit of bravery alive, exploring in his books "the possibilities within death" as a necessary adjunct to living (342).[2]

Ten years later, in the late sixties, Hemingway's capitulation and the ascendancy of technology have weakened the romantic's claim to autonomy, compelling Mailer to reconceive, or at least refashion in a new context, his notions about selfhood, its psychological basis, and its relation to society. Implicit in all his self-characterizations during the sixties was the idea that he could best discern and express the social upheavals and political conflicts of the time by becoming "an egotist of the most startling misproportions, outrageously and often unhappily self-assertive," one who could, if not quite comprehend the age, at least exemplify its larger pattern (*Armies* 66). Now Mailer, "detached this season from the imperial demands of his ego" (*Fire* 6), portrays himself modestly as "little more than a decent spirit, somewhat shunted to the side," using the name Aquarius but knowing that, as we moved into the seventies and the celebrated Age of Aquarius, he had "never had less sense of possessing the Age" (*Fire* 4). His own identity unanchored amid technological forces that seem altogether antithetical, faceless, and impersonal, Mailer finds himself in the position of Henry Adams's confronting the dynamo in the Great Exhibition of 1900; contemplating the moon shot, Mailer can no longer embody or give shape to the social and historical reality.

Mailer's compositional difficulties are real enough, but one should not be taken in by his modesty: like the assumed modesty of Adams in *The Education*, it has its rhetorical uses. Mailer had already evoked Adams in *The Armies of the Night*, his first sustained attempt to speak of himself in the third person, and his subject and mood in *Fire* are even more in line with Adams's self-deprecating irony. For Adams, writing at the dawn of twentieth-century modernity, the third-person narrative provided a way to regain his own place and imaginative coherence in a universe of forces that tended to exclude him—it was a way, that is, both to represent and to participate in the cosmos. Similarly, the authorial persona in *Fire* is essentially a literary device that enables Mailer to become a character in the drama of the space flight with a part equal to the astronaut's.

Throughout the early chapters of the book, Mailer fluctuates in his relation with Aquarius, showing the same sort of ambivalence toward him as he does toward the astronauts and toward space flight and its implications. At times he simply identifies with his alter ego; at other times he keeps this disembodied literary voyager at a humorous distance. In some passages the effect is not much different from the fun Mailer has in presenting the three astronauts:

> So Aquarius began to live without his ego, a modest quiet observer who went on trips through the Space Center and took in interviews, and read pieces of literature connected to the subject, and spent lonely nights not drinking in his air-conditioned motel room ... and by the night before the launch, he was already in orbit himself, a simple fellow with a mind which idled agreeably.... He is beginning to observe as if he were

invisible. A danger sign. Only the very best and worst novelists
can write as if they are invisible.   (56–57)

This all sounds accommodating enough, though in fact one can hardly
overstress Mailer's antithetical purpose here. Though Aquarius would
become "perforce, an acolyte to technology" (56), he undertakes the chore of
mastering the specialized technical material mostly for polemical reasons, as
a prerequisite to attaining the critical distance needed for a credible attack.
In an interview given two years after Mailer had devoted a summer to
studying space technology for the "Apollo" section of *Fire*, his views on
science are unremittingly hostile: "at bottom [the interests of the artist and
the scientist] are opposed and they're enemies. Because the physicist is finally
trying to destroy the fundament of magic, and the artist is trying to blow up
the base of technology" (*Pontifications* 48). So too had he written some years
earlier that "the unendurable demand of the middle of this century" was "to
restore the metaphor, and thereby displace the scientist from his center"
(*Cannibals* 310). Admittedly, any total, unreflective commitment to so
adversarial a position would have reduced his own achievement in *Fire*, an
achievement that depends at least in part on the ability of Aquarius, the
deeper he goes into "these space matters foreign to him," to establish a
complex imaginative sympathy with the astronauts and, at the end of the
book, with the gray rock they had brought back from the moon. But apart
from such moments of honest appreciation (and I am not among those for
whom the ending rings false), Mailer's speculative excursions remain
antithetical; they are, ultimately, bridgeheads into alien territory to rescue
from the engineer and the scientist (as Prometheus steals fire from the gods)
some measure of cultural and imaginative control over reality.

Accordingly, in "The Psychology of Machines" Mailer is interested in
studying primarily those aspects of the machine that are most prone to
breakdown, choosing to interpret malfunctions as evidence not of operator
error, design inadequacy, randomness, or mere entropic decline but of a
psychology inhabiting the inert mechanism. At first glance, this
psychologizing of the machine may appear little more than a way of
enlivening an otherwise straight technical narrative of space rocketry (and
"The Psychology of Machines" is easily the most entertaining chapter in
"Apollo"). But in the light of Mailer's polemical intentions, the theoretical
argument has a greater urgency, amounting to an almost desperate assertion
of human freedom against the threat of total cultural absorption into the
machine. To counter the scientific bureaucrat's supposed reliance on
technology to insulate the self from dread, Mailer would introduce anxiety

into the essential workings of the machine; for every natural cause the technologist might produce to explain mechanical failure, Mailer postulates prior causes beyond the domain of physics. Advancing his ideas in accordance with received conventions of rational argument, he locates his speculative psychology at the point where its existence ceases to be arguable:

> For every malfunction there is a clear cause technology must argue, a nonpsychological cause: psychology assumes free will. A human being totally determined is a machine. Psychology is then a study of the style of choice provided there is freedom to choose. Even a title like The Psychology of Machines assumes that the engine under study, no matter how completely fitted into the world of cause and effect, still has some all but detectable horizon between twilight and evening where it is free to express itself, free to act in contradiction to its logic and its gears, free to jump out of the track of cause and effect.

Mailer is ready to admit that his psychology lacks a scientific basis, but how could it not? "Since such events take place, if they do take place, on those unexpected occasions when no instruments are ready to examine the malfunction, the question is moot. No one alive can state to a certainty that a psychology of machines exists or does not exist" (162). One can ignore the fallacies of reasoning in this assertion. The very fact of breakdown, its persistence in the face of all social, scientific, and technological determinations, is for Mailer solid enough ground on which to build a psychology of machines, one that can be said, however improbably, to apply the ethic of nonconforming autonomy from "The White Negro" to the malfunctioning or conceivable self-functioning of the machine.

Again, for all the "zany theoretical seriousness" of the argument (Poirier 163), Mailer is not the first writer to have thought this way. It was one of Samuel Butler's "Professors of Inconsistency and Evasion" who had argued, in "The Book of the Machines" chapters of *Erewhon*, that spontaneous breakdowns might be taken as proof of a machine's vitality or of some vital spirit manifesting itself through the machine—what we call "spontaneity" being, according to Butler's Erewhonian professor, "only a term for man's ignorance of the gods" (219). Anticipating Mailer's conviction that "dread inhabited the technology of rockets" (*Fire* 169), Butler endows the machine with a consciousness and "a will of its own," meaning that, however much we believe we can understand and control the forces the machine sets in motion, there always remains something "Unknown and

Unknowable" about them (*Erewhon* 215; Mailer uses the phrase "a mind of its own" in *Fire* 162).

Regarded this way, Mailer's psychology can be seen as an assertion—part political, part religious—of what Thomas Pynchon would later describe as "our faith in Malfunction as still something beyond Their grasp," the persistence of freedom and contingency despite corporate efforts to dominate and restrain (*Gravity's Rainbow* 586). But it is more than that. For even as Mailer steps outside the agreed modes of rational argument and scientific debate (where a hypothesis cannot be validated unless it is subject to proof by experiment), he opens discussion to a whole range of irrational human responses that science is obliged to ignore—and these may include the responses of scientists, engineers, and astronauts, as well as those of the laity. Rational argument itself, from his viewpoint, would seem to be a linguistic machine built of interlocking logical components that is unable to accommodate the mystery and nuance inherent in experience, technological or otherwise. Only by taking an imaginative leap or "flight" into metaphor, Mailer seems to imply, can we hope to understand the human dimensions of the flight to the moon.

It is therefore as an expression of our anxiety in the presence of the unknown that his psychology has its first relevance, allowing him to evoke, in defiance of NASA's prosaic rationalism and corporate will to objectify and control, the subtle drama that can exist whenever technological extensions of the human will carry us into regions beyond scientific or rational comprehension. What better way than through a psychology of machines to communicate the tensed activity aboard the lunar module and among the Mission Control engineers during the last four minutes of descent to the moon? It is here, in the brilliantly narrated chapter "The Ride Down," that Mailer's psychology has perhaps its finest application, helping to create for the reader something of the theater that developed when, during the last lunar orbit before the final decision to risk a landing, radio communications began inexplicably to drop out and the display panel flashed the alarm "1202," signaling an information overload in the on-board computer (a development that could have been fatal to the mission).

It is, as Landow has perceived, an existential moment, one that demands more of the astronauts, guidance officers, and Mission Control technicians than the machine alone can give. And yet the feeling conveyed by Mailer's account of the landing is one less of momentary freedom and openness to chance than of greater constriction of will and attention within the binary determinations of the machine. The limits of decision at every stage of the module's flight, GO or NO GO for the mission's continuation, were in place weeks before the warning signal appeared; the navigation and guidance officers were already equipped with established procedures and a clear chain of responsibilities for handling the crisis. All through the landing, flight controllers like mechanical extensions are "screwed to the parameters of the consoles," and the astronauts "come down toward the gray wife of the earth's ages with their eyes riveted to the instruments" (379). Anxiety, an experience of the body and the psyche, resides in the smallest unforeseen occurrence or hint of malfunction, so geared to the machine are the thoughts and emotions of all those involved in the flight. And such anxiety, having originated from the contingency inherent in inert mechanism, has made them more forcefully aware of their own contingent being and of their helplessness to alter it.[3]

Mailer concludes "The Ride Down" with a final reference to the imaginative reaches of the technologist's consciousness:

> And Kranz, who had issued every order to [the flight controller Charles] Duke, and queried his controllers in a voice of absolute calm for the entire trip down, now tried to speak and could not. And tried to speak, and again could not, and finally could unlock his lungs only by smashing his hand on a console so hard his bones were bruised for days. But then if his throat had been constricted and his lungs locked, his heart stopped, he would have been a man who died at the maximum of his moments on earth and what a spring might then have delivered him to the first explorers of the moon. Perhaps it is the function of the dream to teach us those moments when we are GO or NO GO for the maximum thrust into death. They were down, they were on the moon ground, and who could speak?   (381)

The brief but extreme speculation here on the possible depth and function of the dream grows naturally out of the tension in the control room, just as, moments before, a quiet allusion to Armstrong's boyhood dream helps create the mood of descent. But readers familiar with Mailer's earlier work will realize that the conceit of the moon as an angel of death originates not in his immediate involvement in the event but in prior speculations and psychological representations in his fiction. In the first of many such moments in *An American Dream*, for example, Steven Rojack, standing with both feet over the balustrade of a tenth-floor apartment in Manhattan, feels the moon urging him to jump: "My body would drop like a sack, down with it, bag of clothes, bones, and all, but I would rise, the part of me which spoke and thought and had its glimpses of the landscape of my Being, would soar, would rise, would leap the miles of darkness to that moon." Rojack, no less than Kranz, is held immobile within a set of binary determinations: the voices he hears as though from separate compartments of his psyche send contradictory commands ("Instinct was telling me to jump.... Which instinct and where?"), and as he releases one hand from the rail, the other tightens its grip (12).

In citing these resemblances to the fiction, which could be multiplied, I do not mean to suggest that Mailer is *simply* repeating himself, although one recent critic, Stacey Olster, has pointed out that Mailer would return at least twice more in the fiction to the figure of the isolated male consciousness daring the heights. Such repetitions may be a sign of Mailer's "imagistic deprivation," as Olster argues, or they may be the inevitable recourse of any novelist who would sustain a single coherent vision over the course of a long career (407). More interesting than the repetition, however, is the reticence with which these late speculations are presented, suggesting that Mailer could not finally bring himself to insist on his own prior metaphorical flights.[4] His largest claims for the dream continue to be couched in the subjunctive mood ("*Perhaps* it is the function of the dream ..." [my emphasis]), and he has done little with the idea of a psychic journey since his first conjectures about the astronauts' secret belief that "the gamble of a trip to the moon and back again, if carried off in all success, might give thrust for some transpostmortal insertion to the stars" (*Fire* 35). Such last-minute reflections, recalling as they do Mailer's earlier thoughts on interpsychic communication, creative orgasm, and the perception of death, presume a fictional development that *Fire* never realizes. Still less is Mailer able here to extrapolate an inclusive social psychology from the psychology of astronauts. That he had not even made an approach to the high society within NASA, "a group as closed to superficial penetration as a guild of Dutch burghers in the Seventeenth Century," had been the subject of his meditations just a few pages before his account of the moon landing:

> [N]o one but the men in that room would ever begin to know the novels and dramas of conflict, the games of loyalty, and what captures and frustrations of power had played back and forth among these men in the last ten years—it was another of the great novels of the world which would never be written. And was the world a little more polluted for that? (366)

Such are the limitations of Mailer's dream psychology—limitations that Mailer himself recognizes and admits to. What he does achieve, however, in chapters like "The Psychology of Machines" and "The Ride Down," is a compelling meditation on technology's existential dimensions, its shaping influence on the ways that we perceive reality and imagine for ourselves an authentic personal identity. In a concrete sense, Mailer shows how dread might inhabit the technology of rockets, not as magic but as the life experience of individuals who in their daily collaboration with complex and not always predictable machinery might come ultimately to discover their own contingency.

But beyond this achievement, unmatched in the journalistic accounts and histories, there is a particular "great novel" of American technology that Mailer abandoned to the discarded drafts of "The Psychology of Machines." These drafts represent his unprecedented attempt, more ambitious in conception than what survives in the published text, to rid himself of the standard liberal-intellectual objections to the space program, to pare down his own personality, and to internalize the objects and methods of space technology. In the drafts, we can more closely follow Mailer's attempt to narrate the stratifications and lineaments of American society and can begin to distinguish more sharply between possibilities still available to the romantic ego and those that no longer seem to be.

MAILER'S ALPHA-AND-BRAVO UNIVERSE: EARLY DRAFTS FOR "THE PSYCHOLOGY OF MACHINES"

In the Sixty-Second Street warehouse in Manhattan where Mailer's papers are kept, six large boxes contain a late draft and source material for *Of a Fire on the Moon*.[5] One of these boxes contains a half dozen science texts, issues dating from July 1969 of the *New York Times Magazine* and the daily *Times*, lightly annotated copies of *Science* (20 July 1970) and *Scientific American* (May 1968), "more than one technical manual" (Mailer's understatement [*Fire* 152]), hundreds of photocopied NASA press releases and flight transcripts, and some forty double-spaced pages labeled "ALPHA AND BRAVO. Section written for OF A FIRE ON THE MOON, ... not included in the final text of the book." Essentially a meditation on the "grace and economy of communication" between the two halves of a divided psyche, "mythical Alpha and Bravo" (57), this section dovetails quite coherently with the published text: one key passage, for example, on the purported split personalities of the astronauts Armstrong, Aldrin, and Collins, recurs in its entirety in "The Psychology of Astronauts" (46.18–48.7); and another sequence, in which Mailer first hit on the idea of the unconscious as a kind of memory bank, appears in revised form in segment 2 of "The Psychology of Machines" (156.3–157.8).

Although obviously written in haste, and at a time when Mailer had not yet found his theme, these pages read well, and the numerous penciled insertions in his hand suggest that he had gone over the original typescript twice.[6] Except for a wholly mechanical, transitional appearance or two, the Aquarius persona plays a muted role in this chapter, Mailer having crossed out every personal reference to himself and to his dream life. In effect all that remains of Aquarius is the psychological profile of a compositional self, an abstract mental apparatus that in "The Psychology of Machines" would become the conscious "Novelist" and the subconscious "Navigator." In the published text, as in "Alpha and Bravo," Mailer depicts the novelist as that part of the psyche which is forever drawing and redrawing the charts on which the navigator will base a "huge and great social novel" (157). So too does he speak of "that great novel in the map rooms of the self" in a 1967 *Esquire* article on film, parts of which may be regarded as a rough draft for the more extensive psychology Mailer creates in *Fire* (*Existential Errands* 113–14). But nowhere in the published text or in any prior work do the outlines of such a novel take shape quite so explicitly as in the "Alpha and Bravo" manuscript, and in few chapters of *Fire* is the loss of ego so nearly complete or the narrative consciousness rendered so detached and impersonal. It would seem that Mailer is trying to absent himself from the narrative, as he had begun to do in earnest in the Brevard County passages early in *Fire* and as he would do again to brilliant effect in *The Executioner's Song* (1979), so that he can range more freely among the many characters and voices that make up the social and political life of America.

In this way, contrary to our stereotypical view of him, Mailer deemphasizes art as an expression of personality and admits, at least implicitly, that one cannot challenge the repressions and sterility of the contemporary technological age merely by imposing one's ego on the world. And yet (as always), Mailer approaches such total representations by way of the self, seeking to embody the nation's many levels and contradictions within the individual psychic apparatus. Even here, however, before he has properly begun to define his new psychology, he is cautious in his proposal, acknowledging that "a social scientist who draws any relations promiscuously between the psyche of a man and a nation is no poet" (57) and recognizing that "the metaphor can be violating more reality than it illumines." So when he does venture a political metaphor for the double psyche of America, he is as much concerned with the "near indigestible variety within the left and within the right" as he is with the evident fact of polarity:

Left and Right. If in Europe they were born as in separate millennia, as profoundly opposed philosophical ideas of social balance and justice, now in America they symbolize our schism. On the left are hippies, weathermen, SDS Communists, Trotskyites, liberals, social democrats, trade unionists, democrats, blacks, militants, consumer groups, TV commentators, ad agencies, student peace groups, academics, half or more of the working class, and an enormous swatch of the urban middle class.... On the right is the marine corps, the pentagon, the aerospace industries, professional athletes, corporate executives, bigots, squires, country gentry, philosophical conservatives, radical reactionaries, minutemen, farmers, veteran organizers, astronauts, rednecks, small-town high-school principals, state troopers, city police, the majority of dioceses in the church, the other half of the working class, a near unanimity in the small town middle class.... What is immediately apparent is the near indigestible variety within the left and within the right. Such ingredients in a human being would produce a personality doubtless hysterical, vomitous, disoriented, psychopathic, psychotic, wealthy, manic depressive, feverish, yet with it all productive, powerful and possessed of extraordinary funds of unforeseen energy.   (58)

The strategy of this passage, written in 1969, will seem familiar—perhaps overfamiliar—to readers of *The Armies of the Night* and *Miami and the Siege of Chicago*. Indeed, the extensively elaborated lists originated in Mailer's writing as far back as 1957, with "The White Negro," and in the political journalism of the late sixties it became one of his stock devices for massing diverse social and political groups. Whether he is marshaling the forces for and against the war in Vietnam or arraying supporters of Eugene McCarthy against those in favor of Humphrey at the 1968 Chicago convention, the accumulation of conflicting elements on each side serves not merely to traverse a spectrum but to suggest how vulnerable to breakdown the opposing categories are and to prepare for later engagements, transferals, and exchanges within and across the lines of battle.

These unforeseen crossings, for Mailer, give life and significance to the historical moment; they provide the vital mechanism for political change. At the close of *The Armies of the Night*, for example, Mailer foresees a revolution growing out of the extreme psychological differences that had separated the warring "armies" on the steps of the Pentagon during the antiwar demonstration of 21 October 1967: "Whole crisis of Christianity in America that the military heroes were on one side, and the unnamed saints on the other!" (316). Throughout the book the Mailer hero, as a "left conservative," tries to probe the contradictions "at war" in his own personality in order to mediate between the embattled halves in America. The effort can be compelling, as when he considers the number of home, church, and media implantations that must be overcome before the most independent of Americans—not excluding himself—might allow themselves to cross a military line; or it can be altogether despairing, as when, riding a school bus through a prosperous shopping street in Virginia on the way to sentencing soon after his arrest, Mailer listens to the student activists with him yelling out slogans at random uncomprehending teenagers. Recalling himself to "that long dark night of the soul when it is always three o'clock in the morning," Mailer attributes both his present and F. Scott Fitzgerald's past depressions to the evident fact that, despite all literary efforts,

> the two halves of America were not coming together, and when they failed to touch, all of history might be lost in the divide. Yes, there was a dark night if you had the illusion you could do something about it, and the conviction that not enough had been done. Or was it simply impossible—had the two worlds of America drifted irretrievably apart?   (*Armies* 177)

For Mailer, such sad reminders of American demographics translate all too readily into systematic, psychological terms. "We live in an American society," he would say with ever greater frequency during the waning years of the sixties, "which can remind you of nothing so much as two lobes of a brain, two hemispheres of communication themselves intact but surgically severed from one another" (*Existential Errands* 121).

To negotiate a path of communication that would bridge the gap and liberate the energies contained within a polarized society had become perhaps the primary political motivation for Mailer as an author. Yet by the time he wrote "Alpha and Bravo" he seems to have realized that the country's supposed drifting apart was more the result of an overly simple model for the American psyche than a reflection of an actual breakdown in communication among individuals. In *Armies*, Mailer's large formulations and binary groupings are never so convincing as are his encounters, both private and public, with participants in the event: the liberal intellectuals and writers who organized the march, literary friends and strangers on the way to the Pentagon who recognize him as the celebrity "Norman Mailer," and the unlikely collection of marshals, hippies, American Nazis, and professional revolutionaries he comes to know on the bus and in prison. Gradually and cumulatively, without his ever having to insist on his own totalizing systems, these meetings create for the reader a full sense of the many contentions and partial social reconciliations within the larger confrontation in Washington.

At the start of *Fire*, Mailer attempts a similar mediation among the many separate personalities who come together to witness the launch of *Apollo 11*. But here the very magnitude of the event and its near certain success, no matter how well or badly the spectators understand the technological details involved, make such personalities seem irrelevant. Except for a vague awareness among the journalists, spectators, and corporate executives that their own accomplishments are shoddy in comparison with the undisputed accomplishment of *Apollo 11*, it cannot be said that the social, economic, and racial strata come together compellingly in Mailer's imagination, any more than Armstrong seated in the commander's seat of the lunar module can be said consciously to comprehend the "whole congeries of Twentieth Century concepts and forces which have come to focus that this effort may fly to the moon" (182). From so wide a range of classes, interests, and technical expertise does NASA draw its power that no single consciousness could possibly contain it all within itself, not and remain sane.[7]

Hence the compositional strategy of "Alpha and Bravo" is to approach incompatibles such as these not through Aquarius's singular perspective but through the metaphor of a double psyche. In this respect, too, the essay is characteristic of earlier work by Mailer. For even as he had once conceived the hipster as a "philosophical psychopath" who exists at the margins and embodies "the extreme contradictions of the society which formed [the hipster's] character" (*Advertisements* 347), so does he attempt here to embody the political Left and Right in America, indeed all imaginable paired opposites, within the separate domains of a schizophrenic personality.[8] Thus he creates a psychological allegory of conflict, enactment, and cure that he ultimately hopes will extend beyond the individual psyche to American society as a whole.

At hand are any number of models for describing the open converse between Alpha and Bravo, models that range from the legislative drift between opposing factions in a parliament to the formal exchange of "two actors on a stage who speak to one another across the air between," from the stereotyped conflict in the self torn by powerfully conflicting desires (the pillar of society who "might live for years with a full closet of vices") to the recurrent analogy of a marriage in conflict. (Mailer's own marriage to his fourth wife was breaking up even as he wrote this material.) Then there is the schizoid marine who, if he is daily to sustain that part of himself based on "loyalty to outfit, cleanliness, sharp soldiering, weapon efficiency and love of America," must let "the other part live on Saturday," that is, he must give expression to the split side of his psyche by getting into a bad fight ("Alpha" 67). Mailer had likened himself once before to "a drunk marine who knows in all clarity that if he does not have a fight soon it'll be good for his character but terrible for his constitution" (*Presidential Papers* 84), and something of this marine is also evident in Bone Smasher in *Ancient Evenings*. There, as in "Alpha and Bravo," the narrative traverses continuously between low and high life, but whereas Mailer facilitates such transitions in the novel by having one character enter another's head, in "Alpha and Bravo" he often allows the profuse personalities to degenerate into mere lists, as if he were letting his mind idle for a time (like Aquarius's in *Fire* 57), waiting to find an appropriate technological metaphor to contain the many separate and often discordant voices. That metaphor, however, was not forthcoming here.

As in the earlier discussion of the political schism in America, Mailer is interested less in the fact of a mind's division than in the mind's manifest ability to "support personalities of real difference" and so conceivably to reflect or embody the social, political, sexual, and philosophical bifurcations of the age ("Alpha" 64–65). More intriguing yet, and holding for him the highest potential creative value, is the possibility that the two psychic halves exist not simply as separate lobes in the brain but in a communicative relationship of the most complex intimacy. What fascinates Mailer most about the psychology of astronauts is that they should live, more intensely even than the personalities just mentioned,[9]

> with no ordinary opposites in their mind and brain. On the one hand to dwell in the very center of technological reality (which is to say that world where every question must have answers and procedures, or technique cannot itself progress) yet to inhabit— if only in one's dreams—that other world where death, metaphysics, and the unanswerable questions of eternity must reside, was to suggest natures so divided that they could have been the most miserable and unbalanced of men if they did not contain in their huge contradictions some of the profound and accelerating opposites of the century itself.   (*Fire* 47)

It is not enough that the individual psychic apparatus should passively contain such contradictions; what distinguishes the psychology of adventurers is the depth of communication and experiential interchange by which Alpha and Bravo can establish meaningful relations. This is for Mailer the true measure of the astronauts' bravery, their ability to achieve an inner communion comparable in magnitude to their lunar adventure. Unlike the open converse that occurs within the psychopathic personalities described above, the psychic communication Mailer posits within astronauts is not conscious; what makes them exemplary is that their deepest motivation, like the dominant tendency of the age, remains unconscious, unknown to them.

The thesis Mailer originates here eventually appears only slightly revised in the final text of "The Psychology of Astronauts": by exploring the unconscious life of the astronaut one might eventually come to comprehend the age's unknown "metaphysical direction" (*Fire* 48). What in the published version is left unstated, however, and what Mailer perhaps only suspects might be ineffable, or even nonexistent, is the hidden form of that internal communication by which astronauts might contain within themselves "some of the profound and accelerating opposites of the century." We may also suspect such grandiose rhetoric of excluding more possibilities than it opens. It would seem to exclude, for example, the possibility that Henry Adams perceives in his own attempt to postulate "a dynamic theory of history": "The Universe that had formed him took shape in his mind as a reflection of his own unity, containing all forces except himself" (475). The precise dialectic joining and separating the self and these prior self-creative forces eludes Mailer, for however much he may limit his own role within the Alpha-and-Bravo system, he has not yet been willing, with Adams and such literary heirs of Adams as Pynchon, McElroy, and DeLillo, to allow a system of technological forces to take shape in his mind without first imposing his own imaginative structures on them.

It is not surprising, then, that the argument of "Alpha and Bravo" begins to falter at just this point: "To push any further on these lines," Mailer writes immediately after introducing the idea of the unconscious, "is to recognize that talk of Alpha and Bravo will no longer suffice" (70). The psychic apparatus, to be true to his model, must possess not one but two unconsciouses, Alpha id and id Bravo; and the health of the communication between the halves depends on the ability of Alpha id to speak not only to Alpha ego but across to "the ego of Bravo, just as the id of Bravo must in its turn be able to reach the consciousness of Alpha" (73). There follows an elaborate scenario of psychic division, conflict, and conciliation, promising to rival Freud's tripartite division of the psyche into the ego, the id, and the superego; but Mailer pulls up short of a detailed exposition and concludes segment 12—after having made a number of false starts, deletions, and simplifications—with a nearly audible sigh of relief:

> If love, health, and art [are] in large degree dependent upon the unconscious life of Alpha or Bravo being able to speak across to the ego of the other, what is one to make of that more arcane communication from depth across to depth, from Alpha id to id Bravo? Can it be as rare as the passage between planet and satellite? But in fact, suppose that on this thought we have come into sight at last of the lady with the silver mirror who dwells between passion and death. Can she be the true incarnation of the dream? Have we arrived at the harbors of the moon? (73)

The phrase "the harbors of the moon" catches attention, for it is the title image of the opening chapter of *An American Dream*. Yet if the echo suggests again that what Mailer has been seeking all along is a fictive embodiment of the Alpha-and-Bravo configuration, it also indicates how far he has come from the technological reality of the moon shot. At this stage in the composition the dream, for all its theoretical complication, has certainly fallen short of the overarching metaphor projected early in *Fire*. The romantic's desire for unconscious wholeness reclaimed and made complete in the creative imagination remains apart from his subject, and the Alpha-and-Bravo configuration comes to express a purely invented reconciliation where none exists.

Mailer still falls back on prior imaginative connections when he could be building a real system—for there *were* other connections for him to build on, even though he does not allow himself to see them. The dream, for example, has historically been likened to a machine in ways that are not incompatible with the Alpha-and-Bravo concept. If we think of a machine, as Freud may have thought of it late in the nineteenth century, as "a system of opposed parts so arranged as to transform raw energy into 'work'" (Leed 42), then Mailer's dream is, like Freud's, a psychic machine, a structure of entities in conflict arranged to transform libidinal energies into sources of value—"love, health, and art." Of course, Mailer's dream metaphor differs from both the Freudian dream-work and nineteenth-century conceptions of the machine in being a scenario or theater of simulation where existential possibilities are enacted; there is no mechanical certainty about how the various parts of the psyche interact, none of the technologist's limiting of communication to a measurable exchange of information. Mailer's unconscious is not the unconscious of Freud but the romantic unconscious "of imaginative creation, ... the locus of the divinities of the night" (Lacan 24). And Mailer is not about to admit a technological or psychoanalytic definition that might in any way reduce the mystery of creativity, the ineffable psychic core around which his fiction is built.

This opposition between a living and mysterious psyche and more rational modes of structuring the world is of course solidly in the tradition of the Romantic rebellion against the sciences. Yet I cannot help feeling that here Mailer loses more than he gains from the tradition. In "Alpha and Bravo" and the published chapters on psychology, Mailer seems almost willfully ignorant of work being done by practicing scientists and therapists that might have deepened and advanced his own style of existential psychoanalysis—Jaynes's study of bicameral brain economies, for example, or R. D. Laing's passionate researches into schizophrenia and other psychic disturbances.[10] Mailer can, of course, ignore or make use of what he wants to—the choice is his, surely. But by resisting any inclusion of current scientific approaches to psychology, with all the inherently technological metaphors that contemporary researchers often do create in describing the workings of the mind, Mailer would appear to have limited his ability to engage technology. And without this engagement, he can find no way to reconcile the imagined structures of dialogic love and war with the technological subject matter of *Fire*.

This limitation suggests one possible reason for Mailer's having chosen a mostly pretechnological world as the setting for *Ancient Evenings*, the novel that represents the fullest realization yet of the Alpha-and-Bravo psychology. In the Egypt of the twelfth century BC, Mailer could imagine a total organic society in which profoundly human interactions—between minds living and dead, male and female, human and animal, and even at times animate and inanimate—could proceed without the intervention of modern technologies. If *Ancient Evenings* should prove to be among the most fully realized of Mailer's fictions (as I expect that it will), it will not owe this distinction to what it includes—encyclopedic though it may be. Instead, its imaginative coherence seems to depend on the technological influence it ignores.[11] That Mailer himself recognizes something unsatisfactory in this exclusion is suggested by his stated intention to follow up *Ancient Evenings* with a technological novel "about a spaceship in the future" (*Pontifications* 170). But it remains to be seen whether the full "Alpha and Bravo" trilogy, should it ever be completed, will fulfill the intentions that Mailer postponed while writing *Fire*.[12]

NOTES

1. In *An American Dream*, for example, Mailer writes, "[T]he spirits of the food and drink I had ingested wrenched out of my belly and upper gut, leaving me in raw Being, there were clefts and rents which cut like geological faults right through all the lead and concrete and kapok and leather of my ego, that mutilated piece of insulation, I could feel my Being ..." (11–12). Not coincidentally, the subject here, as in the Hemingway passage in *Fire*, is the breakdown of the masculine ego that may occur at the point of suicide.

2. In commenting that "people who had nearly died from wounds spoke of death as offering a sensation that one was rising out of one's body" (*Fire* 35), Mailer would appear specifically to have in mind the near death of Hemingway's protagonist in *A Farewell to Arms*.

3. A passage in *Gravity's Rainbow* makes explicit the feelings that may arise whenever one's fate is given over wholly to the inert mechanisms of technology. Enzian, leader of the South-West African commando devoted to assembling and firing a rocket like the German V-2 (originally designated Aggregat 4 or A-4), describes the engineer's bodily and psychic identification with the weapon:

> One reason we grew so close to the Rocket, I think, was this sharp awareness of how contingent, like ourselves, the Aggregat 4 could be—how at the mercy of small things ... dust that gets in a timer and breaks electrical contact ... a film of grease you can't even see, oil from a touch of human fingers, left inside a liquid oxygen valve, flaring up soon as the stuff hits and setting the whole thing off—I've seen that happen ... rain that swells the bushings in the servos or leaks into the switch: corrosion, a short, a signal grounded out, Brennschluss too soon, and what was alive is only an Aggregat again, an Aggregat of pieces of dead matter, no longer anything that can move, or that has a Destiny with a shape.   (362; Pynchon's ellipses)

4. Held argues convincingly that Mailer's personification of the moon as a "platinum lady with her silver light," though "crucial to the design of *An American Dream*," is hard to sustain in the face of the astronauts' actual flight to the moon (321–22). One other novelist given to repetitive imagery is Don DeLillo, whose novels, Molesworth points out, "begin, again and again, with a solitary man being propelled headlong in a sealed chamber" (382).

5. I was able to study this material through the courtesy of Robert Lucid, Mailer's archivist and biographer.

6. Mailer's first draft of *Fire*, like the initial drafts of all his books after *The Deer Park*, was written in longhand, in pencil. The "Alpha and Bravo" typescript on which this study is based is split up into four segments labeled 10 through 13. While portions of segments 11 and 13 survive in the published text and to a certain extent bridge the gap between "The Psychology of Astronauts" and "The Psychology of Machines," the precise location of "Alpha and Bravo" in the original draft awaits further textual study.

7. Mailer has better success in his fiction, where a character's sanity may come to depend on "the ability to hold the maximum of impossible combinations in one's mind" (*American Dream* 158).

8. I retain the words *schizoid* and *schizophrenic* for sane and psychopathic personalities, respectively, even though Mailer may at times use the terms interchangeably.

9. To avoid awkwardness, I have cited this passage from the published text rather than from the uncorrected draft. Mailer's revisions in this case were entirely mechanical, not substantive.

10. Mailer, I am told, once appeared on television with Laing after having read only seventy pages of Laing's *Divided Self*. In a letter of 3 July 1989, Joseph McElroy recalls that Mailer met Laing "as a rather pontificating equal."

11. Technology is not, of course, the only modern influence that *Ancient Evenings* purposefully excludes. As Lennon points out, Mailer selected Egypt because he "wanted to recreate a society unaffected by Western culture's ruling beliefs—Judaic monotheism, Christian compassion, Faustian progress, romantic love, and Freudian guilt" (18).

12. I am grateful to T. H. Adamowski, Michael Millgate, and Eric Domville of the University of Toronto for comments on earlier drafts of this essay and to the National Society for Literature and Science for awarding its 1990 Schachterle Prize to the essay.

Works Cited

Adams, Henry. *The Education of Henry Adams.* 1905. Boston: Houghton, 1961.

Butler, Samuel. *Erewhon.* 1872. New York: Penguin, 1987.

Goldstein, Laurence. *The Flying Machine and Modern Literature.* Bloomington: Indiana UP, 1986.

Held, George. "Men on the Moon: American Novelists Explore Lunar Space." *Michigan Quarterly Review* 18 (1979): 318–42.

Kernan, Alvin B. "The Taking of the Moon." *The Imaginary Library: An Essay on Literature and Society.* Princeton: Princeton UP, 1982. 130–61. Rpt. in *Norman Mailer,* ed. Harold Bloom. New York: Chelsea, 1986. 143–65.

Lacan, Jacques. "The Unconscious and Repetition." *The Four Fundamental Concepts of Psycho-analysis.* New York: Norton, 1981. 17–64.

Landow, George P. *Elegant Jeremiahs: The Sage from Carlyle to Mailer.* Ithaca: Cornell UP, 1986.

Leed, Eric. "'Voice' and 'Print': Master Symbols in the History of Communication." *The Myths of Information: Technology and Postindustrial Culture.* Ed. Kathleen Woodward. Madison: U of Wisconsin Center for Twentieth-Century Studies; Coda, 1980. 41–61.

Lennon, J. Michael, ed. *Critical Essays on Norman Mailer.* Boston: Hall, 1986.

Mailer, Norman. *Advertisements for Myself.* New York: Putnam, 1959.

——. "Alpha and Bravo." Unpublished manuscript, 1969 or 1970.

——. *An American Dream.* New York: Dial, 1965.

——. *Ancient Evenings.* Boston: Little, 1981.

——. *The Armies of the Night.* New York: NAL, 1968.

——. *Cannibals and Christians.* New York: Dial, 1966.

——. *The Executioner's Song.* Boston: Little, 1979.

——. *Existential Errands.* Boston: Little, 1972.

——. *Of a Fire on the Moon.* Boston: Little, 1970.

——. *Miami and the Siege of Chicago.* New York: NAL, 1968.

——. *The Naked and the Dead.* New York: Rinehart, 1948.

——. *Pontifications.* Boston: Little, 1982.

——. *The Presidential Papers.* New York: Putnam, 1963.

McElroy, Joseph. "Holding with *Apollo 17.*" *New York Times Book Review* 28 Jan. 1973: 27–29.

Molesworth, Charles. "Don DeLillo's Starry Night." *South Atlantic Quarterly* 89 (1990): 381–94.

Olster, Stacey. "Norman Mailer after Forty Years." *Michigan Quarterly Review* 28 (1989): 400–16.

Poirier, Richard. *Mailer.* New York: Modern Masters, 1971.

Pynchon, Thomas. *Gravity's Rainbow.* New York: Viking, 1973.

ROBERT MERRILL

Mailer's Tough Guys Don't Dance *and the Detective Traditions*

Norman Mailer has been threatening to write a novel about
Provincetown, Massachusetts, since the late 1950s. "Advertisements for
Myself on the Way Out" (1959), the prologue to a since-abandoned eight-
volume novel, is set in Provincetown (see *Advertisements for Myself* 512–32).
Provincetown provides the title for Mailer's 1962 essay on Jackie Kennedy,
"An Interview with Jackie Kennedy, or The Wild West of the East" (*The
Presidential Papers* 81–98). (In *Tough Guys Don't Dance*, Alvin Regency twice
refers to Provincetown as "the Wild West of the East" [32, 36–37]). Mailer
writes at length in *Of a Fire on the Moon* (1970) about his experiences in
Provincetown and describes a novel that he planned in 1967 "about a gang
of illumined and drug-accelerated American guerrillas who lived in the wilds
of a dune or a range and descended on Provincetown to kill" (461). The
novel Mailer finally published in 1984 is a very different project, a murder
mystery completed in two months to fulfill a contractual obligation. The
extremely hostile critical reaction suggests that the time spent on the book
and the form chosen are equally to blame for another of Mailer's disastrous
experiments.[1]

Mailer himself refers to *Tough Guys* as "one of my favorites"
(*Conversations* 335), and I think Mailer's critical judgment is superior to that
of his critics. Certainly there has been little correlation between the time

From *Critique* 34, no. 4 (Summer 1993): 232–46. © 1993 by the Helen Dwight Reid Educational
Foundation.

Mailer spends writing something and the quality of the finished product. Mailer wrote *The Armies of the Night* (1968) in two months and *Why Are We in Vietnam?* (1967) in four, in each case writing to fulfill a contract much as Faulkner did when he wrote *As I Lay Dying* in four months.[2] The obvious contrast is with *Ancient Evenings* (1983), to which Mailer devoted ten years, and I must wonder whether *Tough Guys* is not the better book. Nor is Mailer's novel to be despised because it employs the conventions of detective fiction. As John Cawelti points out, many major literary works achieve their effects by playing against the expected or formulaic (18), and so it is in *Tough Guys*, a novel in which Mailer successfully synthesizes the conventions of classical detective fiction, the American hard-boiled detective novel, and *film noir*. The literary result may be "Mailer's least ambitious novel," as Joseph Wenke suggests (229), but a novel in which Mailer manages to emulate the "narrative drive" that he admires in Raymond Chandler (*Pontifications* 133) while embodying themes less successfully developed in earlier novels such as *An American Dream* (1965).

I

> "I love design," [Wardley] said. "That may be what it's allabout."
> —Norman Mailer, *Tough Guys Don't Dance*

Mailer's "murder mystery" may seem so thoroughly hard-boiled as to preclude any serious connections with the detective school identified with Agatha Christie, Dorothy Sayers, John Dickson Carr, and Ellery Queen. Indeed, Mailer might seem to share Chandler's contempt for the classical detective's "futzing around with timetables and bits of charred paper and who trampled the jolly old flowering arbutus under the library window" (Chandler "The Simple Art of Murder" 225). Surely Mailer would agree that "the fellow who can write you a vivid and colorful prose simply won't be bothered with the coolie labor of breaking down unbreakable alibis" ("The Simple Art of Murder" 225). No one's style is more vivid and colorful than Mailer's, and there is as little time spent on breaking down alibis in *Tough Guys* as in any of Chandler's novels. Nonetheless, Mailer does manage to make good use of one or two classical conventions, thus justifying his own use of the phrase "mystery novel" (*Pontifications* 188).

    The first point to be made is that Mailer does make use of "the novelistic machinery of the whodunit," as Wenke calls it (Wenke 232).

Mailer's plot is worthy of an Elizabethan revenge tragedy, filled with violent deaths and strange reversals, but the narrative pattern is recognizably that of a murder investigation. At the end of chapter 1, Mailer's narrator-protagonist, Tim Madden, awakens to find blood on the seat of his car; the rest of the book charts his efforts to explain what lies behind this stain. Soon Madden is looking to explain the deaths of Jessica Pond, a woman he met the night before, and Patty Lareine, his estranged wife; indeed, his goal is to discover whether he is responsible for either murder. (Like so many of Mailer's heroes, Madden suffers from temporary amnesia, in this case the product of excessive drinking.) Eventually, through his inquiries, Madden finds out how each woman died. His investigation is not strewn with clues, nor does he offer an elaborate explanation of his "solution" to the crimes. Nonetheless, his efforts allow Mailer to offer a reasonable facsimile of the classical detective narrative as Cawelti defines the formula: (a) introduction of the detective; (b) crime and clues; (c) investigation; (d) announcement of the solution; (e) explanation of the solution; (f) denouement (82).

Like the best hard-boiled novelists, Mailer declines to embrace the more stylized features of the classical formula. For example, he does not provide Madden with the dozen or so suspects that Agatha Christie loves to develop, and the clues by which Madden resolves his problem would engage Sherlock Holmes or Hercule Poirot for a chapter or two, not an entire novel. Madden does have his suspects, however, and, periodically, in classical fashion, he reviews how plausible each one is. When he finds the first severed blonde head in his marijuana stash, for instance, he narrows the "list" of suspects to those who knew of his burrow in nearby Truro (70). And when he visits the home of police chief Alvin Regency and Madeleine Falco, formerly Madden's mistress and now Regency's wife, Madden takes special note of Regency's framed military photographs, his elaborate gun collection, and Madeleine's admiring description of Regency as a man who beheaded a Viet Cong with one stroke of a machete (107–09). Indeed, Mailer's play with such clues is not unworthy of a Christie or a Margery Allingham, for it turns out that Regency decapitated one of the dead women but not the other and actually murdered neither one. Mailer makes such limited use of the classical formula's suspects and clues, however, that we might wonder why he even bothers to invoke the classical pattern.

I think there are two good reasons for Mailer's decision. The first is that it allows him to cast Madden in the role of detective. Unlike the classical prototypes, Madden is anything but the gifted amateur detective when he finds himself involved in a murder "case." Indeed, Madden at first flounders about as most of us would do, which recalls Mailer's determination to write a mystery with a hero only slightly braver than the rest of us (*Conversation* 330), but also reflects the lack of direction or purpose in Madden's life before this crisis. Nothing in Madden's experience prepares him to take charge of his life as he must finally to enact the detective's part successfully. Now a fledgling but unsuccessful writer, formerly a bartender, Madden is approaching forty with no finer feature to his life than refusing to become a "punk" during a three-year stint in prison (156). Madden's deep involvement with alcohol and drugs (the source of his jail sentence) points up the failure of will all too characteristic of his generation as Mailer understands it. In Mailer's words, Madden must "strive" to be honorable," "to regain his self-respect because he is ashamed of his life until now" (*Conversations* 333, 332). This effort takes the form of beginning to think like a "sleuth" about half way through the book (99) and, more important, beginning to act like the investigator central to any detective plot. From this point of view, the key moment in the novel is Madden's decision to start looking into the people and events so bizarrely intertwined in Jessica's and Patty's deaths. Thus, as his father takes on the grisly task of deep-sixing the women's heads, Madden calls the airport (171), speaks with a local real estate agent (172), examines Patty's gun (174), and forces open the trunk of Regency's car to find the chief's still-bloody machete (181). At no point does Madden control events as decisively as a Holmes or a Peter Wimsey, but his active engagement with the detective's role measures his growth in what one critic calls "this story of self-regeneration" (Wenke 230).

The second reason for Mailer to embrace the formula of classical detective fiction is his desire to engage the themes of coincidence and uncanny "design." Indeed, coincidence plays as conspicuous a role in this novel as in Christie's most convoluted tales. Repeatedly the characters themselves remark "the powerful signature of coincidence," as Madden calls it (197). Madeleine turns out to be married to the very man Madden must outwit to regain his self-respect and avoid arrest for murder; Madden fancifully places Patty's ex-husband, Meeks Wardley Hilby III, in the very house in Provincetown that Wardley is plotting to purchase; Jessica Pond's real name is Laurel Oakwode; Madeleine is known to Madden as Laurel; and the name Madden has tattooed on his arm during the night that he cannot remember is (of course) Laurel. The chain of coincidence is usually a brutal one, as no fewer than seven people die within a week, and at one point Madden discovers not one but two severed blonde heads in his marijuana stash. "I had long been a believer in the far reach of coincidence," Madden understandably remarks. [I]ndeed I went so far as to think one must always expect it when extraordinary or evil events occur" (118). Later Madden tells his father that people come out of their "daily static" when "big" things are about to happen (161): "Their thoughts start pulling toward one another. It's as if an impending event creates a vacuum, and we start to go toward it. Startling coincidences pile up at a crazy rate" (162). I'm tangled up in coincidences," Madden laments (162), and the network of events that he must unravel is indeed worthy of the classical detective at his most ingenious.

Do the novel's coincidences reveal anything like a meaningful design? If so, is it a "design of darkness," as in Frost's famous sonnet, or is it providential, as the patterns in classical detective fiction tend to be? Wardley tells us that he loves design and that the essence of life may be found in such patterns (189). Many of Mailer's earlier characters entertain similar ideas: among others, Cummings in *The Naked and the Dead* (1948), Rojack in *An American Dream* (1965), D. J. in *Why Are We in Vietnam?*, Gary Gilmore in *The Executioner's Song* (1979), and Menenhetet I in *Ancient Evenings*. In Mailer's more naturalistic first novel, Cumming's ideas are exposed as the grandiose illusions of a megalomaniac. In the more recent fictions, however, Mailer takes such thinking much more seriously even if he falls short of endorsing his characters' conjectures about topics such as magic and life after death. In *Tough Guys*, Mailer refuses to "explain" the uncanny network of coincidences constituting his hero's world and his novel's plot, but he also declines to ratify the occult and abandon altogether more common notions of cause and effect. The seven deaths described here are anything but coincidental, for example, as one act of violence leads to another in an all too common human "pattern." The second blonde head is placed with the first as a deliberate act of psychological malice directed at Madden and is, of course, suggested by the first decapitation. Nor does Mailer seem to endorse the notion that all is "fate" or design here, for the very real acts of volition by Madden and his father Dougy expose what is going on and bring things to their admittedly troubling, even inconclusive climax. By means of his extraordinary plot, Mailer renews his insistence on the problematic nature of reality. Mailer loves design as much as Wardley does, but Mailer is a good deal less sure of its standing in the cosmos.

The novel's coincidences thus contribute to Mailer's more serious themes. This is not to excuse the more improbable features of Mailer's plot. In *Tough Guys*, good (or bad) examples include Regency's remarkably arrogant (and implausible) decision to take Jessica's body to Spider Nissen for disposal and Patty's never-explained decision to remove Jessica's severed head from Madden's burrow. Perhaps we are to accept such irrationalities as evidence of the lack of design that everywhere contests whatever is providential in the scheme of things. If so, this is one of the many resemblances between Mailer's fictional world and that of the hard-boiled detective novelists.

II

> In short, the hard-boiled detective is a traditional man of virtue in an amoral and corrupt world.
> —John Cawelti, *Adventure, Mystery, and Resources*

> I always wanted ... to write a detective story with a hero a little braver—just a little—than thee or me.
> —Norman Mailer, *Conversations with Norman Mailer*

The epigraphs to this section are meant to point up the contrast between Mailer's intentions and those of the major hard-boiled detective novelists. Indeed, in the passage quoted above Mailer goes on to speak of the reader's reliance on the all but incorruptible private detective and the risk Mailer is taking by focusing on a "a man of average bravery" (*Conversations* 330). Important as this contrast is, however, there can be little question that *Tough Guys* reveals Mailer's affinities with the hard-boiled novelists. Dashiell Hammett and Raymond Chandler were among the writers that Mailer read during World War II (*Conversations* 190), and as late as 1979 Mailer was rereading all of Chandler's works in one summer (*Pontifications* 133). Whereas the classical detective writers present "mysteries made only to be solved," in Dorothy Sayer's famous phrase (72), Hammett, Chandler, and their compatriots offer relatively realistic fictions much more to Mailer's taste. "Hammett gave murder back to the kind of people that commit it for reasons, not just to provide a corpse," Chandler noted in "The Simple Art of Murder" (234), and Mailer's narrative interests fall into the same tradition. Chandler also insisted that the serious detective story should stress "the gradual elucidation of character" (236). Mailer suggests that writers of reputation don't do detective stories because "the characters in the typical detective story *have* to behave for the sake of the plot"; like Chandler, Mailer refuses to sacrifice characters to the story line: "I wanted a murder mystery that was recognizable as such, that had characters as complex as those in non-murder books" (*Conversation* 331–32). Mailer's literary relations with his hard-boiled predecessors involve many similarities but also a few key differences, as we should see in reviewing their fictional worlds, detectives, and narrative structures.

The world of hard-boiled detective fiction is one in which evil is virtually pervasive. According to George Grella, "All hard-boiled novels depict a tawdry world which conceals a shabby and depressing reality beneath its painted facade" (112). This world is distinctly urban, "a place of wickedness" (Grella 112), the home of "empty modernity, corruption, and death" (Cawelti 141). One thinks of Hammett's Personville and San Francisco, Chandler's Los Angeles, or, more recently, Robert Parker's Boston and Sara Paretsky's Chicago. Whereas the classical detective novel offers cities and country estates temporarily besmirched by the atypical villainy of one or two individuals, the hard-boiled novel presents a social panorama in which virtually everyone seems tainted by greed, ambition, and some other modern "sin," and the novel's killer, once identified, seems no more culpable than many of the other characters and sometimes much less so. Mailer's Provincetown shares much with this depressing fictional landscape. Here, too, the fictional world is filled with so-called respectable sorts more corrupt than the more obvious criminals; lowlifes such as Spider Nissen must finally be credited with none of the novel's many murders, while the book's wealthiest figure (Wardley) and its highest-ranking civic representative (Regency) are responsible for much of the bloodshed and general havoc. Mailer has long stressed the common bonds between criminals and police, a theme he might have inherited from Hammett's *Red Harvest* (1929) or almost any Chandler novel, especially *Farewell, My Lovely* (1940). In *Tough Guys*, the breakdown of conventional distinctions is all but absolute, as the chief of police smokes pot during an interview in his own office and a former policeman helps conceal the remains of no fewer than six murder victims. Mailer's world nonetheless differs from the hardboiled setting described by Grella and Cawelti in two significant ways: (1) it is filled with supernatural portents that Mailer takes far more seriously than anyone writing in this tradition previously; (2) it is not really urban in nature, especially as the novel is set in the November off-season when Provincetown's thousands of tourists are missing. The evil spirits in *Tough Guys* are as American as Hammett's or Chandler's, but they are not confined to the so-called urban jungle.

The hard-boiled detective is all but defined by his resistance to this inhospitable world. Apparently more "common than his classical counterpart, the "detached eccentric" such as Holmes or Wimsey (Cawelti 95), the hard-boiled detective is in fact a very uncommon figure, "a man of honor and courage in a corrupt and hypocritical society" (Cawelti 69). Cawelti notes this detective's penchant for violence, his alienation from society, his rejection of conventional values while adhering to a personal code (59); Grella stresses his "keen moral sense," manifest in his insistence on a

moral code, his "stoic resistance to physical suffering," and his determination
to pursue what he defines as justice ("Nothing, not even love, must prevent
the detective from finishing his quest") (106-10). Chandler offered the most
famous apotheosis of this figure: "... down these mean streets a man must go
who is not himself mean, who is neither tarnished nor afraid.... He is the
hero, he is everything. He must be a complete man and a common man and
yet an unusual man. He must be, to use a rather weathered phrase, a man of
honor ("The Simple Art of Murder" 237).

If Chandler's Philip Marlowe is sometimes less noble than this
description makes him sound, Mailer's Tim Madden is considerably less
heroic. Like the hard-boiled detective in Cawelti's account, Madden briefly
faces "assault, capture, drugging, blackjacking, and attempted assassination
as a regular feature of his investigations" (143). Like this detective, Madden
seeks something like "an escape from the naturalistic consciousness of
determinism and meaningless death" by solving the mysteries he investigates
(Cawelti 161). But ultimately Madden is nothing like the fearless paragon
celebrated by Chandler and his academic critics. What we learn of Madden's
past, highlighted by episodes of wife swapping and cocaine selling, confirms
his own judgment that he was (and still is) "a collection of fragments" (91), a
man very much in search of the identity that he might achieve by
reestablishing his self-respect. His primary response to the "problem" that
he awakens to is one of fear, the same paralyzing fear that he felt when trying
to climb the Provincetown Monument (60-62), the fear he experienced
during a séance when Patty and Spider Nissen "saw" Patty with her head cut
off (72), the fear he feels in driving slowly toward his marijuana stash (45) and
again when he realizes he must return to the stash to identify the blonde head
from which he instinctively fled (72, 81). Far from being the fearless ideal
invoked by Chandler, Madden is all but defined by his various fears and the
self-pity that accompanies them (116). Never a hero, as he acknowledges
(47), Madden finally achieves something like the hardboiled detective's
fearlessness when confronted by Wardley's gun (191). This discovery that he
is no longer afraid comes after his belated but successful efforts to investigate
his situation. At this point the classical and hard-boiled conventions merge
in the figure of the truth if not perfect justice.

The hard-boiled detective's quest defines the narrative structure Mailer
shares with Hammett and Chandler. The nature of this quest is sometimes
obscured by the form's relentless violence, which is associated with
unvarnished melodrama. "When in doubt," Chandler once advised the
authors of tough-guy short stories, "have a man come through a door with a
gun in his hand" (*Trouble Is My Business* ix). In hard-boiled novels, however,

the detective and the narrative alike seek justice rather than the "solution" to the crime, and the narrative focus is the detective's effort to define what Cawelti calls "his own moral position" (146). This is also the case in *Tough Guys*, a novel that proceeds much like the hard-boiled paradigm. Here too the detective's search for the answer to an initial problem leads to the discovery of other problems at least as serious and ultimately implicates most of the dramatis personae rather than a single culprit. Indeed, *Tough Guys* exhibits "the rhythm of exposure" that Cawelti sees everywhere in hard-boiled fiction (147), for Madden's investigation produces discovery after discovery (or is it body after body?), until literally all the characters of any note are either dead or implicated in the death of at least one victim. The resulting structure minimizes the value (perhaps even the relevance) of a single solution to the mystery, so it is wrong headed of Wenke and others to complain that Mailer's solution is "anticlimactic" (233). The same is true in classic hard-boiled novels such as Chandler's *The Big Sleep* (1939) and especially *The Long Goodbye* (1953), in which the murderess is identified fifty pages before the novel ends. Here Mailer begins the explanation of whodunit and why in chapter 8, about forty pages before his conclusion. Throughout this chapter, as Wardley talks at length with Madden, we learn more and more about what happened the night that Madden cannot remember; then, more than thirty pages after Wardley begins to talk about the deaths of Spider Nissen and his companion Stoodie, Regency confirms that it was Patty Lareine who shot Jessica Pond, and the "explanation" of six deaths is finally complete. (We get our seventh body in the epilogue when Madeleine kills Regency [226]). By this point, if not much earlier, we are primarily concerned with the moral position Madden manages to achieve (however precariously) amidst the numerous "exposures" that highlight the narrative structure. This structure exists so that Madden can develop his "position" under conditions of great stress. Its success or failure, like that of Hammett's or Chandler's novels, turns not on its author's ingenuity but on his ability to tell a certain kind of story, one in which the narrator's investigation leads him to discover who killed whom but also—and more important—the sort of person he is capable of becoming.

I would argue then, that *Tough Guys* perpetuates the spirit of the hard-boiled novels even if its fictional world and detective (who is not even technically a detective) depart from traditional models. *Tough Guys* feels like a hard-boiled detective novel because of its pervasive violence but also because the narrative pattern is very like that of the best-known hard-boiled novels. We have already seen that the book also incorporates classical features, however, and I hope to show that the stylized world of James Cain and *film noir* is at work in Mailer's fictional brew as well.

III

It's more fun to pick up a mystery novel and read it, if early in that book you decide that you and the author share a perception that no one else has.

—Norman Mailer, *Pontification*

I do not mean to argue that Mailer and James Cain share an altogether common "perception" of the world. So far as I know, no one has tried to connect Mailer and Cain except Tom Wolfe in his devastating review of *An American Dream* (see "Son of Crime and Punishment; Or, How to Go Eight Fast Rounds with the Heavy-weight Champ—and Lose," 1, 10, 12–13), and the differences between the two writers are profound. Nonetheless, in his venture into detective fiction, Mailer turns to ingredients long before associated with Cain and *film noir*.

One of Mailer's comments on Cain points to their affinities. Musing on the voice of the private detective in hard-boiled fiction, Mailer notes that "the voice of Jake Barnes in *The Sun Also Rises* could have been that of a private eye in a detective story.... Hemingway, James Cain, and Dashiell Hammett understood that special world in which gesture has enormous importance." "This canon on gesture," Mailer adds, "is crucial to the tough-guy murder mystery" (*Conversation* 330–331). Hammett did create private detectives, and Hemingway might have done so; Cain and Mailer create narrator-protagonists who function like detectives even if they are not private eyes. Mailer's comment suggests that his Cain is essentially the author of *The Postman Always Rings Twice* (1934) and *Double Indemnity* (1935), the first-person narratives in which Cain evokes the world of hard-boiled fiction without resorting to literal private detectives. (Even in *Double Indemnity*, it is not Walter Huff but his colleague Keyes who functions as an investigator). Cain also provides parallels both general and specific with Mailer's fiction. A book such as *The Postman Always Rings Twice* includes literary contrivances or "coincidences" beyond even Mailer's imagination, and Cain's "narrative speed" far surpasses Chandler's or Mailer's. The scene in which Frank and Cora make love immediately after Frank kills Cora's husband and just before the police arrive must remind Mailer's readers of the notorious sexual encounter between Rojack and Ruta in *An American Dream*, perhaps most interestingly in our sense that neither author means to condemn his lovers. As Paul Skenazy notes about Cain's novel, "There is no stable moral basis, no middle ground of sympathy, from which to condemn the lovers. Frank and

Cora are all one has left" (Skenazy 30). So it is with Rojack and his sexual partners in *An American Dream*, and so it is with Madden and Madeleine, even at the end of the novel when Madeleine shoots Regency. In the worlds of Cain and Miller, such acts seem all too common, if not finally inevitable.

Cain and the *noir* filmmakers offer visions darker than those to be found in Hammett and Chandler, without the supremely realistic Sam Spade or the knightly Philip Marlowe to contest the evil drift of things.[3] Nor is "their black vision of despair, loneliness, and dread" (Appel 196) tempered by the comforting conclusions of traditional melodrama. Whereas melodrama attempts to resolve the most perilous problems, the *noir* work is much more ambiguous at the end, "leaving a sense of continuing, persisting *malaise* in its wake" (Tuska 151). The typical *noir* protagonist is someone "set down in a violent and incoherent world" with which he must somehow deal, "attempting to create some order out of chaos, to make some sense of the world" (Porfirio 217). This effort invariably fails, however, as the *noir* world proves to be one in which there is "no way out," as J.P. Telotte puts it (Telotte 53). In *film noir*, we observe "sudden upwellings of violence in a culture whose fabric seems to be unraveling" (Telotte 2), with nothing available to repair the design. Such is the fictional world projected in Cain's best-known novels and typical *films noirs* such as Billy Wilder's *Double Indemnity* (1944), Anatole Litvak's *Sorry, Wrong Number* (1948), Rudolph Maté's *D.O.A.* (1949), John Huston's *The Asphalt Jungle* (1950),[4] and Orson Welles' *A Touch of Evil* (1958). A more recent example would be Lawrence Kasdan's *Body Heat* (1981). In all these works, the tidy resolutions of classical detective fiction are virtually inverted and even the ironic, anticlimactic "solutions" of the hard-boiled novels are made to seem wildly optimistic.

The ties between *Tough Guys* and *film noir* will seem especially close to those who have seen Mailer's 1987 film adaptation of his novel, for there he adopts several of *film noir*'s most distinctive features. *Film noir* is almost always retrospective, for example, usually relying on flashbacks and voice-over to explain how the protagonist has arrived at his or her fated moment. Mailer's film employs this technique, beginning with Madden's reunion with his father (the last sentence of chapter 6 [152]) and going on to dramatize many episodes only briefly mentioned in the narrative (or not mentioned at all, as the film's plot differs from the book's). *Film noir* typically conveys the sense of "a mind meditating on the past" (Telotte 13) and finally presents its hero as "morally ambiguous" (Tuska 154). Mailer's film technique almost exaggerates these already stylized features, for Ryan O'Neal's voice-over stresses Madden's sensitive re-engagement with his past, and the almost sinister laughter of Madden and Madeleine at the end underlines the extremely ambiguous moral credentials of our hero and heroine. The connections between Mailer's novel and the *noir* world are somewhat more complex, however, for Mailer's "perception" of reality is not easy to categorize.

Mailer's book is filled with the kind of stylized excess that we associate with *noir*. Compare Mailer's seven bodies with the eight children Phyllis Nordlinger helps to kill in Cain's *Double Indemnity* (a detail so grim Wilder deleted it in the film version). And Mailer's women, especially Patty Lareine and Madeleine Falco, recall *film noir*'s characteristic *femmes fatales*, played most memorably by Joan Crawford and Barbara Stanwyck. But the ambiguities of Mailer's conclusion (if not the laughter at the end of the film) should remind us that, dark as *Tough Guys* is, Mailer does not share the deterministic bent of Cain and *film noir*. The retrospective point of view in *film noir* and the confessional mode of Cain's more famous novels serve to reinforce the despairing notion that indeed there is no way out, no real alternatives to what has already happened. Mailer's decision to adopt this technique in his film is an odd one, for his novel tells a very different kind of story in which Madden's fate and character are in doubt until the very end. Indeed, it seems reasonable to surmise that Mailer was attracted to the mystery rather than the confession because the mystery format permitted him to leave Madden's fate as undetermined as possible. The first-person point of view, coupled with the mystery Madden seeks to penetrate, effectively stresses the series of decisions Madden must make as he gradually becomes the detective of Mailer's chosen genre(s). In the novel, then, Mailer makes occasional but limited use of flashbacks (principally those touching on Madden's marriage to Patty Lareine, his attempt to climb the Provincetown Monument, and a very select set of moments from his affair with Madeleine). Emphasis falls on Madden's efforts in the present to do something about his plight, not simply to meditate upon it. Mailer's unwillingness to concede the deterministic implications in Cain and *film noir* is most obvious in the novel's conclusion, in which Madden roughly succeeds and Mailer seems to be devising what his critics uneasily see as a "happy" ending (see especially Wenke 235–36).

I do not think the novel's ending is really a happy one, as we can see by comparing Madden's situation with Rojack's at the end of *An American Dream*. But the way in which this ending departs from Mailer's *noir* antecedents should again remind us that *Tough Guys* is an eclectic combination of features drawn from classical detective fiction, the hard-boiled detective novel, and *film noir* because none of these forms precisely mirrors Mailer's complex beliefs. The interplay of narrative features is almost always fruitful, for the emergence of the detective-like protagonist alerts us to the fact Mailer is not a classical determinist, yet the overwhelmingly *noir*-like fictional world amply fleshes out the problems that Madden must face in trying to survive or, better yet, turn his life around in some believable form. As we pursue the parallels with *An American Dream*, I believe we will see that in this later book Mailer manages to combine detective traditions in a way that sustains rather than comprises his own distinctive voice and themes.

IV

> I don't consider myself moral at all. I see myself as a man who lives in an embattled relation to morality.
> —Norman Mailer, *Pontifications*

I am hardly the first to see strong parallels between *An American Dream* and *Tough Guys*. Wenke notices general parallels (Wenke 229), Peter Balbert comments on the parallel between Rojack's walk on the parapet and Madden's attempt to climb the Provincetown Monument (Balbert 70), and a number of other critics echo Michael Ventura's characterization of *Tough Guys* as "an overworked rehash of the critically salvaged, badly underrated *An American Dream*" (*Conversations* 380). It is hard to see why Ventura thinks *An American Dream* is "badly underrated," as most of Mailer's critics rate the book at or near the top of his canon. It is easier to see why *Tough Guys* seems a "rehash" of the earlier novel, for there are a number of crucial similarities. In my view, however, the "rehash" is a successful reconstruction of earlier themes and characters.

The two books do share fundamental plot elements and themes. Each novel focuses on a middle-aged narrator-protagonist whose estrangement from his wealthy, domineering wife has brought him to the verge of a nervous breakdown or even suicide. In each case, the wife is killed and our hero is accused of killing her (justly in *An American Dream*, unjustly in *Tough Guys*). In each novel the narrator engages in lengthy conversations with a policemen (Roberts/Regency) and enters into a sexual relationship with someone (Cherry/Madeleine) immediately after the death of the wife. Each novel telescopes a remarkable number of violent, transforming events into a short period of time (less than two days in *An American Dream*, a somewhat more credible seven days in *Tough Guys*). The cathartic effect of personal violence is a common theme, expressed most conspicuously in Rojack's attacks on his wife Deborah and Shago Martin, Madden's seemingly mindless attack on Spider Nissen's car (150–52), and the remission of Dougy's cancer after he involves himself in the after effects of murder (179, 223, 228). The primary thematic parallel is also the principal dramatic one, as the two narrators undergo similarly life-defining experiences in which they must reject their former selves if they are even to survive. In the conditions of this survival we discover, in each case, Mailer's most fundamental beliefs about human existence.

Given these parallels, the differences between the two books and especially the two narrators are extremely revealing. In *Tough Guys* Mailer again insists on the personal voice of the man whose experiences are at issue, and the book records the sometimes subtle, sometimes conspicuous moments of confrontation as Madden faces existential decisions not unlike Rojack's. Like the book itself, however, Madden is a much more believable character whose conversion, partial as it is, compels our belief as Rojack's does not. Significantly, Madden's history is one of repeated failure, whereas Rojack's is Kennedy-like in its trajectory and even its specifics. If Rojack is a prominent national figure as a politician, author, and public personality, Madden is an ex-con who wants to be a writer but can't get published. Rojack's history fits the parabolic form of his novel, in which the American success story of rags to riches is reversed and the protagonist must learn that he was losing all the time that he thought he was winning. Madden's reversals are far more modest but, perhaps for this reason, far more plausible. Similarly, the tests he must pass are rather more internalized than in *An American Dream*. Where Rojack has to strangle Deborah, sexually dominate the "evil" Ruta, do psychic battle with a series of cops and hoods, fight with Shago, and walk a parapet in the presence of his corrupt father-in-law, Madden must learn to deal with his feelings, his fears, and evasions. The contrast is not absolute, for Madden also fights on one occasion and parries Regency much as Rojack duels with Roberts. But the differences are telling. The physical challenge of walking a parapet is for Rojack the climactic test of his newfound courage; the attempt to climb the Provincetown Monument is for Madden an earlier act of bravado that he does not repeat in his week of crisis. Rojack's fears are objictified in the specific people who threaten his safety throughout the novel; Madden's fears involve his own deep reluctance to accept responsibility for his condition and to act, whatever the outcome of his actions. Madden slays no dragons, then, but his movement from the drifting figure we first meet to the man who confronts Regency at the end is much more moving as well as more believable than Rojack's evolution. Madden's "resurrection" is less startling, but perhaps for that reason it is more affecting. Like Mailer, Madden does not become a moralist so much as a man with an embattled relation to morality—a relation Mailer traces in unusually persuasive detail.

The differences between Rojack and Madden point to a formal difference as well. As I argue elsewhere (Merrill 66–86), *An American Dream* constantly vacillates between the formal ends of realistic and didactic fictions, the novel as action, and the novel as apologue. *Tough Guys* seems to me to avoid this kind of formal confusion, perhaps because Mailer's aims are more clearly defined as well as more modest. Madden's fears and failures are developed in the context of a more plausible history and a fictional world as richly textured as any Mailer has created. The spirits of Provincetown may be ghostly or actual ghosts, but they are firmly rooted in Madden's psychological experience as we would expect them to be in any novel with realistic pretensions. Stylized as it is, the detective form provides the necessary shape for Madden's psychomachia or test. The form offers the occasion, indeed the need, for personal involvement and decisive action, for Mailer the essentials of a meaningful life. In tracing Madden's gradual engagement, Mailer gives realistic life to a form often disparaged if not ignored and joins Hammett, Chandler, Ross Macdonald, and John le Carré as at least a one-time master of the realistic detective novel.

This mastery is most evident in Mailer's conclusion. His development of Madden's story is almost always deft, and other characters such as Wardley, Regency, and especially Dougy ("the best thing in the book probably" [*Conversations* 372]) testify to Mailer's desire to create characters "as complex as those in non-murder books" (*Conversations* 331–32). But other characters, especially the women, are somewhat sketchily handled, as Mailer only partially transcends problems inherent in the detective format. Nor is Mailer's control of the detective apparatus without its problems, as when characters such as Wardley all but magically appear to explain matters that would otherwise remain all too mysterious. At the end, however, Mailer's basic command of his form is very much in evidence. For Madden and Madeleine life goes on, neither happily nor unhappily. Unlike Rojack, however, they do continue to deal with their new life together in America (not the "territory" of Guatemala or Yucatan to which Rojack escapes). Their fate is neither comic nor tragic but a tragicomic mixture that seems, in context, very nearly heroic. The novel's conclusion thus eschews the superficial neatness of the classical resolution but also the pervasive gloom of the hard-boiled novel and especially *film noir*. It fits very well the concoction that Mailer has made from these diverse sources and provides for once the kind of satisfying conclusion that Mailer has sought in his fiction for more than forty years now. Those who value this career will of course hope that Mailer continues to provide such conclusions in works even more significant than this extremely successful "murder mystery."

NOTES

1. For Mailer's remarks on how quickly he wrote *Tough Guys*, see *Conversations* 365. J. Michael Lennon documents the hostile response to *Tough Guys* in his unpublished "A Ranking of Reviews of Mailer's Major Works." The average "score" for *Tough Guys* is the lowest for any Mailer book.

2. For the writing of *Armies*, see *Pontifications* 152. For the writing of *Why Are We in Vietnam?*, see *Conversation* 106. Faulkner's motives for writing *As I Lay Dying* are discussed by Dianne L. Cox, "Introduction," *William Faulkner's* As I Lay Dying xi–xv.

3. For this point, see Tuska xxi.

4. Mailer cites *The Asphalt Jungle* as a "very good" film in *Maidstone* 144. He goes on to praise Huston's *The Maltese Falcon* (1941) as well; see *Maidstone* 145.

WORKS CITED

Appel, Alfred, Jr. *Nabokov's Dark Cinema*. New York: Oxford UP, 1974.

Balbert, Peter. "From *Lady Chatterley's Lover* to *The Deer Park*: Lawrence, Mailer, and the Dialectic of Erotic Risk." *Studies in the Novel* 22 (Spring 1990): 67-81.

Cawelti, John G. *Adventure, Mystery, and Romance*. Chicago: U of Chicago P, 1976.

Chandler, Raymond. "Introduction," *Trouble Is My Business*. New York: Ballantine, 1972, vii-xi.

——. "The Simple Art of Murder," in *The Art of the Mystery Story*. Ed. Howard Haycraft. New York: Carroll, 1983, 222–37.

Conversations with Norman Mailer. Ed. J. Michael Lennon. Jackson: UP of Mississippi, 1988.

Cox, Dianna L., ed. *William Faulkner's* As I Lay Dying: *A Critical Casebook*. New York: Garland, 1985.

Grella, George. "The Hard-Boiled Detective Novel," in *Detective Fiction: A Collection of Critical Essays*. Ed. Robin W. Winks. Woodstock, Vermont: Foul Play, 1988, 103–20.

Lennon, J. Michael. "A Ranking of Reviews of Mailer's Major Works." Unpublished study.

Mailer, Norman. *Advertisements for Myself*. New York: Putnam, 1959.

——. *An American Dream*. New York: Dial, 1965.

——. *Maidstone: A Mystery*. New York: New American 1971.

——. *Of a Fire on the Moon*. Boston: Little, Brown, 1970.

——. *Pontifications*. Ed. J. Michael Lennon. Boston: Little, 1982.

——. *The Presidential Papers*. New York: Putnam, 1963.

——. *Tough Guys Don't Dance*. New York: Random, 1984.

Merrill, Robert. *Norman Mailer*. Boston: Twayne, 1978.

Porfirio, Robert G. "No Way Out: Existential Motifs in the Film Noir." *Sight and Sound* 45 (1974): 212–17.

Skenazy, Paul. *James M. Cain*. New York: Continuum, 1989.

Telotte, J.P. *Voices in the Dark: The Narrative Patterns of* Film Noir. Urbana: U of Illinois 1989.

Tuska, Jon. *Dark Cinema: American* Film Noir *in Cultural Perspective*. Westport, Conn.: Greenwood, 1984.

Wenke, Joseph. *Mailer's America*. Hanover, N.H.: U of New England, 1987.

Wolfe, Tom. "Son of Crime and Punishment; Or, How to Go Eight Fast Rounds with the Heavyweight Champ—and Lose." *Book Week*. 14 March 1965, 1, 10, 12–13.

KATHY SMITH

Norman Mailer
and the Radical Text

Historical narration without analysis is trivial,
historical analysis without narration is incomplete.
                    —Peter Gay, *Style in History*

CROSSING FRONTIERS

In order to oppose the state's power over the control and production of words, PEN, the international writers' organization, established a charter that expressed the need to protect writers from potential political oppression resulting from what they wrote. "Literature," reads the charter, "national though it be in origin, knows no frontiers, and should remain common currency between nations in spite of political or international upheavals."[1] To many PEN members, it must indeed have seemed like crossing new frontiers into enemy territory when their 1986 president, Norman Mailer, invited U.S. Secretary of State George Schultz to deliver the keynote address at the forty-eighth PEN conference in New York.

As Ronald Reagan's State Department chief, Schultz could not very well have been regarded as a facilitator of liberal thought. It was Schultz's public relations charge to rationalize spending cuts in arts and education

From *Cohesion and Dissent in America*, edited by Carol Colatrella and Joseph Alkana. © 1994 by the State University of New York.

programs while increasing the military budget. His rhetorical weapon was an un-self-consciously ironic one—government noninterference in the private sector. Moreover, the administration's desire for control of words and information for ideological purposes was manifested, for example, in tacit support of attempts to have certain works of literature banned from public schools. Perhaps the most direct affront to the spirit of PEN's charter was the administration's decision to revive and enforce the Mc-Carran-Walter Act, which denies individuals, including writers who are considered politically dangerous, entrance into the country. Mailer thus risked embarrassment, scorn, and political confrontation by asking Schultz to speak to a group that was alienated from that state's political acts and expressions.

Mailer, it seemed, was forcing the literary community to accept the state's chief administrator in order to dramatize the PEN topic of the day, "The Imagination of the Writer and the Imagination of the State." By so doing, he introduced and promoted a carnival quality in the literary-cum-political event; by inviting this confrontation he thereby made an appropriately incongruent spectacle. I say "appropriately" incongruent for two reasons. First, because Mailer's choice of speakers seemed calculated to create a disturbance, and that impulse is in keeping with Mailer's controversial public persona as a troublemaker. Second, because Schultz's being there raised two interesting speculations in relation to the imaginative connection between writing and the state: How would Schultz's voice, narrated in a traditional space of literature, call into question the "facticity" of state truth or institutionalized media truth? And what cultural effects proceed from the expansion of literary space to include the state as an author?

It seems likely, given the self-consciously political context of so much of his works and activities, that Mailer staged the event in a deliberate effort to politicize the literary and, conversely, to narrate the state's story in a literary setting. This act is clearly consistent with his criticism of the "cult of professionalism," which standardizes and opposes "fields" of cultural practice. He seems to share Edward Said's conviction that

> culture works very effectively to make invisible and even 'impossible' the actual affiliations that exist between the world of ideas and scholarship, on the one hand, and the world of brute politics, corporate and state power, and military force, on the other.[2]

By this grossly unpopular gesture, Mailer meant to make the invisible visible, the impossible, possible. Mailer also capitalized on a certain rhetorical freedom gained by another, nonaffiliative position in respect to PEN in order to test the literary forms that the group was willing to embrace. His connection with the press corps (PEN's purview extends to poets, playwrights, essayists, editors, and novelists) kept him "strange." Mailer the novelist converged with Mailer the journalist when he invited a media show at a conference that had meant to limit its politics to a *literary* discussion of the state's imagination. This freedom jeopardized his position as president of the organization, who, it was assumed, would speak for PEN with a certain measured, liberal authority. But it also allowed him to take up a position from which speculation on the notion of the writing "frontier" could take place.

Mailer's and Schultz's positions as "outsiders" and irritants at the conference did little to disguise their differences, which were glaringly obvious when they spoke. Schultz expressed predictable loyalty to, if not total agreement with, the rhetoric of the Right when he declared himself aligned with a government that upheld the autonomy of the private sphere:

> and that is why I am proud to represent an Administration that more than any in this century is committed in philosophy and in fact to reducing the intrusion of government into the lives, minds and livelihoods of the individual.[3]

Such claims serve a cultural history that continues to affirm, either through romance or parody, its ineluctable ties to the notion of rugged individualism as well as such prevailing dualities as head/heart, state/individual, public/private, and totalitarian/free. In his essay on ideology and American literature, Sacvan Bercovitch makes the important observation that the American experiment—its errand into the wilderness—has itself been a symbol of such affirmation.[4] According to its paradoxical logic, free choice and dissent appear to be the natural handmaidens of democracy. Individual difference, freedom, and opportunity are rhetorically championed, despite, and of course because of, our insistence on consensus. Bercovitch suggests that a peculiar feature of our cultural history is that the need for consensus is played out in a vital interchange between politics and culture:

> What could be a clearer demonstration of ideas in the service of power than the system of beliefs which the early colonists imposed on the so-called New World? What clearer demonstration of the shaping power of ideology than the

procession of declarations through which the republic was
consecrated as New Israel, Nature's Nation in the Land of
Futurity? 'America' is a laboratory for examining the shifting
connections between politics ... and cultural expression.[5]

Bercovitch's discussion of ideology and literature has a particular relevance
here, since Schultz failed to satisfy Mailer's desire for border crossing in one
important regard: He refused to recognize the rhetoric of consensus—"We
the People"—or privileged exclusion—"The New Israel"—as part of a
mythology that could break down when its fundamental assumptions were
tested. Schultz would have Mailer believe that our "city on the hill" is
protected by a truth that simply emerges from common sense and nature.
The functional state metaphors could not be perceived as anything other
than a natural outgrowth of Truth, Justice, and the American Way. The real,
then, in the context of state imagination, is never allowed to be an
unaccommodating or unwilling subject; rather, it is legitimized in the
oxymoronic structure of the "true story."

Schultz's rhetoric rests on the oppositional structure that can, by
consensus, replace one abstraction with another (individual vs. state) without
admitting any overlap. These values operate within a system that produces a
dichotomy between art and politics in order to, as Bercovitch suggests,
"enforce the separation of 'spheres of influence.'"[6] While Schultz would
keep those spheres discrete and uncontaminated, Mailer would like to run
the "laboratory" where their shifts and collisions are produced. Schultz's
division of individual and state into two neat and separate categories opposed
Mailer's sense of movement between them. While in his speech to PEN
Schultz expresses his conviction that the state must not be personified and
that it has no imagination, Mailer's response on this occasion is to remark
that this very imagination of the state and its intrusion into, and production
of, our historical consciousness is what necessitates keeping records:

> I might go so far as to suggest that if the State does not possess
> imagination, then we are left with no need to write history ....
> When states begin to perceive themselves as protagonists, that is
> to say, as embodiments of a creative vision, we may be entitled to
> speak not only of the imagination of the state, but to perceive of
> such states as actors in a scenario, or characters in a novel.[7]

In his assigning imagination to the state, Mailer seems to agree with Hegel's
proposition that the state shapes the historical consciousness out of which
form takes meaning:

it is only the state which first presents subject-matter that is not only *adapted* to the prose of History, but involves the production of such history in the very progress of its own being.[8]

While for Mailer the state acts as a dynamic organism, not only selecting and disseminating a particular history that will conform to its own needs but actually producing it, Schultz characterizes the state as a kind of passive engine of the collective peoples' wills. If for Mailer the state is a living, breathing body, for Schultz it is a kind of shadow. Schultz's conception of statehood does not work for Mailer, because, in his view, politics take place in shifting narrative scenes whose true stories change with the telling.

COHESION AND DISSENT IN *ARMIES OF THE NIGHT*

Bercovitch writes that in creating America, the Puritans adopted a style of rhetoric capable of establishing a social contract that held forth the promise of fulfillment through a process that would continually invest the secular with the sacred.[9] Bercovitch "reads" America as a symbol of that fusion, and what attracts him to the living mythology of the American dream is the notion that the country,

> despite its arbitrary territorial limits, could read its destiny in its landscape, and a population that, despite its bewildering mixture of race and creed, could believe in something called an American mission, and could invest that patent fiction with all the emotional, spiritual, and intellectual appeal of a religious quest.[10]

In his Pulitzer Prize-winning novel, *Armies of the Night*, Mailer prompts his readers to examine that fiction by forcing political interference in the literary and vice versa. By reconstituting the connections between events and narrative interpretations of history, he thereby seeks to challenge the rhetoric of the American social contract.

By challenging the conventional workings of both narrative and cultural symbology, Mailer's aim is twofold: to produce change in the way we come to knowledge and to avoid being disarmed and commodified by the ideological machine of consensus. If, as Bercovitch claims, the paradoxical logic of the American dream reveals that "progress and conformity stand ... as the twin pillars of the American temple of freedom," and that "process and essence merge in the symbols of the Revolution,"[11] it is all the more interesting that Mailer should choose a seemingly subversive historical moment, the 1967 civil disobedience at the Pentagon, to test how he and other culture makers reshape history.

Rhetoric thematizes the individual *will* to truth or the desire to make sense of history. In *Armies of the Night*, Mailer implies that the history of his subject, America, is increasingly difficult to recognize, not only because of the absurdity of events, but because the historian must place himself in an ambiguous position when he attempts to record them:

> Either the century was entrenching itself more deeply into the absurd, or the absurd was delivering evidence that it was possessed of some of the nutritive mysteries of a marrow which would yet feed the armies of the absurd. So if the event took place in one of the crazy mansions, or indeed the crazy house of history, it is fitting that any ambiguous comic hero of such history should be ... very much to the side of the history ... thrusting itself forward the better to study itself ... at home in a house of mirrors.[12]

Mailer makes the perhaps obvious but compelling point that if history does indeed inhabit a crazy house, and if the historian himself resides in a house of mirrors, the better to reproduce the craziness, it will be difficult to determine just where the missing center of history can be placed.

In journalism, the play on "center" and "self" is doubly interesting, because the codes built up by the profession act as a deterrent to the forbidden play of ego in the text. Mailer's strategy throughout *Armies of the Night* is to question the authority of the newspaper text and to discover the limits of the reporter's narrative practices by counterposing a more imaginative recorder of events:

> an eyewitness who is a participant but not a vested partisan is required, further he must be not only involved, but ambiguous in his own proportions, ... is he finally comic, a ludicrous figure with mock-heroic associations; or is he not unheroic, and therefore embedded somewhat tragically in the comic? Or is he both at once, and all at once? (*Armies of the Night*, 67–68)

Mailer's ruminations proceed from a constant shifting of subject positions throughout the text. One of the effects of this shifting is to offset the conceptual associations that accumulate around and cling to the notion of "center." Of course, in the two passages quoted above, it is easy to locate a structural bias in Mailer's construction of history. He positions himself, for example, off "to the side" of history. Spatial metaphors are grounded in a structural philosophy whereby meaning can be permanently fixed (in a center, to the side). Their use here indicates Mailer's need to ground his provisional remarks in the language of authority. But that authority is contradicted by the house-of-mirrors metaphor and the unstable self as it mutates in an effort to make order out of confusion.

Mailer implies elsewhere that it is bad fiction to historicize events by claiming to have determined their natural boundaries. His purpose is certainly not to defer all judgments. Indeed, it is clear that Mailer is finally against the war in Vietnam that the "armies" have come to protest. It is more to his purpose to uncover connections where none seem to exist and to find differences "within" logical formations that the state imagination and media practices obscure by insisting on objective writing as truth rather than as metaphor for truth.

In the fun-house mirror, the subject watches the transmogrifying self observing the self-observing subject. What Mailer has come to know as history is reflected in this metaphor of the distorted images created by the act of looking. The metaphor is a rich one, inviting distortion of meaning, inviting the preemption of the event by the self, whose difference from itself requires a reexamination of the true story. For Mailer, the viewing subject's eye is the only legitimate mediator between the word and the event, but this eye is no longer "sanctified."

The assumption of the eye's sanctity is, of course, a major feature in the paradigm of the American dream, in the ideology of objectivity, and therefore in the rhetoric of the state and the media. For truth in history, the most credible and sought-after form of evidence has always been the eyewitness account. In *Armies of the Night*, the self's preemption of the story, the self *as* story, is the only strategy that can precipitate a radical rethinking of how history provides cohesive explanations of ambiguous events. If Mailer succeeds in disrupting the logic behind the truth of history, then he has corrupted, too, the equation by which the secular and sacred can fuse.

Within the context of the antiwar movement, Mailer develops the reader's wariness by distorting his own political views, calling himself a "Left Conservative." It is with this label in mind that Mailer wants us to receive his impressions about why we are in Vietnam. They are presented in such a way as to complicate apparently polarized positions: you are either for the war or against it. By way of condemning the war in Vietnam, he suggests that he will think "in the style of Marx in order to attain certain values suggested by

Edmund Burke" (*Armies of the Night*, 208). He sets up several criteria by which a good war can be differentiated from a bad. As a Left *conservative*, Mailer finds that there are "roots" worth fighting for even at the cost of full-scale war: the preservation of a world in which justice, patriotism, and equality, for example, are valued in practice over genocide, colonization, class oppression, and exploitation. As a *Left* conservative, he also understands that these concepts do not operate in a vacuum. Supporters of the war in Vietnam use this rhetoric of worthy causes to support the very things they purport to fight against. A hidden agenda of the pro-Vietnam War rhetoric of making the world safe for democracy was spreading what Mailer calls the "cancer" of corporation land, a symptom of the colonizing adventure.

Mailer is not merely reciting whimsical, equal-but-opposite opinions that cancel each other out; those same opinions are marked by change and movement between contradictory positions. The bad war in Vietnam, ironically enough, is also a source of energy for him. Because it is a physical manifestation of the American sickness that he has been talking about for so long, he experiences the fulfillment of his prophetic ideas. According to Mailer, the war is also energizing for the country, because it allows what Bercovitch has argued is at the very heart of the American experiment—a convergence of state acts and cultural expression.

In Mailer's contextualizing of the war, objectivity is not reduced either to pure relativism or to absolute truth. He works the border between. And like the fun-house image of himself, the border is an impersonation, a mythical form that he wants to rewrite continually. Even when he pronounces upon specific social phenomena, the conclusions are apt to partake of a symptomatic inconclusiveness. It is not that he gives no clear message, but rather the message is itself clearly contradictory:

> He had come to decide that the center of America might be insane. The country had been living with a controlled, even fiercely controlled, schizophrenia which had been deepening with the years ... Any man or woman who was devoutly Christian and worked for the American Corporation had been caught in an unseen vise whose pressure could split their mind from their soul. For the center of Christianity was a mystery, a son of God, and the center of the corporation was a detestation of mystery, a worship of technology. (*Armies of the Night*, 212).

The deep-seated affliction of the schizophrenia indicates that the effects of both the war and the demonstration on the national psyche will be difficult to assess. On the one hand, "the good Christian Americans needed the war or they would lose their Christ," assuming that Christianity is predicated on sacrifice and purification. By a strange convoluted logic, the Christian supporters of the war wanted it so that they could get their payback on the middle class, whose identification with "technology land" and the corporation targeted it as the oppressor. The war presented for the working class the possibility for a potential destruction of technology in an all-out war that would signal a new beginning, a return to the roots. Being hopelessly victimized by his own schizophrenia, however, the average American did not resist the war in Vietnam, for precisely the opposite reason: to join the protest was to fight "the cold majesty of the corporation," which had come to be regarded as another promise of peace:

> The Corporation was what brought him his television and his security, the Corporation was what brought him the unspoken promise that on Judgment Day he would not be judged, for Judgment Day—so went the unspoken promise—was no worse than the empty spaces of the Tonight Show when you could not sleep (*Armies of the Night*, 212–13).

The absurdity of the march thematized in *Armies of the Night* makes sense to an historian who understands how the events of history serve as media fetishes, that is, how events are made to act as symbols of events or spectacles of themselves. One aspect of the absurdity of the protest march on the Pentagon, for example, is that it was negotiated in advance, on the one hand so that it could remain controlled, predictable, and safe, and on the other so that it would receive the kind of media coverage that would reflect its radical departure from the everyday. The march is a wonderful example of Bercovitch's claim that cultural symbols do the work of ideology by pushing continually for consensus. The potential subversive quality of the march was undercut before it began by everyone involved in its orchestration. The one chance for what Yippie leaders called "revolution by theatre and without a script" (*Armies of the Night*, 249) was summarily squashed, not only by armed National Guardsmen but by the protest organizers themselves.

One can only give lip service to the forms of dissent already destined to be absorbed into the consensual language of American politics. The march's revolutionary aesthetic, as David Eason suggests, turns on the protest organizers' "absorption in the techniques of media production that threatens to transform protesters into actors."[13] The house-of-mirrors metaphor calls attention to this imminent transformation and suggests that a critical self-reflexivity could act as a corrective to what Eason calls the "disjunction between the symbolic and the real that pervades modern culture."[14] It is the historical "lie" that results from the perceived *conjunction* between real and symbolic that Mailer's book is about.

In the process of writing, Mailer feeds into the narrative something like a confession of the author's entrapment from within; characters and witnesses are unable to break from the "tower" of their egos, and that creates a vague awareness that choice is mere illusion. Mailer senses, too, that the massive institutions of America have an independent life of their own that he cannot check or change regardless of what he writes. Moreover, he is frightened by the ambiguous episodes of history that force him to question his fractured memory: at these moments he can never be sure of the clarity of his own record. Society, represented as a thing with its own dynamics, quite beyond human control, keeps expanding to accept more towers, and as the towers proliferate, they all begin to look alike.

The metaphor of the tower is one that appears often in our literary culture. It is manifested as prison, asylum, and privileged vantage point. As in the Rapunzel myth, the tower imprisons the subject and keeps it from the broad possibilities of experience. It keeps us safe from our own "bad" desires, creating the illusion of a natural fate and an appropriate end. It is both safety and confinement. It also commands a superior view of the forest and the liberating hero, the one fate that may make escape from the tower possible. However, despite one's having made eye contact with a world that appears separate and outside the tower, the suspicion remains that it is the tower itself that creates the special illusion of pattern. The meaning we assign reality and from which we gain control and assurance, the meaning that conditions choices, is a function of the tower, and escape may thus be impossible.

Is the tower all? This question remains strategically posed between the text's two books, "History as a Novel" and "The Novel as History." The first book, which reads like a novel, is the only accurate "firsthand" version of the march that Mailer can produce. It is a more "reliable" account because it does not make claims to truth but instead shows a grim determination to record his own participation in the event even at the risk of appearing unreliable. The second book, which reads like a journalistic account, is really a "condensation of a collective novel" in which every bit of information is gathered from other sources and then remodeled. (*Armies of the Night*, 284)

The word "as" in the titles of Books 1 and 2, respectively, "History as a Novel" and "the Novel as History," operates by displacement. That is, "as" denotes a metaphorical relationship between history and fiction, implying not only that history is *like* fiction, and vice versa, but that one always contains the other even when the writing does not happen to be overtly metaphorical or self-conscious. Mailer uses "as" to complicate the terms, allowing them to merge into one another. The disturbing relativity that threatens public truth when it is made up of only individual truths is held off by the parameters of the historical event and the self-conscious positioning of the author in a specific place in respect to that event.

So, rather than produce a stabilized version of history through what looks like a balanced presentation of the event in two separate books, Mailer disrupts his own scheme by constantly reinterpreting his observations. His provisional contexts have the effect of uniting the writing act and the event, but the union is always fraught with tensions—between text and context, and between his direct experience of the event and its subsequent reproduction as text. For example, in book 1, Mailer describes his arrest after deliberately crossing a military police line at the demonstration in the Pentagon parking lot. He is taken by a U.S. marshal to await his incarceration and notes that while he is being escorted away, the marshal's hand, which now encircles his arm, is trembling. For Mailer the incident is worth noting in the context of the march and subsequent arrest precisely because, added up, such details describe and limit the way in which the event can be interpreted. However, the significance of this detail cannot clearly be determined from Mailer's account. It must be held in suspense, and consequently it colors the event, which vibrates with possibilities:

> Mailer's arm was being held in the trembling grip of a U.S. Marshal ... Whether this was due to a sudden onrush—quote Freud from a letter to Fliess—of "unruly latent homosexuality" or whether from a terror before God that they judged other men sufficiently to make arrest, or whether simply they were cowards, or if to the contrary they trembled from the effort it cost them to keep from assaulting the prisoner, whatever, Mailer could not quite decide—he had sometimes even wondered if it had to do with the incongruities of his own person. (*Armies of the Night*, 156)

Mailer directs us to a story that is *as* true as author is *as* self, both story and self are composites of an indistinct meaning constructed with unreliable tools. More important, however, is Mailer's message that once one comes to recognize the true story as a replica of or metaphor for truth, then history becomes a more reliable record, capable of being distinguished from ideological practice.

The problem for Mailer's readers, in trying to access history through an historian who "is not one," corresponds with the conflicts Mailer encounters when he explores the nature of communication itself. He finds that those official media channels one relies on for recognizable representations of reality are the less reliable the more they are seen as institutionalized information centers that claim to tell the facts but do not add, as Carlin Romano convincingly demonstrates in his essay, "The Grisly Truth about Bare Facts," that these facts are really statements "based on inferences from traces of the events."[15]

Mailer's advertisement is always for a self that is different from what it says it is, and these personae eventually clash with the historian who wants to recreate the world in its own image. Traditionally, the historian tries to silence these other voices so that his masterpiece might be purified of any romantic taint of subjectivity. Mailer, of course, encourages those personae to speak. For example, in the penultimate chapter of book 1, "The Communication of Christ," Mailer ministers to the waiting crowd after just having been released from a night in jail:

> ' ... You see, dear fellow Americans, it is Sunday, and we are burning the body and blood of Christ in Vietnam. Yes, we are burning him there, and as we do, we destroy the foundation of this Republic, which is its love and trust in Christ.' He was silent. Wow. (*Armies of the Night*, 239)

One of the things that Mailer should *not* say here is that he is a Jew. His positioning of himself as a member of a group whose foundation was not the love of Christ would have nullified his speech and made him appear not himself, an impostor, insincere and ridiculous. And it is precisely in this "existential" moment that Mailer wants to appear most sincere, most docile, most responsible. In fact, though, Mailer starts the speech by mentioning that he is not a Christian. He hopes to give the impression, perhaps, that his Jewish self is subsumed or assimilated in his American one. He emphasizes his participation in the demonstration in order to ground his evocation of mystery and faith in Christ (whom he refers to as a "revolutionary") in concrete political acts that could identify hopeful change. Because he senses that his audience needs some sense of closure after the events of the march, he calls up the most reassuring associations of love, forgiveness, and regeneration. Moreover, he cleverly connects Christ with America, again multiplying associations between state and cultural practice, associations he reinforces throughout the text, for example, when he compares Christ and Jerry Rubin as revolutionaries.

The speech testifies to Mailer's capacity to understand what Bercovitch calls the centrality of the Puritan errand of revolution in the wilderness to American culture. At the same time, he is very much aware of the incongruent spectacle he makes when he envelopes the last words of perhaps his finest hour of the weekend in a romantic rhetoric at odds with an earlier harsh and obscene speaking stint at the Ambassador Theatre. Rather than ignore the contradiction between his previous public speech act as the "beast" and this "modest" Judeo-Christian version, he interrupts his speech twice precisely to call attention to his masquerade. His speech, therefore, is another "act" of speech. Twice referring to himself in the third person, he establishes an effective literary distance between his writing and speaking self, a strategy he uses throughout the text. He is only able to *say* the difference that would negate the Christian self—"I am Jewish"—by creating separate personalities that coexist, and, at the same time, have in common the trait that they are aware of themselves as incomplete and unreliable.

Mailer ends book 1 with a report from the *Washington Post* based on this same Sunday speech on America and Christianity. Mailer's words are effectively undercut in the context of the report, which ends as follows:

> Mailer said he believed that the war in Vietnam 'will destroy the foundation of this republic, which is its love and trust in Christ.' Mailer is a Jew. (*Armies of the Night*, 240)

Clearly the *Post* cannot be faulted for deliberately "misrepresenting" the facts. What the newspaper story has kept silent, however, is that those facts have been arranged in such a way as to produce a calculated response. Because the newspaper business operates on the assumption that provisional truth is no better than a lie, "salience" must substitute for complexity as a measure of understanding history. Of course, it is this very desire for salience that often causes an important context of historical events to go unrecorded. Also, the expectation of salience is a convenient screen for editorializing even when the "facts" seem to speak for themselves. By beginning the *Post* story with thelead, "Novelist Norman Mailer using a makeshift courtroom to deliver a Sunday sermon on the evils of the Vietnam war ... ," the writer sets up for a satirical treatment of the subject. Readers might bring a more serious consideration to the subject had the report begun, for example, with "Arrested demonstrator, novelist Norman Mailer ..." Beginning with "Novelist Norman Mailer" and ending with "is a Jew" gives the report a neat balance: We are invited to take Mailer's modest comments about Vietnam and Christianity with a grain of salt because he is, first of all, a novelist prone to fictionalizing, as he himself has taken pains to show, and, second of all, a Jew, who, perhaps, lacks the authority or conviction to proselytize for Christianity. The newspaper account, then, *also* calls attention to Mailer's speech as a speech *act*. But it is a one-dimensional account that offers no counter to the sarcastic tone with which Mailer is treated.

Clearly, *Armies of the Night* includes other journalistic reports in it so that readers can compare texts and intertexts and make their own judgments about reliability. Indeed, Mailer's invitation to Schultz tested the PEN event's capacity to bear such intertextuality. It is to be expected, perhaps, that in a style-conscious city like New York, in the midst of politically conscious writers like Grace Paley, it was difficult even for Schultz to take his role as author seriously. He opened his speech with a glib remark about his lack of artistic credentials: "I can only regard Norman Mailer's invitation to me as another shining example of that charitable spirit for which New York literary circles have long been famous."[16] Indeed, his presence there makes little sense if we continue to regard the domain of narrative as a strictly novelistic one. But the power of story and narrative to "assist" truth is not an exclusively novelistic practice. The fear of the state's misuse of the power of language to construct cultural truths occasioned the establishment of PEN in the first place.

Since Mailer is so self-consciously directing our own reading event, it is perhaps fitting to end with a final note on his own style of dissent. As he is being arrested, Mailer reveals that he has made a deal with the BBC to photograph his every move during the demonstration. How, we are invited to ask, has the BBC's role in filming Mailer "meddled" in the playing out of history and increased, if that is possible, Mailer's already "disproportionate" egotism and self-consciousness? Mailer's confession emphasizes once more how he comes to terms with doubt and uncertainty about the real. By agreeing to have himself filmed, he once more complicates the fun-house-mirror metaphor and forces us to question the image (in this instance the one that depicts Mailer as moral hero) he desires to be true and natural.

For politicians and journalists, narrative's capacity to challenge the notion of the real as a bare fact presents a theoretical crisis of monumental proportions, if only because the codes for guaranteeing accuracy and protection against the invasion of fiction are so firmly entrenched in cultural practice. The crisis remains an issue for the state and the media because ideology breaks down under the skeptical scrutiny of central symbols like "the City on the Hill." The city cannot be replaced by a faulty tower.

Mailer's nonfiction novel introduces a critique of the value system based on an ahistorical, Aristotelian notion of immutable forms, and commensurability between the logos and the real. Read as literature, texts conventionally received as nonliterature can be reassessed in light of a metaphorical play. By reinvesting nonfictional discourse with literary possibilities, Mailer disturbs carefully drawn categories, and the consequent convergence of historical, novelistic, and ideological practices undermines consensual logic.

NOTES

1. Richard Stern, "Penned In," *Critical Inquiry* 13 (Autumn 1986).

2. Edward Said, "Opponents, Audiences, Constituencies, and Community," in *The Anti-Aesthetic: Essays on Postmodern Culture*, ed. Hal Foster (Port Townsend, Wash.: Bay Press, 1983), 145.

3. George Schultz, "The Writer and Freedom," Current Policy No. 782, (Washington D.C.: Department of State, Bureau of Public Affairs), 2.

4. Sacvan Bercovitch, "The Problem of Ideology in American Literary History," *Critical Inquiry* 12 (Summer 1986): 641.

5. Ibid., 635.

6. Ibid., 636.

7. Norman Mailer, "The Writer's Imagination and the Imagination of the State," *New York Review of Books*, 13 February 1986, 23.

8. G. W. F. Hegel, *Lectures on the Philosophy of History*, trans. J. Sibree (New York: Dover, 1956), 63.

9. Sacvan Bercovitch, *The American Jeremiad* (Madison: University of Wisconsin Press, 1978).

10. Ibid.

11. Ibid., 149.

12. Norman Mailer, *Armies of the Night: History as a Novel, the Novel as History* (New York: Signet, 1968), 68.

13. David Eason, "The New Journalism and the Image-World: Two Modes of Organizing Experience," *Critical Studies in Mass Communication* 1 (March 1984): 62.

14. Ibid., 60.

15. Carlin Romano, "The Grisly Truth about Bare Facts," in *Reading the News*, ed. Michael Schudson and Robert K. Manoff (New York: Pantheon Books, 1986), 77. In his discussion of truth as historically conditioned concepts, Romano is referring specifically to Richard Rorty's *Philosophy and*

the Mirror of Nature and to the work of Hans-Georg Gadamer and Michel Foucault.

16. Schulz, "The Writer and Freedom," 1.

MICHAEL K. GLENDAY

The Hot Breath of the Future:
The Naked and the Dead

'P robably still the best novel about Americans at war, 1941–1945.'[1] So wrote critic Alfred Kazin in 1974 about his subject, Mailer's first published novel, *The Naked and the Dead*. Set on the Pacific island of Anopopei—a fictional setting, though Mailer himself saw action on the Philippine islands of Luzon and Leyte in 1945—the novel inaugurates some of Mailer's most enduring themes. In its main characters, particularly the American commander, Major General Edward Cummings, and his junior officers Lieutenant Hearn and Sergeant Croft, the reader is forced to consider the pathology of power in a military context as Hearn and Croft lead a reconnaissance platoon on their trek towards Mount Anaka. The novel was a considerable popular and critical success for the young author, and Kazin's judgement of it remains secure today. Power, and its relationship to violence in both the individual and the state, leads to Mailer's first dramatisation of totalitarianism in American life, with Cummings finding in Hitler the 'interpreter of twentieth century man'.[2] The novel's concerns thus extend beyond 'Americans at war, 1941–1945' to address Mailer's fear that with Truman's election in 1945 the United States would emerge from 'the backwaters of history' (321) to inherit its full share in the fascist dream. 'America is going to absorb that dream', says Cummings, 'it's in the business of doing it now' (321).

From *Norman Mailer*. © 1995 by Michael K. Glenday.

Diana Trilling was right to feel what she called 'the hot breath of the future' brooding over Mailer's vision in *The Naked and the Dead*.[3] The army world is 'a preview of the future' (324), a microcosm of the political reaction which would threaten the democracies unless a more potent liberal challenge could be developed. But in the novel's political plot the 'bourgeois liberal' Lieutenant Hearn is easily disposed of by both Cummings and Croft, showing the inadequacy of the liberal alternative. However, Mailer's conclusion dramatises his view that the political future belongs not to dangerous mystics like Cummings, but rather to the system's slaves, men like Major Dalleson. He has no wish to transcend the prevailing order, only to be its obedient servant. Fifteen years after the publication of his first novel, in *The Presidential Papers*, Mailer looked back on the intervening decade, the 1950s, years of organisation-man good manners and coercive conformity in American life, years in which the machine mentality of those like Dalleson would flourish: 'America was altered', Mailer wrote, and became 'a vast central swamp of tasteless toneless authority whose dependable heroes were drawn from FBI men, doctors, television entertainers, corporation executives, and athletes who could cooperate with public relations men'.[4] As totalitarianism pervaded almost everything American, it was Dalleson, not Cummings, who epitomised the safe mediocrity of American decline.

Unlike most readers and critics, Mailer is able to see some brighter colours in the bleakness of the novel's tones:

> People say it is a novel without hope. Actually it offers a good deal of hope. I intended it to be a parable about the movement of man through history. I tried to explore the outrageous propositions of cause and effect, of effort and recompense, in a sick society. The book finds man corrupted, confused to the point of helplessness, but it also finds that there are limits beyond which he cannot be pushed, and it finds that even in his corruption and sickness there are yearnings for a better world.[5]

In Mailer's army all are victims, either of each other or of the deterministic trap within which they are boxed almost as soon as they are born. 'My Sam is a mean boy', boasts Jesse Croft of his son, 'I reckon he was whelped mean' (156). In 'The Time Machine' interchapters, we are presented with grim vignettes of American lives in distorted development, and as Jean Radford rightly concludes, 'the result is a systematic indictment of the racialism, sexual neurosis and economic insecurity in American society'.[6] In such conditions idealism does not endure, or if it does, as with Cummings and

Croft, it is tainted with inhumanity and contempt for others. 'I HATE EVERYTHING WHICH IS NOT IN MYSELF' is the inner voice screaming from Sam Croft's being. It is difficult to see just where that good deal of hope exists in this novel's representation of futile striving.

Mailer borrows style and technique from his early literary influences; it is most clearly a first novel in its compliant naturalism, its debts to American novelists of the 1920s and 1930s such as John Steinbeck and John Dos Passos, from whom Mailer took the flashback device of 'The Time Machine':

> I didn't have much literary sophistication while writing *The Naked and the Dead*. I admired Dos Passos immensely and wanted to write a book that would be like one of his. My novel was frankly derivative, directly derivative ... I had four books on my desk all the time I was writing: *Anna Karenina, Of Time and the River, U.S.A.*, and *Studs Lonigan*.... The atmosphere of *The Naked and the Dead*, the overspirit, is Tolstoyan; the rococo comes out of Dos Passos; the fundamental, slogging style from Farrell, and the occasional overrich descriptions from Wolfe.[7]

In his reliance upon such models, Mailer demonstrated for the first and last time in his writing career an 'all-bets-covered caution'[8] with respect to the form his novel took. Critics have also been quick to point out the political and philosophical correspondences between the novel and its antecedents in the leftist American literary scene of the 1930s. In its stress upon deterministic views of human behaviour, and its realisation of a world in which the individual is dehumanised and subjected to the efficient functioning of entrenched systems of control, *The Naked and the Dead* may seem a somewhat stale recapitulation of a vision and a style inappropriate to a changed postwar world. However, as Nigel Leigh has argued, one should not be misled by the novel's dated style since Mailer's concern is not primarily retrospective, 'not a historical preoccupation with the war itself', but is rather prophetic, to do with 'the crises of the post-war United States'.[9]

In the shadow of the Holocaust, Mailer, like Saul Bellow, a Jewish-American contemporary whose first novel, *Dangling Man*, appeared in 1944, saw America's future, humanity's future, as tending towards the cancellation of freedom and creative individualism. There are intriguing similarities to be found in these first novels by two writers who were to dominate American literature in the post-war period. Both Bellow and Mailer conclude their novels ironically; the war fought for freedom and democracy has somehow contrived to undermine the appeal of these ideals, and in Bellow's novel we see his central character, Joseph, fleeing freedom and self-consciousness to embrace the regimentation of the Army. In view of Mailer's later exaltation of 'American existentialism' in the figure of the hipster, it is also interesting that at the end of the narrative Joseph is what might be termed an exhausted existentialist who has found freedom to be disabling. 'To be pushed upon oneself entirely put the very facts of simple existence in doubt',[10] he concludes. With underscored irony Bellow presents his character as an existential failure, deep in the bad faith of his gratitude that with the Army to save him he would no longer 'be held accountable' for himself; he is willing to explore the route down which Mailer's broken soldiers go, to open himself to war's means—'perhaps the war could teach me, by violence, what I had been unable to learn during those months in the room'.[11] In both novels, then, we witness the demise of liberal humanism as it succumbs to the leash of military structure. The efforts of individuals to reach their goals end in defeat. Croft fails to lead his platoon to the summit of Mount Anaka—'he had failed, and it hurt him vitally' (709), while Cummings's strategy to breach the Toyaku line from Botoi Bay is overtaken by Dalleson's unplanned breakthrough overland. The latter's emergence as mock-hero looks forward to many such types in that other, rather delayed American novel of the Second World War, Joseph Heller's *Catch-22*, where again we see the military as a paradigm of inhuman totalitarian bureaucracy.

Both Heller and Mailer, like Hemingway before them, offer us war as a metaphor for much else besides. In its structures and effects on men it represents Mailer's view of the modern social order. As Richard Poirier has noted, '"war" was the determining form of his imagination long before he had the direct experiences of war that went into his first big novel'.[12] Yet if war was the specific and figurative context of *The Naked and the Dead*, the novel has very little to say about the military enemy, the Japanese, whose forces, led by General Toyaku, the Americans need to overcome if they are to take Anopopei. As Leigh remarks, 'no attempt is made to write about the international nature of the war: there are few allusions to Japan (the single Japanese character, Wakara, is given only a few pages); Germany and Italy are merely mentioned in passing'. Mailer is concerned 'with the enemy located within ... the United States'.[13] As we become more familiar with the platoon members we find that what they most despise and fear is rooted in their prior experience of life in America. As mentioned previously, in 'The Time Machine' Mailer cuts a cross-section of American life and finds there the ugly reality behind the American Dream of success and fulfilment. 'No

Apple Pie Today' is the title of Brown's 'Time Machine' chapter, and soon enough he and his colleagues learn to give up on deferred dreams, and to hope instead for a minimal survival. As Red Valsen knows,

> You carried it alone as long as you could, and then you weren't strong enough to take it any longer. You kept fighting everything, and everything broke you down, until in the end you were just a little goddamn bolt holding on and squealing when the machine went too fast. (703–4)

In Lieutenant Hearn's view, only General Cummings seemed capable of transcending what he calls 'the busy complex mangle, the choked vacuum of American life' (85). This is the America out of which Mailer's soldiers struggle. In contrast to it the Army may even have its attractions—order, a certain place in the hierarchy, and the hope, however baseless, that soldiering would not be without its satisfactions. On board the landing craft taking them back from Mount Anaka the platoon members found 'a startled pride in themselves ... "we did okay to go as far as we did"' (708). Against this Mailer puts the America of 'The Time Machine', one that chokes and mangles individual effort, an ironic reverse of the mythical land of untrammelled possibility, the Dream America.

Much of the critical commentary on *The Naked and the Dead* has focused upon the problematic relationship between the novel's critique of totalitarianism and Mailer's representation of the fascist mentality. Readers are right to see the novel as an extensive political allegory through which Mailer dramatises for the first time in fiction his enduring belief that America is being destroyed by totalitarianism. The difficulties arise when we begin to consider Mailer's characters and the extent to which they embody this political vision. Cummings, Croft and Hearn have often been cast as the main players in an ideological war:

> The central conflict in *The Naked and the Dead* is between the mechanistic forces of 'the system' and the will to individual integrity. Commanding General Cummings, brilliant and ruthless evangel of fascist power and control, and iron-handed, hard-nosed Sergeant Croft personify the machine.[14]

Against these is ranged the 'confused humanism'[15] of Lieutenant Hearn. The problem with this interpretation, as some critics have seen, is that by its logic Cummings and Croft ought to emerge as victors. Yet while it is true that Hearn is unequivocally defeated, effectively murdered by both men, so too both Cummings and Croft are defeated, their individual will to conquer undermined by the absurdities of chance (Croft and his platoon run in panic from a swarm of hornets, when Croft kicks over their nest accidentally; Cummings's plan to outflank the Toyaku line is thwarted by Dalleson's success, which is achieved by accident rather than by design). This conclusion is problematic for those who take the view that Cummings and Croft embody totalitarian values—as creatures of the system their survival would be expected so as to stress Mailer's belief in its hegemony. Instead, the novel's ending appears to confound such expectations:

> The conclusion ... and its total meaning are unclear. The failure of Cummings' and Croft's designs would seem to indicate the failure of the machine to work its will upon man and nature, and to justify reading the novel as a 'parable' of man's refusal to be dehumanized by the forces of mechanized society. Yet Hearn's death and Valsen's shattering humiliation clearly dramatize the defeat of man by the machine.[16]

The flaw in such a reading lies in its assumption that Cummings and Croft simplistically embody the machine mentality of totalitarianism. In *The Presidential Papers*, Mailer confessed to having had a 'secret admiration' for characters like Sam Croft—'behind the ideology in *The Naked and the Dead* was an obsession with violence. The characters for whom I had the most secret admiration, like Croft, were violent people'. While it is true that Croft shares with Cummings much that is evil—he is for the most part inhumane in his dealings with others, and like Cummings, he can kill easily and with relish, he yet possesses certain qualities which make him an enemy, rather than a servant of a totalitarian system. Cummings and Croft, so far from being outright villains, can even be seen as the novel's natural heroes. They are both self-exalting, both visionaries who would impose themselves upon the world. As Nigel Leigh has argued, 'seen as the only source of vitalist power in a naturalistic world, they are not without an heroic dimension ... Cummings and Croft possess a charisma absent from all the other characters'.[17] For Robert Solotaroff, Croft is still 'after four subsequent novels, the most compelling character by far that Mailer has created', and he sees him as 'the novel's true idealist'.[18] Richard Gilman is another critic who argues that 'Mailer was clearly more ravished than a programmatically humanist writer would have been by the ostensible villains of his tale'.[19]

If Cummings and Croft are indeed Mailer's crypto-heroes, we need to consider their relationship to the unquestionable demon of the novel, totalitarianism. To what extent *do* they 'personify the machine'? Mailer's first extended definition of totalitarianism came in 'The Ninth Presidential Paper'. There, he argues that the most insidious aspect of it is that 'it beheads individuality, variety, dissent, extreme possibility, romantic faith, it blinds vision, deadens instinct, it obliterates the past'.[20] In political and social terms, totalitarianism cannot tolerate those who demand to express themselves independently of the system. As a result it produces a culture marked by mediocrity, conformity and the elimination of any human aspiration except as that serves the system. 'It would be the hacks who would occupy history's seat after the war' (718) thinks Cummings ruefully. At the end of the novel Mailer leaves us with Dalleson and his big idea:

> He could jazz up the map-reading class by having a full-size color photograph of Betty Grable in a bathing suit, with a co-ordinate grid system laid over it. The instructor could point to different parts of her and say, 'Give me the co-ordinates.' Goddamn, what an idea! (721)

In Mailer's view, totalitarianism rewards hacks, not heroes. In his next novel, *Barbary Shore*, Mailer's first-person narrator, Lovett, says, 'it's a measure of the disaster that everywhere the bureaucrat has the magic power'. And in *An American Dream* Barney Kelley reinforces the point for Steve Rojack, telling him 'it's the hard-working fellow at the desk who has the real power'. Cummings, for all his insights into the military mind, is blind to his own logic. He tells Hearn that 'in the Army the idea of individual personality is just a hindrance' (180-1), yet fails to see that his own arrogant, even demiurgic personality ('You know, if there is a God, Robert, he's just like me'—183) may be a touch more than the Army can stand. It is important to see that in Cummings's politics, Mailer has domesticated fascism, mobilising its appeal from a European to an American context. As Jean Radford has noted, Cummings's 'is "a peculiarly American" brand of fascism, combining individualism and idealism with a dream of totalitarianism'.[21]

Through such characterisations, Mailer shows that one of the side-roads from the transcendentalist celebration of the self leads to a fascist view of man. It is a short step from Whitman's 'I celebrate myself' to Croft's 'I hate everything which is not in myself'. Cummings believes that man is naturally fascist, and that in Hitler was 'the interpreter of twentieth-century man' (313). However, at the end of *The Naked and the Dead*, Mailer's concern with American capitalism and fascism has shifted to focus instead on the dangers of totalitarianism. In his study of Mailer, Joseph Wenke discriminates between the developing stages of totalitarianism and their treatment of idiosyncratic personality:

> For there is a species of revolution and counterrevolution within totalitarianism itself. Though a totalitarian movement may well have its origin in a powerful and charismatic personality committed to risktaking as a means of achieving power, totalitarian institutions gravitate inexorably toward a consolidation of power and an elimination of personality.[22]

For all that must be said against the fascist disposition of Cummings or Croft, both men possess qualities which fly in the face of the machine mentality. Mailer has said that Melville's *Moby Dick* was 'the biggest influence'[23] on *Naked*, and certainly one can see resemblances between the vaunting ambitions of Captain Ahab and those of General Cummings. Both men are solitary, mystical, fastened to their omnipotent urges:

> Always, he had had to be alone, he had chosen it that way, and he would not renege now, nor did he want to ... Cummings stared at the vast dark bulk of Mount Anaka, visible in the darkness as a deeper shadow, a greater mass than the sky above it. It was the axis of the island, its keystone. There's an affinity, he told himself. If one wanted to get mystical about it, the mountain and he understood each other. Both of them, from necessity, were bleak and alone, commanding the heights. (563)

Cummings does not regard himself as a functionary of the military system, rather as standing outside its means; his ultimate goal is superhuman, to take charge of his island world, to subdue 'whatever lay between Hearn and himself, between himself and the five thousand troops against him, the terrain, and the circuits of chance he would mold' (85). Like Ahab, Cummings tests himself against considerable adversaries; and like Ahab he is finally defeated in his aims. Chance, in the shape of Major Dalleson, defeats him; and so too do his troops who 'resisted him, resisted change, with maddening inertia. No matter how you pushed them, they always gave ground sullenly, regrouped once the pressure was off ... there were times now when he doubted basically whether he could change them, really mold them' (717). Victory over the Japanese, which might have been accomplished by his own grand plan was, he is forced to concede, 'accomplished by a random play of vulgar good luck' (716).

Nevertheless, though both Cummings and Croft fail, their failures are redeemed by heroism. In Mailer's terms, they refuse to be trapped in the conventions of the military machine; they are each examples of extreme individualism, resisting the system's imperative of efficiency. Croft's obsessive desire to scale Mount Anaka has, in the end, no military justification whatsoever; and Cummings's plan to accelerate the Japanese defeat by launching an invasion by the sea route of Botoi Bay involves unnecessary risk, expense (since it can only be carried out with additional naval support), and, more than this, it is conceived not to serve the system but primarily to glorify Major-General Edward Cummings. 'What a conception it was', Cummings congratulates himself, 'there was an unorthodoxy, a daring about it, which appealed to him greatly' (399). He has an intellectual contempt for the officer class, and despises the 'hacks' at GHQ on whom he nevertheless has to depend. With several carefully chosen images, Mailer finally establishes Cummings not as an uncritical agent of, but as a threat to the machine mentality to which he feels superior. In the following passage Cummings reacts to the news that his troops have been gaining ground in a slow advance on the Toyaku line; although this is achieving the military objective, it also threatens Cummings's more flamboyant Botoi Bay plan:

> All day as he had sat in the operations tent, reading the reports that had come in, he had been a little annoyed. He had felt like a politician on election night, he thought, who was watching the party candidate win and feeling chagrined because he had tried to nominate another man. The damn thing was unimaginative, stale, any commander could have mounted it successfully, and it would be galling to admit that the Army was right. (561)

It is very clear that Cummings regards himself as specially gifted, superior to the dull efficiencies of the military machine. This impression is consolidated in another image—where Mailer stresses that for Cummings, the strategies of war imply a creative effort. For victory must carry a personal signature. He is not willing to be a machine operative: 'Cummings was bothered by a suspicion, very faint, not quite stated, that he had no more to do with the success of the attack than a man who presses a button and waits for the elevator' (560).

So, although Cummings is undoubtedly fascistic in his views, he is yet, by nature, an enemy of totalitarianism, which would in Mailer's terms 'behead' his kind of aggressive individualism. As for Sergeant Croft, who in many ways shares Cummings's faults, there would be reincarnation of sorts in Mailer's urban frontiersman, the white negro. As many critics have noted, Croft is in significant ways the prototype of this figure. A psychopath who 'smouldered with an endless hatred' (164), he yet personifies much that is essential to Mailer's 'philosophical psychopath' in the violent radicalism he would advocate a decade later. In his important essay of 1960, 'Superman Comes to the Supermarket', Mailer would trace what he called the 'psychotization' of America back to its frontier history. In a compelling piece of cultural analysis he saw twentieth-century American history as almost fatally split between 'two rivers':

> one visible, the other underground; there has been the history of politics which is concrete, factual, practical and unbelievably dull ... and there is a subterranean river of untapped, ferocious, lonely and romantic desires, that concentration of ecstasy and violence which is the dream life of the nation.[24]

Croft exemplifies this cultural disjunction. His 'Time Machine' narrative tells us of his violent upbringing, explicitly tied to the raw aggression of frontier-breaking ancestors. His father, who literally beats his values into his son, is proud of the issue:

> 'He got good stock in him' Jesse Croft declared to his neighbours. 'We was one of the first folks to push in here, must be sixty years ago, and they was Crofts in Texas over a hunnerd years ago. Ah'd guess some of them had that same meanness that Sam's got. Maybe it was what made 'em push down here.' (15)

Like Cummings, Croft's nature subverts crucial features of the totalitarianism which Mailer abhors, and as such, Croft also acquires some degree of heroism in the narrative. His urges are irrational, instinctive, influenced by the pull of blood from a primitive ancestry; he too owns his ancestors' meanness, their frontiering drive to 'push down' and 'push in' to new, unknown territory. As Solotaroff notes, Croft's violence is atavistic:

> as the prototype of the hipster, Croft instinctively knows what actions will minister to his ailments and enable him to break open

the walls which have held his straining psyche encased. Anaka contains within its bulk all the frontiers that have been closed to Croft.[25]

Totalitarianism, which 'deadens instinct' and 'obliterates the past', would certainly regard Croft's type as tending to undermine its objectives. Nigel Leigh has argued that Croft cannot be described as either totalitarian or fascist:

> He is clearly outside the political categories. Although his nature is decidedly non-liberal ... in a number of ways he is notably non-fascistic: he has no connection with groups on the American right, as might be expected; he is less racist, ethno-centric or anti-Semitic than most of the working-class men in his command; and he is the only person to show affection for the Mexican Martinez.[26]

Neither Leigh nor the other critics quoted in this discussion underestimate the capacity for evil in Cummings and Croft; while resisting the mechanistic efficiencies of the military as tending to degrade his own potentialities, Cummings nevertheless advocates such a reductive standard for most of the rest of humanity. Both he and Croft exemplify the iniquitous relationship between violence and power. Listening to the sounds of war, Cummings experiences a sense of erotic exaltation:

> The war, or rather, *war*, was odd, he told himself ... it was all covered with tedium and routine, regulations and procedure, and yet there was a naked quivering heart to it which involved you deeply when you were thrust into it. All the deep dark urges of man, the sacrifices on the hilltop, and the churning lusts of the night and sleep, weren't all of them contained in the shattering screaming burst of a shell, the man-made thunder and light? ... All of it, all the violence, the dark coordination had sprung from his mind. In the night, at that moment, he felt such power that it was beyond joy. (566–7)

As Richard Poirier noted, in *The Naked and the Dead*, Mailer had 'not yet learned how to suggest any possible heroic resistance to the encroaching forces of totalitarianism',[27] for even though it has been possible to point up manifestations of heroism in Cummings and Croft, this is unquestionably heroism of a very problematic kind. As Joseph Wenke has argued, the novel 'sets Mailer's talent for creating powerful and violent characters at odds with the thematic necessity of placing some limits on the success of totalitarians'.[28] Yet if, as Wenke writes, Cummings and Croft 'prove to be the novel's most dynamic characters',[29] this is mainly due to the weakness of their opposition, provided in the shape of Lieutenant Hearn. Although Hearn is often seen as his spokesman, Mailer has referred to Hearn as 'a despised image of myself'.[30] The author's friends recall that after publication of the novel, he seemed more drawn to Croft's character—'we'd all read *The Naked and the Dead* in galleys. I'm sure of this, because when we took our trip to Mont-Saint-Michel we were already playing a game called "The Naked and the Dead." Bea was usually Wilson, and Norman always wanted to be Croft.'[31] The image of Mailer 'doing Croft ... running around yelling, bullying'[32] and shouting in a Croft-like southern accent on a beach near Mont-Saint-Michel is not prepossessing, except that it may confirm his natural dislike of the officer mentality represented by Hearn. 'The hatred of officers went over to the minor characters, the minor officers', he has said.[33] Creating Croft's character in the novel 'came naturally ... but Hearn and Cummings drove me crazy'.[34]

Nigel Leigh provides one of the best studies of Hearn's role in the novel's structures, both thematic and technical. With regard to the latter, Leigh notes that:

> In the unfolding narrative Hearn cements the disparate elements of the book together and remains the only character rendered with both realistic authority and psychological depth. He provides the nearest thing in the text to a constant point of view. ... His world view provides a positive point of resistance to the fascism of Cummings and Croft and to power in a much more generalized sense.[35]

He contends that Hearn 'not only represents a broad inclination towards Marxist values but also carries much of Mailer's personality' and then advances the unusual proposition that Mailer's connection with Hearn 'is coded in the text through Hearn's peculiar role as a Jew'.[36] Hearn, of course, is not Jewish, but rather a WASP. Still, Leigh argues that Mailer's portrait of Hearn as a 'pseudo-Jew' is consistent with the author's own unwillingness to be closely identified with a Jewish sensibility. As noted above, he has acknowledged Hearn as 'some extension of myself, a despised image of myself', and Leigh's remarks may consolidate Leslie Fiedler's assessment of

Mailer as in many respects an 'anti-Jew'.[37] But if Hearn can be described as a pseudo-Jew, suggesting Mailer's own ambivalence with regard to ethnic identity, so too can he be described as a pseudo-liberal. His political affiliations are the cause of some critical disagreement. While many are content to describe Hearn as a liberal, Leigh stresses that he should certainly be seen as 'a radical liberal', while Robert Merrill believes that 'Hearn does not so much represent liberalism as the *desire* to be liberal ... temperamentally, Hearn is an aristocrat'.[38] I cannot agree with those critics who regard Hearn as an effective counterforce to the values represented by Cummings or Croft, for Hearn's liberalism is often seen to be a soft target, easily collapsing in the face of Cummings's theoretical rigour, and proving no match for Croft's manic single-mindedness. Far from having created in Hearn a force that can 'counteract the personal and political excesses of the other two major characters', one who 'provides a positive point of resistance to the fascism of Cummings and Croft',[39] the overwhelming impression for me is of a man without stable convictions. When in Cummings's orbit, Hearn feels himself to be 'basically like Cummings ... they were both the same' (392); when in Croft's presence, Hearn realises he has to leave since 'if he stayed he would become another Croft' (586). So while Leigh is correct to say that with Hearn's death 'the most enlightened position in the novel has been shown to be insubstantial', this is due to more than 'the conspiracy of values between Cummings and Croft'.[40] As their ideological opponent, Hearn fails to convince because as a character he lacks those qualities Mailer has always deemed admirable. When he looks at Mount Anaka, all he can see is an image of defeat—'it was the kind of shore upon which huge ships would founder, smash apart, and sink in a few minutes' (498). In contrast to Hearn's 'fear' of the mountain, Croft in looking at its bulk is exalted by its beauty—'the mountain and the cloud and the sky were purer, more intense, in their gelid silent struggle than any ocean and any shore he had ever seen' (497). Had Mailer been fully behind Hearn's politics he would have surely sought out the kind of objective correlative which Anaka provides in Croft's case. Instead we have in Hearn a feeble ideologue whose final decision is to retire from the struggle, to resign his commission.

The most astute analysis of Mailer's politics in *The Naked and the Dead* is still that offered by Norman Podhoretz in 1959. For Podhoretz, the novel shows Mailer discovering 'that American liberalism is bankrupt' because:

it is animated by a vision of the world that neither calls forth heroic activity nor values the qualities of courage, daring, and will that make for the expansion of the human spirit ... ultimately what Mailer was looking for—and has continued to look for—is not so much a more equitable world as a more exciting one, a world that produces men of size and a life of huge possibility, and this was nowhere to be found in the kind of liberalism to which he committed himself in the earliest phase of his literary career.[41]

In his first novel Mailer represented war as an incubator of totalitarianism in American life. In his next, *Barbary Shore*, American idealism is all but gone, replaced by the cold grip of political reaction.

NOTES

1. *Bright Book of Life*, p. 71
2. *The Naked and the Dead*, (London, 18949) p. 313.
3. D. Trilling, 'The Moral Radicalism of Norman Mailer', in R. Lucid (ed.), *Norman Mailer: The Man and his Work* (Boston, Mass., 1971) p. 116.
4. 'The Ninth Presidential Paper—Totalitarianism', in *The Presidential Papers*, p. 183.
5. Quoted by Randall H. Waldron, 'The Naked, the Dead and the Machine', in H. Bloom (ed.) *Modern Critical Views: Norman Mailer* (New York, 1986) p. 118.
6. Jean Radford, Norman Mailer: A Critical Study (London, 1975) p. 345.
7. P. Manso, *Mailer: His Life and Times* (Harmondsworth, Middx., 1986) p. 101.
8. Marvin Mudrick, 'Mailer and Styron: Guests of the Establishment', *Hudson Review*, vol. 17 (1964) 353.
9. N. Leigh, *Radical Fictions and the Novels of Norman Mailer* (Houndmills, Hampshire, 1990) p. 7.
10. *Dangling Man* (London, 1946) pp. 190-1.
11. Ibid., p.191.
12. R. Poirier, *Mailer*, (London, 1972) p. 28.
13. Leigh, *Radical Fictions*, p. 7.
14. Waldron, 'The Naked, the Dead and the Machine', p. 118.
15. Ibid., p. 119.
16. Ibid., p. 125.
17. Leigh, *Radical Fictions*, p. 21.
18. R. Solotaroff, *Down Mailer's Way* (Urbana, Ill., 1974) pp. 30, 38.

19. R. Gilman, 'Norman Mailer: Art as Life, Life as Art', in his The *Confu- sion of Realms* (London, 1970) p. 98.

20. *The Presidential Papers*, p. 84.

21. Radford, *Norman Mailer*, p. 48.

22. J. Wenke, Mailer's *America* (Hanover, NH, 1987) pp. 9-10.

23. In Manso, *Mailer*, p. 397.

24. 'The Third Presidential Paper—The Existential Hero: Superman Comes to the Supermarket', in *The Presidential Papers*, p. 38.

25. Solotaroff, *Down Mailer's Way*, p. 27.

26. Leigh, *Radical Fictions*, p. 26.

27. Poirier, *Mailer*, p. 33.

28. Wenke, *Mailer's America*, p. 9.

29. Ibid., p. 9.

30. Manso, *Mailer*, p. 101.

31. A. Adams, in Manso, *Mailer*, p. 114.

32. M. Linenthal, in Manso, *Mailer*, p. 114.

33. Ibid.

34. Manso, *Mailer*, p. 101.

35. Leigh, *Radical Fictions*, p. 15.

36. Ibid., p. 13.

37. L. Fiedler, *Love and Death in the American Novel* (London, 1970) p. 406.

38. R. Merrill, *Norman Mailer* (Boston, Mass., 1975) p. 38.

39. Leigh, *Radical Fictions*, p. 15.

40. Ibid., p. 20.

41. N. Podhoretz, 'Norman Mailer: The Embattled Vision', in *Norman Mailer: The Man and his Work*, pp. 67-8.

JOHN WHALEN-BRIDGE

The Myth of the American Adam in Late Mailer

Let us begin with the problem of Adam. Lewis's 1955 study, *The American Adam*, explored a variety of nineteenth-century American writings to show that "the American dialogue" has largely been about notions of American innocence, about whether the American self is Adamically new, fallen into the corruption of history, or fortunately fallen. This notion of innocence has been much criticized for its political effects. American identity has long been predicated on the absence of class-conflict. Cultural myths such as the American Adam have been blamed for the specifically American refusal to examine class-conflict that is sometimes called "American Exceptionalism." The American self-concept, the argument goes, masks over class-conflict, since "the simple genuine self against the whole world," to use Emerson's phrase, is by definition a being without class affiliation. Critics of Lewis (and of similar theorists of American culture and identity) have insisted that myths of American innocence function to narrow the American horizon of expectation, specifically excluding political conflict, such as when Russell Reising accuses Lewis of segregating politics from literature in *The Unusable Past: Theory and the Study of American Literature*.

Lewis is faulted for being "ahistorical," since his study of the American dialogue pays no attention to nineteenth-century controversies such as the slavery debates.[1] Whether or not we would agree that Lewis is guilty as

From *Connotations* 5, nos. 2-3 (1995/96): 304-21. © 1996 by Waxmann Verlag GmbH.

charged, the literary criticism his seminal work fostered certainly acquired a sharply ahistorical rhetoric one generation later. In *Radical Innocence* Ihab Hassan discusses some versions of the American Adam as he is reincarnated in an existentialist, alienated, A-bomb afflicted postwar world. Refiguring the opposition between Emerson's "Plain old Adam, the simple genuine self" and "the whole world" against which that opposing self was defined, Hassan sees the oppositional nature of the American protagonist as essentially "radical":

> His innocence ... is a property of the mythic American self, perhaps of every anarchic Self. It is the innocence of a Self that refuses to accept the immitigable rule of reality, including death, an aboriginal Self the radical imperatives of whose freedom cannot be stifled. (6)

This radicalism has nothing to do with political radicalism, however. The word radical in Hassan's usage means something like "profound," and the imperatives driving Hassan's neo-innocent are rooted entirely in psychological rather than social or political self-definition. An "aboriginal Self" claims an identity prior to law and politics.

The radically innocent Adamic character, remaking himself or herself on a daily basis in a proper existential fashion, can be interpreted as a Self from which to develop a political intelligence, since the American Adam is a social outsider. His, or her, status as one beyond the pale makes this apparition uniquely qualified to comprehend the society within.[2] Thus, Adam is an anarchic self, not one governed by party affiliation or any other sense of communal debt. But at the same time, this Adam is most definitely on the outside looking in, an apparently ideal culture critic. For Hassan radical innocence is an indispensable political credential precisely because it offers transcendence of traditional styles of political engagement (those styles that became an embarrassment during the Cold War, it so happens).

The "noble but illusory myth of the American as Adam" functions as a kind of "false consciousness" in the skeptical criticism that follows that of Lewis and Hassan. The image of the American Outsider has in recent years lost authority for those who charge that the tendency to "transcend" quotidian history is "one of the major political effects that the work of American ideology as a whole helps to reinforce" (Kavanagh 313). Leo Marx begins *The Machine in the Garden* with criticisms of American ideologies such as that of the American Adam and cites Richard Hofstadter and Henry Nash Smith to demonstrate ways in which "this ideal has appeared with increasing frequency in the service of a reactionary or false ideology, thereby helping to mask the real problems of an industrial civilization" (7). The pastoral fantasy has of course been a common mode of escape from the pressures of the real world, and Marx goes on to point out how American Renaissance writers employed the mode as a springboard to escape social and political conflicts that endangered their sense of artistic detachment:

> Our writers, instead of being concerned with social verisimilitude, with manners and customs, have fashioned their own kind of melodramatic, Manichean, all-questioning fable, romance, or idyll, in which they carry us, in a bold leap, beyond everyday social experience into an abstract realm of morality and metaphysics. (343)

American literary mythology, in sum, has often been used as an escape from the clash of the world. It directs our attention to the problems of the individual rather than toward the obligations of the individual to the community, and Ihab Hassan's identification of Lewis's Adamic self with the "Anarchic self" certainly suggests the sort of individual entitlement that American literary myths can be made to support.

With these charges in mind, it may be a surprise to remember that Lewis called for a kind of Adamic resistance to Cold War containment: "Ours is an age of containment; we huddle together and shore up defenses; both our literature and our public conduct suggest that exposure to experience is certain to be fatal" (Lewis 196). Lewis's epilogue, "Adam in the Age of Containment," is an explicit consideration of the relationship between American literary myths and political culture. While it is certainly true that some writers "light out for the territory" to escape political conflict in their work, there is also a political strain within the Adamic tradition.

Postwar critics and novelists alike have celebrated the freedom of the individual over any sense of group affiliation that individual might feel. Unlike the Popular Front writers of the 1930s, postwar writers who have used fiction as a mode of political resistance have tended to fashion "parties of one," and Norman Mailer's Left Conservatism of the mid-1960s, like Henry Adams's earlier "Conservative Christian Anarchism," can hardly be said to have broken the "one man, one party" rule.[3] No postwar fiction was more committed to a group political action than Mailer's *Armies of the Night*—even though that book expends half of its energy distancing its author from the social movement with which it is inextricably linked! Mailer's career exemplifies the ways in which the postwar American Adam is very much a divided self.

It is a commonplace of Mailer criticism to note that he follows in the Adamic tradition as defined by Lewis.[4] Readers of Mailer's work have noted his tendency to regenerate typically American voices in a book-by-book fashion, but so far there has not been a satisfactory theory to explain what this tendency means when regarded as an overall design.[5] If we note that Mailer consistently takes ahistorical American selves and transfers them to explicitly political situations, we recognize that there is a method to his stylistic derangements.

In *Harlot's Ghost*, Mailer reworks the supposedly apolitical Adamic mythos to reveal the "invisible government" of the CIA. Adamic ideology, it has been argued, stands between American novelists and political fiction of the first rank. Whether it is referred to as Adamic ideology, American individualism, or pastoralism, the argument is that the American insistence on the primacy of the individual experience and the measurement of that experience in terms of "innocence" will inhibit or thwart the creation of political novels.[6]

The American narrative in its cruder forms has often expressed the belief that we Americans are somehow not to blame for the fallenness and impurity of history.[7] There is always a time, further back, when there was entitlement without condition and when one could name the world with assurance.[8] It is currently fashionable to condemn authors who uncritically reflect this belief, and Donald Pease has recently accused Mailer of presenting "official American history" in his novels rather than something subversive like New Historicism (Pease 1990). This is a fairly odd claim, since in Mailer's writings there is never a clear line between the fictions and myths with which we construct our national identity and the political ideologies that struggle for prevalence in our society. In this way Mailer is often doing what Richard Slotkin has said the literary critic must do: "We can only demystify our history by historicizing our myths—that is, by treating them as human creations, produced in a specific historical time and place, in response to the contingencies of social and personal life" (80).

It would be a mistake simply to read Harry Hubbard as Adam-before-the-Fall, and the CIA as the fallen world, strewn with apple cores, although Harry Hubbard does begin his career as a spy from a position of *naïveté*. At the beginning of his autobiographical narrative Hubbard knows little or nothing about the inner workings of the CIA, and in this sense he is Adamic, but this phase is very brief. When he quickly gets caught in an internecine bureaucratic struggle, his patron Harlot gets him out of trouble by changing his code-name so rapidly that Harry's antagonized superior officer will never know who to blame. Harry Hubbard's introduction to CIA life is, then, an inversion of the simple, referential language of Adam before Apple. Agency life trains Hubbard to suspect every memo, every individual word, of falsehood or indirection. In complicating his Adamic protagonist's innocence, Mailer has moved beyond the fictions of pure opposition, of narcissistic antipathy toward the fallen world of political reality.

In placing his American Adam within "the Company," Mailer reveals the ideological similarities between the myth of the American Adam and that of the American Century: both are organized groups of ideas that entitle and empower *American* activity. Both sets of ideas necessarily conceal the self-interest behind this activity, instead creating the belief that an "unfallen" motive underlies the endeavor. On the individual level, the self-concept of Adamic innocence promotes individualistic activity by freeing the simple genuine individual from the consequences of social corruption: the individual is an exception to social rules. On the national level a similar idea is at work: the American nation is capable of its greatest political debauchery when it believes itself to be the simple genuine democracy against the whole world (Steel 5). As Noam Chomsky and other radical critics of American foreign policy have pointed out repeatedly, the American media will always depict American invasions of other countries (Nicaragua and Grenada are recent examples) as a *defense* of an American value rather than an offensive attack (59-82). The cameras will focus on a simple American self (a medical student from Grenada, a lone soldier drinking coffee), rather than the enemy dead. Adamic ideology is typically used to portray the American agent as underdog, and Mailer is short-circuiting just such an ideological construction when he makes his latest American Adam a CIA agent.

During the Cold War, it has sometimes seemed that the American Adam is a double-agent in the garden. The degree to which a protagonist has individual freedom determines how much "agency" that character has, and thus how much a character may represent a general resistance to institutions that threaten individual freedom such as the Central Intelligence Agency. The individual is political agency in its most decentralized form. At the same time, the containment of dissent within the Adamic individual insures that no collective resistance to institutions such as the CIA may form. Mailer has attempted to comprehend this figure, the harlot in the garden. His fictional interpretation of American intelligence work does more than any other work of literature to help readers gain access to "the imagination of the State."[9]

In *Harlot's Ghost* ends and beginnings become indistinguishable, confounding the simple myths of origins on which the American national identity is founded. Two manuscripts form *Harlot's Ghost*, and of course Omega precedes Alpha. The Omega manuscript has a gothic urgency that accelerates until a mansion actually burns down in romantic fashion. The narrative which ends up in the land of Poe begins in the Garden of Eden: "Even guidebooks for tourists seek to describe this virtue: 'The island of Mount Desert, fifteen miles in diameter, rises like a fabled city from the sea. The natives call it Acadia, beautiful and awesome'" (4). Harry parodies the language of guidebooks in this tongue-in-cheek description to demonstrate his own complex attitude: America is at once a land where great purity can be seen and experienced, but it is also a cultural landscape that sustains almost invincible dreams of innocence in spite of great evidence to the contrary—a land where almost any wrong can be forgotten. The island under Hubbard's Keep is haunted by the memory of the Abnaki Indians of the Algonquin tribe, reminders in the first pages of *Harlot's Ghost* that the Adamic myth can be a cloak of innocence to hide a more sinister history: "The ghosts of these Indians may no longer pass through our woods, but something of their old sorrows and pleasures join the air. Mount Desert is more luminous than the rest of Maine" (4). The opening pages of the novel, so reminiscent of the travel guide's tone of innocent enjoyment, is troubled by ghosts, specifically ghosts that precede Adam, be he American or Hebrew. *Ancient Evenings* and *Harlot's Ghost* both travel back to a time before Adam to indicate the historicity of the Adamic mythos.

Just when it seems that Mailer's narrator is going to see the CIA through Acadia-shaded glasses, the chapter ends with an italicized passage in which Harry Hubbard, in March of 1984, is fleeing from the United States to Moscow, where he hopes to find a still living Harlot: "*Due for arrival in London in another few hours, I felt obliged to read the rest of Omega, all of one hundred and sixty-six pages of typescript, after which I would tear up the sheets and flush away as many of them as the limited means of the British Airways crapper on this aircraft would be able to gulp into itself*" (11). The stylistic shift (reminiscent of the shift from the well-cured style of the first book of *Ancient Evenings* to the obscene gravy of the second book) conditions our reading of any Adamic or otherwise idealized perceptions in the manuscripts that follow.

By carefully separating earlier and later perspectives in this way, Mailer's CIA novel introduces the Adamic self into Cold War America. The Adamic myth must of course be adapted to the realities of CIA life. "'Oh, darling, I love giving people names. At least, people I care about. That's the only way we're allowed to be promiscuous. Give each other hordes of names'" (21). Kittredge, Harry Hubbard's wife, comments on the penchant for nicknames, acronyms, and code-names in Agency life. Naming is, for Kittredge, a compensation for the sexual power she has given up to obtain her position in society and in the CIA. This sublimation of sex into language is one of many reflections of the Protestant ethos that shapes life in the Agency.

The Adamic power to name is the privilege of agents in general, but higher ranking namers approach the Biblical power of the original Adam: "It was Allen Dulles who first christened him thus" (21). In naming each other, Mailer's characters partially manifest the Adamic entitlement of the Garden of Eden. They are people who presume they have political power: "Did people in Intelligence shift names about the way others move furniture around a room?" (22).

R. W. B. Lewis described the Parties of Hope, Despair, and Irony as the choices available to the American writer who wished to take a position in the American dialogue, but Adamic entitlement in the CIA is a more slippery affair. When Harry Hubbard, who has just spun out on an icy road, calls home to his wife Kittredge, she says "'Are you really all right? Your voice sounds as if you just shaved off your Adam's apple'" (24). Unbeknownst to Kittredge, Harry has betrayed her sexually and is returning from a visit to his mistress. Just after Harry's car went into a skid and then mysteriously righted itself, Harry quotes *Paradise Lost* to himself, as if to say Adamic entitlement and paradise lost exist side-by-side in the CIA. The ideology of American innocence is precisely what underwrites American transgression.

The coexistence and interdependence of good and evil runs through Mailer's work but receive supreme expression in *Harlot's Ghost*. Mailer begins this theme with the name of the novel, as we note from "Harlot." The word apparently has nothing to do with the "innocence" that we usually associate with American Adamicism, but if we track it to its root, we see that Mailer's Harlot and Lewis's American Adam have some rough similarities. The word harlot descends from the Middle English *herlot*, meaning "rogue" or "vagabond." In this sense, the harlot has a freedom from ethical, economic, or other kinds of historical constraints, and in this freedom the harlot resembles the adventurous Adam whose absence Lewis laments in the final pages of *The American Adam*.

The coexistence of Adam-before-the-Fall and Adam-Fallen is a puzzling theme in Mailer's work, since to understand it we must fuse Adamic linguistic confidence and existential dread. Mailer insists that our moral action is predicated on a Kierkegaardian uncertainty, and his novels develop this moral insight in a variety of ways.[10] As uncertainty is the defining condition of the individual, Mailer shows it to be the formative condition of the CIA; it is certainly at the heart of *Harlot's Ghost*, a thirteen-hundred page novel that ends with the words "TO BE CONTINUED." This is a shocking way to end the novel. The reader confronts a formal uncertainty, since we do not know if the narrative is over, if Mailer is pulling our collective leg, if he is in fact continuing and planning to finish the trilogy he began with *Ancient Evenings*, or if he will simply write a sequel to *Harlot's Ghost* that will take us from the Kennedy assassination, through Watergate, and up to the Iran/Contra scandal and beyond. The formal uncertainty reverberates throughout the novel, since, at the novel's inconclusive conclusion, Harry wonders from inside his Moscow hotel room if he will find Harlot alive or not. Has Harry Hubbard defected? The novel denies us all the assurance provided by the insider-formulas and neat conclusions of spy thrillers. Mailer maintains uncertainty after Harry becomes a fully-initiated member of the organization, which is the only way Harry can still be a "simple genuine self against the whole world" after he has been an integral part of attempts to assassinate a head of state.

Uncertainty is one way to keep the idea of innocence alive; the problems of writing and interpretation are another. That is, he can fashion an innocent self, though that self is clearly guilty of crimes against civil liberty, if he becomes a writer. On the written page he can deploy selves at will. He can begin in youth (as he does in the Alpha manuscript) and approach the complex world of the CIA as a beginner. Despite prohibitions, Harry has written about the CIA. Thus, the prohibition against writing about the CIA becomes another source of innocence, since it pits Harry (simple genuine self) against the CIA (Harry's whole world):

> I had navigated my way across half of a large space (my past) and if I put it in that fashion, it is because I did not see how I could publish the manuscript, this Alpha manuscript as I called it— working title: *The Game*. Of course, it did not matter how it was christened. By the pledge I had taken on entering the Agency, it was simply not publishable. The legal office of the Agency would never permit this work to find a public audience. Nonetheless, I wished *The Game* to shine in a bookstore window. I had simple literary desires. (35)

Simple literary desires. The simple, genuine writer against the legal office does not even claim power to name (christen) the manuscript. He resigns himself to the fact that he must be a secret writer, that is, one whose discourse can be neatly divided into public and private. Writing is the perfect expression of Harry's double-consciousness, since the individualistic and defiant act of writing gives him claim to innocence even as he writes the story of his own complicity in matters such as political assassination. Mailer at once engages in and subverts Adamic ideology.

However cynical it may seem to speak of American innocence in the midst of the CIA, Mailer's choices are guided by his belief in a far worse alternative to this semi-cynical situation. The best argument for the Adamic viewpoint that Mailer offers the postwar world is that it is an alternative to cynicism. Cynicism as a world-view is ultimately contemptuous of history, and this is especially true of political fiction. For this reason Mailer rejects cynicism, the absurd, and other broadly ironic world views. Mailer's literary and political choices may be understood in part as a life-long refusal to accede to the postmodern condition that Mailer refers to as "the Absurd." This refusal is the key to any understanding of Mailer's uncertain influence on contemporary American literature, his fluctuating political attitudes, and his sometimes startling artistic choices. To postmodern critics Mailer often seems naive precisely because he refuses the ironic pleasures that are, say, Nabokov's main harvest, but Mailer has given much thought to the philosophical implications of authorial irony. While his position has altered over the years, it has always been consistent with his literary and political aims. That is to say, Mailer has always resisted the temptations of irony as a full-blown world view for reasons that are inherently political.

The thoroughly cynical political novel offers an imaginary stairway to transcendence. Because it results so frequently in a morally crude vision of history, Robert Alter dismissed the cynical tendency of recent American political fiction:

> If the conventional political novel tends to assume that, despite troubling agitations of the surface, all's well with the Republic, what the adversary political novel of the past two decades has generally assumed is that the Republic is rotten to the core. (Alter, *Motives* 39)

If one *knows* that government is "rotten to the core," why detain oneself with the messy details of history or the delicacies of art? Alter's complaint suggests a new meaning to Adorno's notion that poetry after the Holocaust is barbaric. We can understand the comment aesthetically rather than ethically if we believe, after the death camps and the totalitarian organization of modern societies, that History has revealed its apocalyptic face. If we *know* the meaning of history in an absolute sense, fine distinctions, formerly the poet's province, have become outdated. The only appropriate poetry in this barbaric age will be barbaric poetry.

In the days of "apocalypse now," the argument continues, artistic subtlety is a form of nostalgia. In the days of Moloch, poets may howl. Mailer evokes Nazi genocide to justify the excesses of the hipster in the first sentence of "The White Negro," and he howls against Cold War conformity when he writes, in *Advertisements for Myself*, that "the shits are killing us." Mailer's collection of essay, short story, semi-poetry, and less classifiable forms of self-awareness is a "Howl" in prose. Like Ginsberg's early poetry, Mailer in the 1950s adopted the attitude of the outraged outsider.[11] It can be considered true that the writer's barbaric yelp from the rooftops is the sweet and fitting response to the age if and only if the historical backgrounds of which we speak can properly be called "apocalyptic." In America, where we have economic slumps, periodic foreign wars, and above-average scores in terms of old age, sickness, and death, we see writers oddly scrambling for personal affliction. We all know that "writers need to suffer," and this notion follows directly from the entitlement granted to the Storyteller who has suffered. We pause to hear the story of the car accident or the dramatic fall. Catastrophe confers authority.

In the post-war period the apocalyptic mood has received its greatest support from the revelations of Auschwitz. Against such horrors, what can a writer *not* say? Totalitarianism has, in the same manner, been the source of power for many Cold War era political novelists.[12] Willie Stark, ominously, has a forelock in *All the King's Men*. General Cummings predicts an Americanized version of Fascism in *The Naked and the Dead*, and Lieutenant Hearn is proven to be short-sighted in his belief that Liberals will band together to form an adequate response. William Burroughs's anti-heroes are chased across the galaxy by fascistical Divisionists and innumerable other political forces dedicated to exterminating whatever is eccentric or individual. Billy Pilgrim finds a "world elsewhere" in Trafalmador. American versions of the Holocaust and of totalitarian oppression have been adapted to American themes, particularly to the myth of the American Adam. We see this especially in "The White Negro," an essay that justifies the murder of an innocent man by contextualizing an act of violence as an act against corrupt society. The binary logic operating in the essay and many postwar fictions recreates innocence in opposition to corrupt society: the corruption of the world empowers "Adam" to act, and an insane world entitles the opposing self *completely*. Thus, Adamic individualism is, in many 1960s texts, converted into a Faustian hunger for power.

This kind of post-war Adamic entitlement does not sit well with Alter. He expresses irritation with American political fiction in the days after Vietnam and Watergate not because the literary form is a spring of protest, but rather because it is a kind of protest that will settle for nothing less than pure opposition: by casting the Republic in an absolutely diabolical light (Alter argues that Coover does this in *The Public Burning*), the novelist forsakes the moral variegations of history. The aesthetic result is often somewhat melodramatic, a chiaroscuro of good and evil in which the authorial voice is conveniently identified with the forces of Good.[13] Almost never, complains Alter, does the writer have to measure politically offensive policies or practices against more palatable ones. The writer is most content, and most empowered, on the outside. But to judge politics from the outside, to judge without ever taking a positive stand that can itself be subject to criticism, is cynical. Those who agree with Alter's demand that political writers be historically responsible will want to avoid being charmed by the sirens of Cynicism.

Mailer picks up American politics by the "affirmative" handle, though the nature of this affirmation becomes increasingly qualified throughout his work. In strictly political terms, his novels can be shown to profess a belief in the "balance of powers," which is perhaps the most intellectually defensible tenet of American civil religion. Nonetheless, his books hardly suggest that all is right with the republic. Mailer agrees that everything has two handles, one good and one evil, but for Mailer there is no Emersonian confidence about our ability to choose properly between them. Mailer's novels put into play the most unlikely Manichean scenarios—he can find gods battling in the sexual act as well as in a grain of sand—but it is important to realize that the greatest failure of human life is not to enlist on the "wrong side" of the vast moral battle, but rather to refuse to face the Kierkegaardian uncertainties that are the painful foundation of human existence.

Despite his assorted comments about "American schizophrenia" over the years, Mailer's obsession with the self-division in *An American Dream*, *Why Are We in Vietnam?*, and *Armies of the Night*, and more recently in *Ancient Evenings* and *Harlot's Ghost*, does not merely attempt to reflect a multitude of American voices. Mailer is concerned, as Lewis suggested the artist must be, to capture the dialogue of American life. Mailer not only tries to imagine conversations that matter politically, but he also tries to enter into these dialogues. Critics such as Richard Poirier have long ago suggested that we see Mailer's writing as a huge work in progress. This work is a democratic fantasy in which individual citizens engage in a dialogue with power, and this huge, sprawling work is, even now, quite possibly, "TO BE CONTINUED." As the line between life and death is intentionally unclear in novels like *Ancient Evenings* and *Harlot's Ghost*, there is also great uncertainty about the continued health of American democracy. Has the CIA established itself as a power unto itself, free of other governmental checks and balances? Maybe.

Mailer has attempted to communicate with political powers directly, and his imaginary personas have petitioned God, gods, pharaohs, presidents. Thrones, powers, dominions: the Satanic machinery of *Paradise Lost* also has a necessary place in this essentially mysterious world. The puritan division of good from evil is a condition that Mailer has worked through, and his late novels are built on the interdependence of Heaven and slime.

We see this interdependence in that moment in the Omega manuscript where Harry Hubbard almost dies—or may have died. Having almost driven over a cliff—he is not certain that he is still alive—on the way home from his earthy mistress' trailer, Harry Hubbard realizes in great fright that

> "*Millions of creatures,*" I said aloud to the empty car—actually said it aloud!—"*walk the earth unseen, both when we wake and when we sleep,*" after which, trundling along at thirty miles an hour, too weak and exhilarated to stop, I added in salute to the lines just recited, "Milton, *Paradise Lost,*" and thought of how Chloe and I had gotten up from bed in her trailer on the outskirts of Bath a couple of hours ago and had gone for a farewell drink to a cocktail lounge with holes in the stuffing of the red leatherette booths.

Millions of creatures ... Manichean battles. Intolerable to Mailer is the separation of gods and devils, of the high and the low, of the heavenly from the red leatherette. His whole career has been a struggle to discover the meeting place of God and the Devil, to get Ishmael and Ahab to sit at the same table, to get readers to talk back to the "electronic malignity" of the television set. Each one of these conflicts could serve as a metaphor for the others in Mailer's work. His work declares the futility of any search for "a virgin land" or "a world elsewhere" beyond political consequences—even if that world elsewhere is understood only as the private individual in opposition to society.

NOTES

1. In *The Unusable Past* Russell Reising discusses Lewis as one of the "founding fathers" of American literary studies who excludes social and political reality from canonical American literature (107-22).

2. In Carolyn Porter's formulation, Emerson initiates a mode of *detached* pragmatism: "when Emerson becomes a 'transparent eyeball,' joyfully announcing 'I am nothing; I see all,' he articulates the position of both the transcendent visionary poet (to whose role he himself aspires) and the neutral scientific observer (whose role he wishes to counteract). That is, the detached observer, like the visionary seer, appears to himself to occupy a position outside the world he confronts" (xii).

3. Frank Lentricchia makes the generalization that in America "parties of one" have flourished in *Criticism and Social Change* (6).

4. See especially Laura Adams's *Existential Battles: The Growth of Norman Mailer* and Joseph Wenke's *Mailer's America*.

5. Barry Leeds's *The Structured Vision of Norman Mailer*; Michael Cowan's "The Americanness of Norman Mailer"; and Gordon O. Taylor's "Of Adams and Aquarius." Laura Adams argues in *Existential Battles* that Mailer is *not* part of the American tradition as defined by Lewis (13).

6. On the common ground of critics such as R. W. B. Lewis, Leo Marx, Edwin Fussell, and Leslie Fiedler, see Gerald Graff, "American Criticism Left and Right" in *Ideology and Classic American Literature*: "In one way or another, all these theories tend to see American literature in terms of some form of escape from social categories.... these theories of the American element in literature actually make many of the same points in different vocabularies. (Roughly, Adamic innocence equals pastoral equals frontier equals evasion of heterosexual love, over and against which are the machine, coextensive with genteel society, coextensive with women and domestic love, etc. The collision results in tragedy, symbolism, etc.)" (106-107).

7. Consider the mythical American hero in the form of popular culture's most famous Vietnam War veteran, John Rambo. He is a war veteran and has killed many, but he exemplifies what might be called "relative innocence." In one of the *Rambo* film sequels, the hero tricks Vietnamese soldiers into following him into a tall, dry field, which Rambo then torches. The men are burned to death, but since we are watching the lone individual as he defends himself against an angry, superior force, the action of burning the Vietnamese is far more "innocent" than, say, the action of dropping napalm on Vietnamese civilians. When President Bush referred to "the Vietnam Syndrome" during his 1992 re-election attempt, he was calling for a reinvention of American innocence of a similar sort. Relative innocence, like Hassan's radical innocence, is non-innocence given an imaginary form of social sanction.

8. American writing, as distinguished from the songs of this continent before the first contact with Europe, begins with and is characterized by Adamic entitlement. The power to name and political dominion are each assumed by the same poetic flourish: Columbus renamed the rivers without concern that the native people called them by different names. See Bartolomé de Las Casas's "Journal of the First Voyage to America" (70-80).

9. "The imagination of the state" is Mailer's main concern in *Harlot's Ghost*. It is the title of narrator Harry Hubbard's unfinished work within the fictional world of the novel, and it was also the subject of an international conference organized by Mailer during his term as PEN president. While writers such as Donald Barthelme responded positively to the topic, saying that the imagination of the state and that of the writer "are in radical conflict all over the world," the South African novelist Nadine Gordimer objected that the state had no imagination since imagination is "private and individual." But if the writer is alienated from the state precisely because the state is certain "it is always right," as Gordimer claimed, then the state is in some sense an entity with an imagination. For details on the conference and its various controversies, see Rollyson (338-49).

10. George Alfred Schrader has a much more disparaging view of Mailer's Kierkegaardian aspect. His essay "Norman Mailer and the Despair of Defiance" (in Braudy, 82-95) is highly critical of Mailer's existentialism, but I would argue that Schrader's essay describes the early Mailer. First published in 1961, it renders the philosophical corollaries to Mailer's immature Adamicism: "He identifies with the hipster both because the White Negro is in full-scale rebellion against civilization (defiant) and unleashes the life-giving force of primitive emotion. The very notion of the White Negro symbolizes the opposition between civilization (White) and instinctual passion (Negro). It is not only a dialectical but a *contradictory* idea in that rage and rebellion derive their force and meaning from civilized passion and can by no act of violence gain reentry into the innocence of immediacy. Mailer refuses to accept original sin as a fact of human life and would undo the Fall of mankind. He will, if need be, carry the human race back to the Garden of Eden on his own shoulders—even if he must tread upon all the edifices of civilization to do it. The courage he wants is heroic, epic, Promethean, but, also, futile." In later work such as *Ancient Evenings* (1983) and *Harlot's Ghost*, Mailer becomes increasingly aware of the insufficiency of the absolute Adamic separation of individual and society, but this realization does not lead him to abandon the Adamic metaphors through which the specifics of American identity have been constructed.

11. To some readers he seemed to exploit the Holocaust, fifties conformity, and literary gentility for the sense of entitlement he can garner. In his critical yet essentially sympathetic essay (Baldwin calls it a "love letter"), Baldwin points out that Mailer very often plays the "bad boy." By pretending to be an outsider, a "hipster," the misbehaving insider gives other insiders a sense that they know the "real world" of the outside. See "The Black Boy Looks at the White Boy" in Braudy 66-81. Our judgment of Mailer's work as a whole will likely hinge on whether we are convinced that he has gathered power from various sources for ethically honorable or for spurious reasons.

12. For a discussion of totalitarianism as the theoretical anchor of Cold War discourse, see William Pietz's "The 'Post-Colonialism' of Cold War Discourse."

13. Novelists such as E. L. Doctorow have answered Alter's criticism by charging that his (neo-conservative) complaint stems from an inability to tolerate political criticism or dissent when it comes from American authors (Doctorow 85-86).

WORKS

Adams, Laura. *Existential Battles: the Growth of Norman Mailer*. Athens: Ohio UP, 1976.

Alter, Robert. *Motives for Fiction*. Cambridge, MA: Harvard UP, 1984.

————. *The Pleasures of Reading in an Ideological Age*. New York: Simon and Schuster, 1989.

Bakhtin, M. M. *The Dialogic Imagination*. Ed. Michael Holquist. Trans. Caryl Emerson and Michael Holquist. Austin: U of Texas P, 1981.

Baldwin, James. "The Black Boy Looks at the White Boy." Braudy 66-81.

Bercovitch, Sacvan. *The Puritan Origins of the American Self*. New Haven: Yale UP, 1975.

———— and Myra Jehlen, eds. *Ideology and Classic American Literature*. New York: Cambridge UP, 1986.

Braudy, Leo, ed. *Norman Mailer: A Collection of Critical Essays*. Englewood Cliffs: Prentice-Hall, 1972.

Breasted, James Henry. *A History of Egypt*. New York: Charles Scribner's Sons, 1905.

Casas, Bartolome de Las. *The Heath Anthology of American Literature*. Ed. Paul Lauter *et al*. Lexington: D.C. Heath and Co., 1990. 70-80.

Chomsky, Noam. "The Manufacture of Consent." *The Chomsky Reader*. New York: Pantheon Books, 1987. 59-82.

Cowan, Michael. "The Americanness of Norman Mailer." Braudy 143-57.

Doctorow, E. L. Interview with Bill Moyers. *A World of Ideas: Conversations with Thoughtful Men and Women about Shaping Our Future*. Ed. Betty Sue Flowers. New York: Doubleday, 1989.

Elliott, Emory, ed. *Columbia Literary History of the United States*. Columbia UP, 1988.

Ellison, Ralph. *Invisible Man*. New York: Signet Books, 1952.

Graff, Gerald. "American Criticism Left and Right." Bercovitch 91-121.

Hassan, Ihab. *Radical Innocence: Studies in the Contemporary Novel*. New York: Harper and Row, 1961.

Jaynes, Julian. *The Origin of Consciousness in the Breakdown of the Bicameral Mind*. New York: Penguin, 1976.

Kammen, Michael. *Mystic Chords of Memory: the Transformation of Tradition in American Culture*. New York: Knopf, 1991.

Kavanagh, James H. "Ideology." *Critical Terms for Literary Study*. Ed. Frank Lentricchia and Thomas McLaughlin. Chicago: U of Chicago P, 1990.

Kazin, Alfred. "How Good is Norman Mailer?" *Contemporaries*. Boston: Little, Brown, and Company, 1962.

Leeds, Barry. *The Structured Vision of Norman Mailer*. New York: New York UP, 1969.

Lentricchia, Frank. *Criticism and Social Change*. Chicago: U of Chicago P, 1983.

———. "The American Writer as Bad Citizen—Introducing Don DeLillo." *South Atlantic Quarterly* 89 (1990): 239-44.

Lewis, R. W. B. *The American Adam: Innocence, Tragedy, and Tradition in the Nineteenth Century*. Chicago: U of Chicago P, 1955.

Lynn, Kenneth. "Welcome Back from the Raft, Huck Honey!" *American Scholar* 46 (1977): 338-47.

Mailer, Norman. *Advertisements for Myself*. New York: G. P. Putnam's Sons, 1959.

———. *Ancient Evenings*. Boston: Little Brown and Company, 1983.

———. Foreword. *The Best of Abbie Hoffman*. Ed. Daniel Simon with Abbie Hoffman New York: Four Walls Eight Windows, 1989.

———. *The Executioner's Song*. Boston: Little, Brown, and Company, 1979.

———. *Harlot's Ghost*. New York: Random House, 1991.

————. *Of a Fire on the Moon*. New York: New American Library, 1971.

————. Personal communication to author, 22 March 1984. HEH collection.

————. *Pieces and Pontifications*. Boston: Little, Brown, and Company, 1982.

Martin, Jay. *Who Am I This Time? Uncovering the Fictive Personality*. New York: W. W. Norton, 1989.

McHale, Brian. *Postmodernist Fiction*. New York: Methuen, 1987.

Miller, Henry. *A Devil in Paradise*. New York: Signet Books, 1956.

Morrison, Toni. *Song of Solomon*. New York: New American Library, 1977.

————. *Sula*. New York: Plume, 1973.

Pease, Donald E. "Citizen Vidal and Mailer's America." *Raritan* 11 (1992): 72-98.

Pietz, William. "The 'Post-Colonialism' of Cold War Discourse." *Social Text* 19/20.7 (1988): 55-75.

Poirier, Richard. *Norman Mailer*. New York: The Viking Press, 1972.

Porter, Carolyn. *Seeing and Being: the Plight of the Participant Observer in Emerson, James, Adams, and Faulkner*. Middletown, CT: Wesleyan UP, 1981.

Radford, Jean. *Norman Mailer: A Critical Study*. London: Macmillan, 1975.

Reising, Russell. *The Unusable Past: Theory and the Study of American Literature*. New York: Methuen, 1986.

Rollyson, Carl. *The Lives of Norman Mailer*. New York: Paragon House, 1991.

Said, Edward. "Opponents, Audiences, Constituencies and Community." *The Anti-Aesthetic: Essays on Postmodern Culture*. Ed. Hal Foster. Seattle: Bay Press, 1983.

Schaub, Thomas H. *American Fiction in the Cold War*. Madison: U of Wisconsin P, 1990.

Siebers, Tobin. *Cold War Criticism and the Politics of Skepticism*. New York: OUP, 1993.

Slotkin, Richard. "Myth and the Production of History." Bercovitch 70-90.

Steel, Ronald. *Pax Americana*. New York: The Viking Press, 1970.

Taylor, Gordon O. "Of Adams and Aquarius," *American Literature* 46 (1974): 68-82.

Warren, Robert Penn. *All the King's Men*. 1946. New York: Bantam Books, 1973.

Webster's New Collegiate Dictionary. Ed. Henry Bosley Woolf. Springfield: G&C Merriam Company, 1979.

Wenke, Joseph. *Mailer's America*. Hanover, NH: UP of New England, 1987.

White, Hayden. *Metahistory: The Historical Imagination in Nineteenth-Century Europe*. Baltimore: Johns Hopkins UP, 1974.

Whitfield, Stephen J. *The Culture of the Cold War*. Baltimore: Johns Hopkins UP, 1991.

Chronology

1923	Norman Mailer born in Long Branch, New Jersey, to Isaac Barnett Mailer and Fanny Schneider Mailer.
1927	Family moves to Brooklyn, where Mailer attends local public schools.
1939–43	Attends Harvard University, intending to study aeronautical engineering. Wins *Story* magazine's annual college contest for his story "The Greatest Thing in the World" and writes first novel (unpublished). Receives a B.S. in engineering sciences.
1944–46	Elopes with Beatrice Silverman in February, 1944, and remarries her in a traditional Jewish ceremony in March. Enters the Army, and serves at Leyte, Luzon, and with the occupation forces in Japan. Discharged in May, 1946.
1948	Publishes *The Naked and the Dead*. Studies at the Sorbonne on the GI Bill, writes articles for the *New York Post*.
1949	Birth of daughter Susan. Speaks at Waldorf Peace Conference. Works on rejected screenplay in Hollywood. Reads Marx's *Das Kapital* which he later credits for making him a better writer.
1951	Publishes *Barbary Shore*.
1952	Divorces Beatrice Silverman.
1953	Works as a contributing editor for *Dissent*.

1954	Marries Adele Morales. Contract disputes over obscenity in *The Deer Park*; after several rejections from publishers, the manuscript is accepted.
1955	Publishes *The Deer Park*. Founds *The Village Voice* with Daniel Wolf and Edwin Francher.
1957	Daughter Danielle is born. Publishes "The White Negro" in *Dissent*.
1959	Publishes *Advertisements for Myself*. Another daughter, Elizabeth Anne, is born.
1960	Runs for Mayor of New York City on the Existentialist ticket. Stabs wife Adele with penknife, she refuses to press charges. Undergoes observation at Bellevue for a few weeks.
1962	Publishes *Death for the Ladies (and Other Disasters)*. Divorces Adele Morales and marries Lady Jeanne Campbell, a columnist. Their daughter Kate is born in August.
1963	Publishes *The Presidential Papers*. Divorces Lady Jeanne Campbell and marries actress Beverly Bentley.
1964	Publishes *An American Dream* serially in *Esquire*. Son Michael Burks is born.
1965	Publishes a revised version of *An American Dream* in book format.
1966	Publishes *Cannibals and Christians*. Birth of son Stephen McLeod.
1967	Publishes *Why Are We in Vietnam?* Adapts *The Deer Park* for the theater, where the play receives a limited run. Makes two films. Participates in anti-war demonstrations, and is elected to the National Institute of Arts and Letters.
1968	Publishes *The Armies of the Night*, which receives both the Pulitzer Prize and the National Book Award. Covers both political conventions and publishes *Miami and the Siege of Chicago*.
1969	Runs for Mayor of New York in Democratic primary, advocating the city's secession from the state; comes in fourth out of five.
1970	Publishes *Of a Fire on the Moon*. Elected to the American Academy of Arts and Sciences.

1971	Publishes *The Prisoner of Sex*. A daughter, Maggie Alexandra, is born to Mailer and Carol Stevens. Separates from wife Beverly Bentley.
1972	Publishes *Existential Errands*.
1973	Publishes *Marilyn: A Biography*.
1975	Publishes *The Fight*, an account of the famous fight between Muhammad Ali and George Foreman.
1976	Publishes *Genius and Lust: A Journey through the Major Writings of Henry Miller*.
1978	Publishes *A Transit to Narcissus*. Wife Beverly Bentley sues for divorce. Birth of son John Buffalo to Mailer and Norris Church.
1979	Publishes *the Executioner's Song*, based on the life and death of a convicted killer Gary Gilmore. Wins the Pultizer for *Executioner's Song*. Divorces Beverley Bentley.
1980	Marries and divorces Carol Stevens. Marries Norris Church, an art teacher. Publishes *Of Women and Their Elegance*.
1983	Publishes *Ancient Evenings*.
1984	Visits the Soviet Union. Publishes *Tough Guys Don't Dance*.
1984–86	President PEN (American Chapter).
	Publishes *Harlot's Ghost*.
	Publishes *Portrait of Picasso as a Young Man: An Interpretive Biography* and *Oswald's Tale: An American Mystery*.
1997	Publishes *The Gospel According to the Son*.
1998	Publishes *The Time of Our Time*.

Contributors

HAROLD BLOOM is Sterling Professor of the Humanities at Yale University and Henry W. and Albert A. Berg Professor of English at the New York University Graduate School. He is the author of over 20 books, including *Shelley's Mythmaking* (1959), *The Visionary Company* (1961), *Blake's Apocalypse* (1963), *Yeats* (1970), *A Map of Misreading* (1975), *Kabbalah and Criticism* (1975), *Agon: Toward a Theory of Revisionism* (1982), *The American Religion* (1992), *The Western Canon* (1994), and *Omens of Millennium: The Gnosis of Angels, Dreams, and Resurrection* (1996). *The Anxiety of Influence* (1973) sets forth Professor Bloom's provocative theory of the literary relationships between the great writers and their predecessors. His most recent books include *Shakespeare: The Invention of the Human* (1998), a 1998 National Book Award finalist, *How to Read and Why* (2000), and *Genius: A Mosaic of One Hundred Exemplary Creative Minds* (2002). In 1999, Professor Bloom received the prestigious American Academy of Arts and Letters Gold Medal for Criticism, and in 2002 he received the Catalonia International Prize.

ALVIN B. KERNAN has been Kenan Professor of the Humanities at Princeton University. He is the author and/or editor of a number of titles, including *In Plato's Cave*, *The Death of Literature*, and *Shakespeare, the King's Playwright in the Stuart Court, 1603-1613*.

RICHARD POIRIER has been a Professor of English and Chairman of the Department of English at Rutgers University, New Brunswick, New Jersey.

He is the author of a number of books, including *Norman Mailer*, *Robert Frost: The Work of Knowing*, *The Comic Sense of Henry James*, and *Poetry & Pragmatism*.

STACEY OLSTER teaches English at the State University of New York at Stony Brook. She is the author of *Reminiscence & Re-Creation in Contemporary American Fiction*.

GABRIEL MILLER teaches English at Rutgers University, Newark, New Jersey. He is the author of *Screening the Novel* and has also written and/or edited books on Daniel Fuchs, John Irving, and Clifford Odets.

NIGEL LEIGH taught American literature at Catania University in Italy. He has written essays for the *Journal of American Studies* and currently writes for television.

PETER BALBERT is Chair and Professor of English at Trinity University. He has written and/or edited various books on D. H. Lawrence.

MARK EDMUNDSON teaches English at the University of Virginia. He is the author of *Literature Against Philosophy*, *Plato to Derrida: A Defence of Poetry*, and has written other titles as well.

JOSEPH TABBI is Assistant Professor of English at the University of Chicago. He is the author of *Postmodern Sublime: Technology and American Writing from Mailer to Cyberpunk* and *Cognitive Fictions*.

ROBERT MERRILL teaches English at the University of Nevada at Reno. He is the author of *Norman Mailer* in the Twayne's United States Authors series, as well as *Critical Essays on Kurt Vonnegut*.

KATHY SMITH has taught writing at the University of Massachusetts at Amherst and at other universities. She is a published poet. She has been Assistant Director of the New Hampshire Humanities Council.

MICHAEL K. GLENDAY has taught American Studies at the Liverpool Institute of Higher Education. He has written *Saul Bellow and the Decline of Humanism*.

JOHN WHALEN-BRIDGE is Assistant Professor at the National University of Singapore. He is the author of *Political Fiction and the American Self* and has also written on biography, Gary Snyder, and Jaques Lacan.

Bibliography

Algeo, Ann M. *The Courtroom as Forum: Homicide Trials by Dreiser, Wright, Capote, and Mailer*. New York: Peter Lang, 1996.

Alsen, Eberhard. "Norman Mailer (1923-)." *Contemporary Jewish-American Novelists: A Bio-Critical Sourcebook*. Joel Shatzky and Michael Taub, eds. Westport, CT: Greenwood, 1997, pp. 192-203.

Arlett, Robert M. "The Veiled Fist of a Master Executioner," *Criticism* 29, no. 2 (Spring 1987): pp. 215-32.

Balbert, Peter. "Configurations of the Ego: Studies of Mailer, Roth, and Salinger," *Studies in the Novel* 12, no. 1 (Spring 1980): pp. 73-81.

Clendinnen, Inga. "Norman Mailer Meets Jack Ruby," *HEAT* 7 (1997): pp. 49-55.

Escoffier, Jeffrey. "Homosexuality and the Sociological Imagination: The 1950s and 1960s." *A Queer World: The Center for Lesbian and Gay Studies Reader*. Marin Duberman, ed. New York: New York University Press, 1997.

Felty, Darren. "Media Representations of Gary Gilmore in Norman Mailer's *Executioner's Song*." *The Image of Violence in Literature, the Media, and Society*. Will Wright and Steven Kaplan, eds. Pueblo, CO: Society for the Interdisciplinary Study of Social Imagery, University of Southern Colorado, 1995, pp. 141-45.

Gerson, Jessica. "Norman Mailer: Sex, Creativity and God," *Mosaic* 15, no. 2 (June 1982): pp. 1-16.

Hellman, John. *Fables of Fact: The New Journalism as New Fiction*. Urbana: University of Illinois Press, 1981.

————. "Postmodern Journalism." *Postmodern Fiction: A Bio-Bibliographical Guide*. Larry McCaffery, ed. New York: Greenwood, 1986.

Hersey, John. "The Legend on the License," *The Yale Review* 75, no. 2 (Winter 1986): pp. 289-314.

Horn, Bernard. "Ahab and Ishmael at War: The Presence of *Moby-Dick* in *The Naked and the Dead*," *American Quarterly* 34, no. 4 (Fall 1982): pp. 379-95.

Hume, Kathryn. "Books of the Dead: Postmortem Politics in Novels by Norman Mailer, Burroughs, Acker, and Pynchon," *Modern Philology* 97, no. 3 (February 2000): pp. 417-44.

Kar, Prafulla C. "Norman Mailer and the Shift of Fictional Modes," *Indian Journal of American Studies* 14, no. 2 (July 1984): pp. 43-9.

Kellman, Steven G. "Mailer's Strains of Fact," *Southwest Review* 68, no. 2 (Spring 1983): pp. 126-33.

Khan, A. G. "Defiance and Acceptance: Two Modes of Cultural Response in Mailer's *American Dream* and *The Armies of the Night* and Updike's *Rabbit Redux*," *Indian Journal of American Studies* 14, no. 2 (July 1984): pp. 103-109.

Kimball, Roger. "Norman Mailer's American Dream," *New Criterion* 16, no. 3 (November 1997): pp. 4-10.

Koelb, Clayton. "Reading Is Fundamental: Norman Mailer and the Rhetoric of Narrative," *Texte* 8-9 (1989): pp. 203-305.

LeComte, Edward. "'No One in School Could Read or Write So Well as Me': Our Semi-literate Literati," *Greyfriar: Siena Studies in Literature* 26 (1985): pp. 31-48.

Leeds, Barry H. "Norman Mailer: Politically Incorrect?" *English Record* 51, no. 2 (Winter 2001): pp. 10-25.

————. "Tough Guy Goes Hollywood: Mailer and the Movies." *Take Two: Adapting the Contemporary American Novel to Film*. Barbara Tepa Lupack, ed. Bowling Green, OH: Popular, 1994, pp. 154-68.

Leigh, Nigel. "Spirit of Place in Mailer's *The Naked and the Dead*," *Journal of American Studies* 21, no. 3 (December 1987): pp. 426-29.

Lennon, J. Michael, ed. *Critical Essays on Norman Mailer*. Boston: Hall, 1986.

Lennon, J. Michael. "Mailer's Cosmology," *Modern Language Studies* 12, no. 3 (Summer 1982): pp. 18-29.

Lounsberry, Barbara. *The Art of Fact: Contemporary Artists of Nonfiction*. New York: Greenwood, 1990.

Lott, Eric. "White Like Me: Racial Cross-Dressing and the Construction of American Whiteness." *Cultures of U.S. Imperialism*. Amy E. Kaplan and

Donald E. Pease, eds. Durham, NC: Duke University Press, 1993, pp. 474-95.

McCann, Sean. "The Imperiled Republic: Norman Mailer and the Poetics of Anti-Liberalism," *ELH* (Spring 2000): pp. 293-336.

McCord, Phyllis Frus. "The Ideology of Form: The Nonfiction Novel," *Genre* 19, no. 1 (Spring 1986): pp. 59-79.

McLaughlin, Robert L. "History vs. Fiction: The Self-Destruction of *The Executioner's Song*," *CLIO* 17, no. 3 (Spring 1988): pp. 225-38.

Mellard, James M. "Origins, Language, and the Constitution of Reality: Norman Mailer's *Ancient Evenings*." *Traditions, Voices, and Dreams: The American Novel Since the 1960s.* Melvin J. Friedman and Ben Siegel, eds. Newark, DE: University of Delaware Press, 1995, pp. 131-49.

Merrill, Robert. "Mailer's Sad Comedy: *The Executioner's Song*," *Texas Studies in Literature and Language* 34, no. 1 (Spring 1992): pp. 129-48.

———. "Mailer's *Tough Guys Don't Dance* and the Detective Traditions," *Critique: Studies in Contemporary Fiction* 34, no. 4 (Summer 1993): pp. 232-46.

Mierau, Maurice A. "Carnival and Jeremiad: Mailer's *The Armies of the Night*," *Canadian Review of American Studies* 17, no. 3 (Fall 1986): pp. 317-26.

Miller, Gabriel. "A Small Trumpet of Defiance: Politics and the Buried Life in Norman Mailer's Early Fiction." *Politics and the Muse: Studies in the Politics of Recent American Literature.* Adam J. Sorkin, ed. Bowling Green: Popular, 1989, pp. 79-92.

Misra, Kalidas. "The American War Novel from World War II to Vietnam," *Indian Journal of American Studies* 14, no. 2 (July 1984): pp. 73-80.

Mutalik-Desai, A. A. "The Paradox of Norman Mailer." *American Literature and Culture: New Insights.* Laxmi Parasuram, ed. New Delhi: Prestige, 1995, pp. 31-36.

———. "Norman Mailer's *An American Dream*: A Twentieth-Century Fable." *American Literature Today.* Suman Bala, ed. New Delhi: Intellectual, 1994, pp. 114-21.

———. "Norman Mailer's *The Naked and the Dead*: Theme and Technique." *Contemporary American-Jewish Novel*, volume II. Tarlochan Singh Anand, ed. Jalandhar: ABS, 1994, pp. 301-10.

Mylan, Sheryl A. "Love in the Trenches: Images of Women in Norman Mailer's *The Naked and the Dead*," *War, Literature, and the Arts* 6, no. 1 (Spring-Summer 1994) pp. 75-85.

Neilson, Heather. "Jack's Ghost: Reappearances of John F. Kennedy in the Work of Gore Vidal and Norman Mailer," *American Studies International* 35, no. 3 (October 1997): pp. 23-41.

O'Donnell, Patrick. "Engendering Paranoia in Contemporary Narrative," *Boundary* 19, no. 1 (Spring 1992): pp. 181-204.

Olster, Stacey. "Norman Mailer after Forty Years," *Michigan Quarterly Review* 28, no. 3 (Summer 1989): pp. 400-16.

Parker, Hershel. *Flawed Texts and Verbal Icons: Literary Authority in American Fiction*. Evanston: Northwestern University Press, 1984.

Pease, Donald E. "Citizen Vidal and Mailer's America," *Raritan* 11, no. 4 (Spring 1992): pp. 72-98.

Poirier, Richard. *Norman Mailer*. New York: The Viking Press, 1972.

Pops, Martin. "Mailer's Picasso: Portrait and Self-Portrait," *Salmagundi* 116-117 (Fall-Winter 1997): pp. 141-59.

Rosenshied, Gary. "Crime and Redemption, Russian and American Style: Dostoevsky, Buckley, Mailer, Styron, and Their Words," *Slavic and East European Journal* 42, no. 4 (Winter 1998): pp. 677-709.

Schleifer, Ronald. "American Violence: Dreiser, Mailer, and the Nature of Intertexuality." *Intertexuality and Contemporary American Fiction*. Patrick O'Donnell and Robert Con Davis, eds. Baltimore: Johns Hopkins University Press, 1989, pp. 121-43.

Shanmugiah, S. "Norman Mailer and the Radical Hero: A Study of an American Dream." *Indian Views on American Literature*. A. A. Mutalik-Desai, ed. New Delhi, India: Prestige, 1998, pp. 36-43.

Shoemaker, Steve. "Norman Mailer's 'White Negro': Historical Myth or Mythical History?" *Twentieth Century Literature* 37, no. 3 (Fall 1991): pp. 343-60.

Taylor, Gordon O. "Joan Didion and 'Company': A Response to John Whalen-Bridge," *Connotations: A Journal for Critical Debate* 6, no. 2 (1996-97): p. 251-57.

Thornton, William H. "American Political Culture in Mailer's *The Naked and the Dead*," *EurAmerica* 22, no. 1 (March 1992): pp. 95-122.

———. "Stranded in the Sixties: The Politics of Mailer's *Armies of the Night*," *Popular Culture Review* 5, no. 1 (February 1994): pp. 97-105.

Tonn, Horst. "Making Sense of Contemporary Reality: The Construction of Meaning in the Nonfiction Novel." *Historiographic Metafiction in Modern American and Canadian Literature*. Bernd Engler and Kurt Muller, eds. Paderborn: Ferdinand Schoningh, 1994, pp. 197-208.

Widmer, Kingsley. "Lawrence's American Bad Boy Progeny: Henry Miller and Norman Mailer." *D. H. Lawrence's Literary Inheritors*. Keith Cushman and Dennis Jackson, eds. New York: St. Martin's, 1991, pp. 89-108.

———. "Lawrence's Cultural Impact." *The Legacy of D. H. Lawrence*. Jeffrey Meyers, ed. New York: St. Martin's, 1987, pp. 156-74.

Wilson III, Raymond J. "Control and Freedom in *The Naked and the Dead*," *Texas Studies in Literature and Language* 28, no. 2 (Summer 1986): pp. 164-81.

Acknowledgments

"The Taking of the Moon: The Struggle of the Poetic and Scientific Myths in Norman Mailer's *Of a Fire on the Moon*" by Alvin B. Kernan. From *The Imaginary Library: An Essay on Literature and Society.* © 1982 by Princeton University Press. Reprinted by permission of Princeton University Press.

"Norman in Egypt" by Harold Bloom. From *The New York Review of Books* 30, no. 7 (April 28, 1983): pp. 3-5. © 1983 by NYREV, Inc. Reprinted by permission.

"In Pyramid and Palace" by Richard Poirier. From *The Times Literary Supplement* 184, no. 4 (June 10, 1983): pp. 591-92. © 1983 by Times Newspapers Limited. Reprinted by permission.

"Norman Mailer After Forty Years" by Stacey Olster. From *Michigan Quarterly Review* 28, no. 3 (Summer 1989): pp. 400-16. © 1989 by The University of Michigan. Reprinted by permission.

"A Small Trumpet of Defiance: Politics and The Buried Life in Norman Mailer's Early Fiction" by Gabriel Miller. From *Politics And The Muse: Studies in the Politics of Recent American Literature*, edited by Adam J. Sorkin. © 1989 by Bowling Green State University Popular Press. Reprinted by permission.

Nigel Leigh, "Marxisms on Trial: *Barbary Shore*" from *Radical Fictions and the Novels of Norman Mailer.* © 1990 by Nigel Leigh, reproduced with permission of Palgrave Macmillan.

"From *Lady Chatterley's Lover* to *The Deer Park*: Lawrence, Mailer, and the Dialectic of Erotic Risk" by Peter Balbert. From *Studies in the Novel* 22, no. 1 (Spring 1990): pp. 67-81. © 1990 by the University of North Texas. Reprinted by permission of the publisher.

"Romantic Self-Creations: Mailer and Gilmore in *The Executioner's Song*" by Mark Edmundson. From *Contemporary Literature* 31, no. 4 (Winter 1990): pp. 434-47. © 1990 by the Board of Regents of the University of Wisconsin System. Reprinted with permission.

"Mailer's Psychology of Machines" by Joseph Tabbi. Reprinted by permission of the Modern Language Association of America from *Publications of the Modern Language Association of America* 106, no. 2 (March 1991): pp. 238-50. © 1991 by The Modern Language Asociation of America.

"Mailer's *Tough Guys Don't Dance* and the Detective Traditions" by Robert Merrill. From *Critique* 34, no. 4 (Summer 1993): pp. 232-46. Reprinted with permission of the Helen Dwight Reid Educational Foundation. Published by Heldref Publications, 1319 Eighteenth St., NW, Washington, DC 20036-1802. Copyright © 1993.

"Norman Mailer and the Radical Text" by Kathy Smith. From *Cohesion and Dissent in America*, edited by Carol Colatrella and Joseph Alkana. © 1994 by the State University of New York. Reprinted with permission.

"The Hot Breath of the Future: *The Naked and the Dead*," by Michael K. Glenday. From *Norman Mailer*. © 1995 by Michael K. Glenday. Reprinted with permission of Palgrave Macmillan.

"The Myth of the American Adam in Late Mailer" by John Whalen-Bridge. From *Connotations* 5, nos. 2-3 (1995/96): pp. 304-21. © 1996 by John Whalen-Bridge. Reprinted with permission of the author.

Index